ISBN 0-8248-0480-5 $12.95

The Unsteady State
Environmental Problems, Growth, and Culture

Kenneth E. F. Watt
Leslie F. Molloy
C. K. Varshney
Dudley Weeks
Soetjipto Wirosardjono

Critical shortages of food, expanding populations, overcrowded cities, depletion of energy resources, increasing economic instability, unemployment, and crime are among the complex array of problems that threaten all human societies. The current dominant culture, the "technoculture," promises a better life for everyone and contends that for all societies there is one common path of economic development. The authors of the present volume argue that this is the critical error being made by the industrial societies.

In the spring of 1975 a team of physical and biological scientists from Indonesia, India, Japan, New Zealand, and the United States gathered at the East-West Center in Honolulu to study the relationship between culture and environment. This book emerged from that gathering. It illustrates how environmental problems are caused by cultural beliefs and by certain patterns of growth cherished by modern technological society and unquestioned by the conventional wisdom.

Instead of rejecting growth entirely, the authors conclude that development strategies which will provide a kind of organic growth must be worked out. This kind of growth must be oriented to improving the quality of life and to arriving eventually at a condition of environmental equilibrium they call the "dynamic steady state."

KENNETH E. F. WATT is professor of zoology and environmental studies, and research systems analyst at the Institute of Zoology, University of California at Davis. Since 1968 he has been head of a group that builds large-scale computer-simulation models of society. His books include *The Titanic Effect: Planning for the Unthinkable, Ecology and Resource Management,* and *Principles of Environmental Sciences.*

LESLIE F. MOLLOY for the past ten years has been a soil scientist in the Soil Biochemistry and Organic Matter Section of the Soil Bureau, New Zealand Department of Scientific and Industrial Research, Lower Hutt, New Zealand. Dr. Molloy's research subjects have included soil/plant fertility and its influence upon metabolic diseases in ruminants, and the influence of climate on carbon recycling in montane grassland ecosystems.

DUDLEY WEEKS is currently director of the Peace Research Laboratory, St. Louis, Missouri, and has been a teacher and community development organizer in Asia, Latin America, Europe, the Middle East, and North America. Dr. Weeks has served as assistant director of the Center for the Teaching about Peace and War at Wayne State University, and was codirector of the Alternative Futures Program at the University of Hawaii.

SOETJIPTO WIROSARDJONO is the director of the Research Center in Jakarta, Indonesia, and has a degree in statistics. He has been executive secretary of the Inter-Indonesian Municipalities Organization, and a member of the executive board, Pollution Study Group, Petroleum Institut, Jakarta, Indonesia.

C. K. VARSHNEY teaches ecology at the University of Delhi, India. He has also served the government of India as the first secretary of the National Committee on Environmental Planning and Coordination, and of the Indian National Committee for the Man and Biosphere Program.

THE UNSTEADY STATE
Environmental Problems, Growth, and Culture

Kenneth E. F. Watt
Leslie F. Molloy
C. K. Varshney
Dudley Weeks
Soetjipto Wirosardjono

AN EAST-WEST CENTER BOOK
Published for the East-West Center by
The University Press of Hawaii/Honolulu

Library of Congress Cataloging in Publication Data
Main entry under title:

The Unsteady State.

    ''An East-West Center book.''
    Bibliography: p.
    Includes index.
    1. Environmental policy. 2. Economic development—
Social aspects. 3. Technology—Social aspects.
I. Watt, Kenneth E. F., 1929–
HC79.E5U58   301.31   77–3879
ISBN 0-8248-0480-5

Contents

Preface

The East-West Center is a national, nonprofit educational institution established to "promote better relations and understanding between the United States and the nations of Asia and the Pacific through cooperative study, training and research."

Each year the Center brings together more than fifteen hundred people from the many cultures and nations of these regions. Among this number are included small teams of scholars and authorities known as Open Grants Senior Fellows who work together for periods of four to six months on problems of mutual concern to East and West. *The Unsteady State: Environmental Problems, Growth, and Culture* is an outgrowth of the spring 1975 Open Grants project entitled "Cultural Dimensions of Environmental Problems."

The project brought together physical and biological scientists from Indonesia, India, Japan, New Zealand, and the United States to explore the relationships between culture and the environment. To our knowledge, this is the first time an international team has been put to work on this particular topic. Realizing the unique opportunity such a project provided, we set ourselves from the outset the task of weaving together our diverse beliefs and philosophies into a statement that would not only have relevance to the issues of growth, culture, and environmental problems, but that would be presented in a manner capable of reaching the general reading public. Quite naturally, such an undertaking brought both constraints and blessings. Of the constraints, by far the most serious were lack of time (only three months for the bulk of the writing) and scarcity of international data. The shortage of time made it impossible to develop several important themes as thoroughly as we desired. The most obvious of these are the theme of cultural dimension and the vast area of specific proposals for change. Of the blessings, the most rewarding have been the multicultural learning opportunities generated by the diverse backgrounds of the team members, and the insights and contributions of participants from the East-West Center and the Honolulu community.

The working methods we employed provided many lessons for each of us. During the first four months of the project there were many informal conferences and seminars (with a variety of people and groups) that helped expand our thinking. As we began to synthesize this diverse input, lengthy meetings among the authors were held on each chapter, and formal assignments were agreed upon. The process used in producing chapter 1 illustrates the team nature of our effort. Watt wrote an original draft, which was virtually scrapped and then allocated in bits and pieces to other chapters. Then a Molloy-Weeks version of chapter 1 was submitted and discussed, and Watt and Varshney appended certain additions. The entire group then did a logical analysis of the material and assigned Molloy to pull together the final draft. Many chapters have followed this general process. The result is a final product that contains the contributions of all of us and presents a statement we can all support.

Our overall message is twofold and, although quite simple, is also quite challenging. Modern environmental problems cannot be solved unless the beliefs and economic systems giving rise to these problems are thoroughly examined and, in many cases, significantly altered. Society can no longer afford to ignore the fact that rapid economic and technological growth is leading to severe problems in the natural and social environment.

Several reviewers of the final product expressed an interest in knowing more about the internal substantive dynamics of such a diversely constituted team. In general, although we were guided by frequent and intense discussion, we made a conscious effort to cooperate and to reach consensus on as many issues as possible. But even in the midst of efforts at consensus, there were several key issues on which disagreement persisted and eventual synthesis proved difficult. Although it would be far too lengthy and tedious to go into detail, it might prove instructive to summarize a few of the more significant debates.

Perhaps the most recurring discussion centered on "universal" prescriptions. We all agreed on the major criteria of "quality of life," but differed markedly on what *degree* of fulfillment of the criteria each society would choose. We also agreed that various societies and systems must base their own development designs on the needs, beliefs, and total resources peculiar to their own experience. However, some of us (notably Weeks, Molloy, and Watt) felt that heavy emphasis should be put on new structures and priorities with *global* applicability, while others (particularly Varshney and Wirosardjono) consistently argued that we should not go much beyond *national* parameters in our discussion of options.

A second area of lively debate centered on the question of redistribution. Varshney argued that the priority for development is to enlarge the resource base, while Weeks, Molloy, and Watt contended that unless distribution patterns were made more equitable *now*, a growth in resources would not necessarily result in a society's meeting its most desperate needs.

On the issue of population growth, some interesting differences of opinion appeared. More than any of the other authors, Watt emphasized the seriousness of overpopulation, claiming that the optimum level of world population might be as low as five hundred million people. On the other hand, Wirosardjono saw population redistribution as the major priority, and Weeks pointed out the interconnections among population concerns and other social and environmental problems (such as distribution patterns), emphasizing that merely limiting population growth may be of little help to struggling societies unless global structures of inequity are also revamped. Molloy tended to support this last position, emphasizing the relationship between excessive per capita consumption in affluent areas and resource shortages in other locales.

Another area of mutual concern was the large number of specific North American examples. Certain obvious factors, such as data availability, contributed to the imbalance of examples. But perhaps even more important was the fact that the only culture we attempted to examine was the ''technoculture,'' a complex array of beliefs and institutionalized behavioral patterns that is most powerfully exemplified by American activity and institutions in contemporary global society.

In pointing out areas of disagreement, it is also important for us to acknowledge that we ultimately omitted several issues that some or all of us wished to include if time and overall expertise had allowed. We have already mentioned the less-than-adequate space alloted to an in-depth analysis of various cultures. Similarly, we also found it necessary to omit any in-depth treatment of the role specific religious beliefs play in cultural attitudes toward environmental problems.

And finally, on a more political note, we found ourselves enmeshed in a ticklish debate over which examples of alternative policies for the future we should discuss, or perhaps even advocate. Although we considered it definitely unwise and impossible to single out any one society as an example of how to reach qualitative growth, we could not help acknowledging in our discussions the most dramatic alternative models now in existence. As might be expected, how to deal with the People's Republic of China, with its apparent commitment to labor-intensive rather than capital- and energy-intensive growth, and its position as a frequent model of Third World development, became a matter of concern and debate. Weeks strongly advocated a rather extensive discussion of the more significant socioeconomic experiments now taking place in China. Molloy and Watt also favored such discussion, emphasizing, of course, the Chinese cultural context in which the pertinent policies were rooted. In the final outcome, however, the wishes of Wirosardjono, and to some degree, Varshney, prevailed, primarily on the grounds that the substance of alternative policies can be adequately discussed and evaluated without necessarily tying those policies to any one nation.

Throughout these debates we searched for the keys that would make our final product an outgrowth of a dynamic and cooperative multicultural team effort. Although we feel that in most respects this has been accomplished, we hope that the passage of time will make it even more possible and rewarding to conduct interdisciplinary, intercultural team projects such as the one we had the privilege of experiencing.

Although the five authors worked primarily as a team, it seems appropriate to point out specific individual contributions. Ken Watt originally conceived the idea of the book and, more than any other author, his contributions run throughout all chapters. Of special importance, however, are chapters 2 and 5; the sections on stability theory, economic system balance, and planning; and much of the substance and methodology of the data analysis. Les Molloy wrote the section on ecosystem balance, compiled and analyzed significant data for chapters 4 and 5, worked with Ken Watt in the original conceptualization of the book, and did most of the final work on chapter 1. Dudley Weeks authored most of chapter 7, the sections on inequity, and portions of chapters 1 and 6; provided much of the conceptualization and definition for the quality of life paradigm; wrote much of the technoculture versus qualitative growth material; and was responsible for the final rewriting and editing of the entire manuscript. Soetjipto Wirosardjono not only assisted Ken Watt in the statistical analysis portions, but also contributed significantly to chapter 6 and the basic need section of chapter 4. C. K. Varshney contributed portions of the section on ecosystem balance and some of the overall framework for chapter 1; assisted in data compilation, and contributed his share of the critical analysis of all portions of the manuscript.

We are especially grateful for the contributions of John Morgan, a graduate student in urban and regional planning at the East-West Center's Technology and Development Institute, particularly in the writing of portions of chapter 4, and in bringing to our attention additional information on intermediate technology. We are also indebted to Lester Milbraeth, Tai-joon Kwon, Yosaku Hasegawa, Mike Powers, Renton deAlwis, Beverly Knittle, Tian Soo Lim, Raul Berrios Loyola, James McEvoy, and Aspy Palia for valuable assistance to our efforts. In addition, we profited from the ideas and critical analysis of numerous people, including several groups at the University of Hawaii (Rudi Rummel's DON project, John Bardach's marine laboratory group, and the Environmental Center), Murray Ellis, Theodore Herman, O. T. Jones, Pete Bostwick, Henry Makey, Herman Spieth, R. W. Armstrong, Stephen Yeh, Lois Edinger, Joanne Baldine, Genevieve Watt, Sonia Molloy, and Yvonne Hunter.

Absolutely indispensible to the overall project were Sumi Makey, executive officer of Open Grants; Miriam Gould, who coordinated much of the senior fellows' operations and assisted in editing; and Open Grants staff members Gay Yoshida, Fusae Uyemura, Carol Sakai, and Rose Nakamura.

And finally, we express our appreciation to East-West Center President Everett Kleinjans and Vice-President John Brownell for making possible this entire project.

1
Environmental Problems and Quality of Life

INTRODUCTION

The rapid increase in the number and intensity of environmental problems threatens all human societies. Critical shortages of food, exploding populations, and rapid depletion of energy sources are all posing real and present dangers to humanity. But these well-known concerns are only part of the vast and complex range of contemporary environmental problems. The migration of displaced farm workers into already overcrowded cities; the threatened extinction of almost two hundred species of birds and more than one hundred twenty species of mammals; rapidly increasing economic instability, unemployment, and crime—these, too, are part of a far-reaching array of environmental problems that influence almost every aspect of our lives.

The character and intensity of environmental problems vary greatly from society to society, depending on numerous factors such as historical background, life-style, cultural values, and level of socioeconomic development. It is the purpose of this book to trace the origins of man's environmental problems; in particular, to illustrate how they are related to cultural beliefs and to certain patterns of growth cherished by the modern technological society, and unquestioned by the conventional wisdom. We will show how the problems of poverty, resource depletion, economic instability, environmental deterioration, and social disruption are, in fact, related manifestations of conventional beliefs and patterns of growth. For example, we will demonstrate that excesses in commodity consumption and energy utilization join with the profit-maximization motive to increase unemployment. We will show that increased energy consumption does not necessarily lead to a growth in Gross National Product (GNP) per capita, and that growth in GNP may not lead to economic and social stability. And, using a large collection of diverse data, we will suggest other intriguing relationships that can be explored and possibly verified by additional reasearch.

To draw the detailed blueprints for a new enlightened environmental order is beyond the scope of this book. It is our belief that new strategies can be best developed when the majority of mankind realizes where our present beliefs and behavior are leading us. Consequently, it is to solving this problem of perception that the first six chapters of the book are addressed. However, we readily acknowledge that the literature on environmental problems is replete with descriptions of the problem and the reader is often left begging for some solutions. Our final chapter, then, does attempt to discuss some of the changes that will be necessary. Some are simply reforms, but others will require fundamental changes to our society.

THE NATURE OF ENVIRONMENTAL PROBLEMS

To define environmental problems adequately is as difficult as fully understanding and describing human values—a task which has occupied humans for tens of thousands of years. While to one person the clear-felling of a forest of mature California redwood trees may be an act of wanton vandalism, to another it is an act that provides essential materials for human existence and provides employment for the local populace. In a historical sense man has always had a problem with his environment—the problem of survival in the face of the powerful forces of nature. Yet the term *environmental problems* came into fashionable usage only with the rapid development of the environmental movement in the affluent, industrialized countries during the late 1960s. This new emphasis on the environment has given a welcome impetus to the investigation of a major question: Is there any common dimension to the many differing environmental problems, particularly the ubiquitous ones associated with poverty and affluence?

The one most obvious common dimension is survival. Survival for any species depends upon a sustainable relationship with its environment, an environment containing both life-support systems and competitors. For humans, environmental problems basically arise when there is an imbalance between man and the available resources of the environment. The primary focus of these problems is in the inadequate or excessive utilization of the natural resources of the *physical* environment. These physical problems are then often manifested in the related problems of the social environment. This implies a limit to the population that can be supported by these finite resources—the concept of "carrying capacity." To exceed this carrying capacity will bring a reduction in the standard of living. Thus, growth in population and the demand for higher consumption of resources are two of the major driving forces that cause the carrying capacity to be exceeded and environmental problems to result.

This situation can be illustrated in a flow chart (figure 1.1) of the world's interrelated physical and social environmental problems. The problems in the developing countries arise partly from high growth rates of population, inadequate distribution of benefits, dependent economies, and poorly developed or mismanaged resources. Their natural resources are exported to the developed countries to pay for the food, technology, and capital they consider necessary to import. The developed countries, using their superior economic power, arrange to pay low prices for these basic resources, and in so doing make it easier for consumption in their own societies to reach staggering excesses. The expansion of the whole urban/industrial complex not only contributes to pollution but also increases the demand for natural resources. This demand is satisfied by further depleting local resources and/or by importing more resources from developing countries. The resultant overexpansion, pollution, and depletion then contribute further harm to the physical environment through the destruction of agricultural lands and wilderness, two vital contributors to the satisfaction of man's basic needs and the maintenance of biological stability.

For most of mankind, however, the problems become most cruelly apparent in the social environment. The problems of poverty—malnutrition, disease, illiteracy, inadequate housing and clothing—still plague the masses of the more than four billion people of the world. And the affluent minority also has its serious problems. Violence, especially homicide, is increasing at an alarming rate. Symptoms of stress, such as neurosis, alcoholism, drug abuse, suicide, and family breakdown, are common features of the urban/industrial society. Industrial man is becoming increasingly alienated from the fruits of his work and from the natural environment that once nurtured him. In all societies unemployment is on the rise, and a breakdown of traditional values and beliefs is creating a population that is insecure and afraid of an increasingly foreign and unpredictable environment.

GROWTH STRATEGIES AND ENVIRONMENTAL PROBLEMS

These environmental problems did not just appear overnight. Rather, they have developed gradually as the consequences of certain cultural belief-patterns and certain types of economic development. The belief systems underlying environmental problems will be discussed in chapter 2; but it is important to our theme that we delay no further in examining the complex nature of economic development. We will carry out this introductory examination by contrasting two fundamental types of growth that are intimately involved in the past and future development of societies.

The first type is "undifferentiated" growth,[1] a uniform, self-replicating

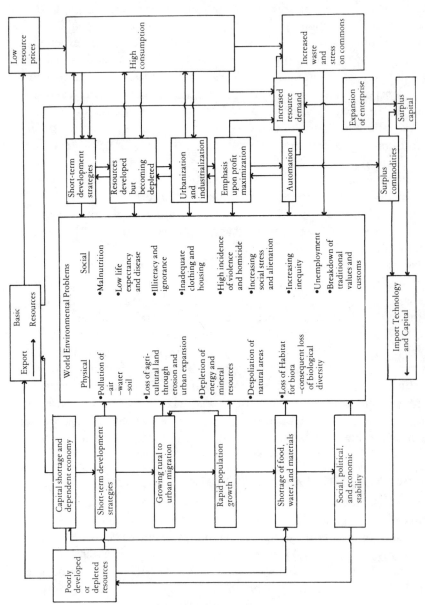

Figure 1.1. Interrelationships of World Environmental Problems

process that occurs at a constant rate and is analogous to the rapid exponential growth of cancerous cells. Quantity rather than quality becomes the primary objective of undifferentiated growth. In the context of the modern political economy this type of growth has been synonymous with the attitude of mind described as "growthmania."

> "Growthmania" is an insufficiently pejorative term for the paradigm or mind-set that always puts growth in first place—the attitude that there is no such thing as enough, that cannot conceive of too much of a good thing.[2]

The alternative to the undifferentiated process is what can be termed "organic" growth. With an emphasis on quality rather than quantity, organic growth envisages a process of differentiation that develops an organism with diverse structures, each with different functions. Such an organism grows to maturity, a state which is not *static* but *dynamic*, since the whole organism is continually being renovated. While this organism, like all others, will eventually die and decay, it will prolong a state of dynamic equilibrium by developing *homeostatic* mechanisms. The achievement of homeostasis or *dynamic steady state* thus becomes the ultimate objective of organic growth. Undifferentiated growth, on the other hand, lacks the negative feedback loops[3] necessary to reach and maintain *homeostasis*. The processes leading to the environmental problems depicted in figure 1.1 are those policies that create surplus production in developed countries, expansion of their enterprise, and consequent increased demand for resources. This demand in turn gives rise to a set of actions which will lead to further environmental problems in both developed and developing countries.

The growthmania paradigm promises a better life for everyone, contending that for all societies there exists one unilinear path of economic development. This path is characterized by several stages, the most significant of which is the well-known "takeoff" period. "The take-off usually witnesses a definitive social, political, and cultural victory of those who would modernize the economy over those who would either cling to the traditional society or seek other goals."[4] Growth of the productive forces, a rise in the rate of production investment, and an increase in capital-intensive development theoretically provide the leap forward that gets a society moving on its way to prosperity. The prime movers in the takeoff are the leading sectors of the economy, the owners and managers of the forces of production. As they grow and prosper, the benefits of this growth then spread to the other sectors of society until finally the ultimate stage of development is reached: the mass high-consumption society. More production, more technological development, and more consumption continue, allowing a society to finally conquer its "backwardness" and realize the fullness of its human potential. This classical model of economic development envisages a constant growth of overall GNP sufficient enough to provide benefits, benefits which ultimately "trickle down" to all groups in the society.

A close examination of the reality of this model of *undifferentiated* economic growth reveals several disturbing features. First, the assumption that all societies must follow the same path to development ignores the great diversity of physical resources, culture, and demography that characterizes today's world. Second, to categorize traditional values that do not support the "production-consumption" ethos as "backward" indicates the limited cultural perceptions of the modern technological culture.

Third, we find that in spite of the influx of more aid, more investment, and more industrialization (all of which are promised as the main sources of capital necessary for takeoff), many societies have not "taken off." The more perceptive of the proponents of the old urban-based, capital-intensive development model now admit that the causes of underdevelopment cannot be explained by simply pointing to a lack of capital or to a society's "backward" traditions.[5] Rather, the strategies of the urban-based, capital-intensive model have failed to recognize that "sustained growth cannot take place by transplanting modern technology in small areas while neglecting the mass of traditional producers."[6]

The third disturbing feature is the failure of the model to anticipate the detrimental ecological consequences that undifferentiated economic growth brings. Under this model, there have been numerous examples of serious ecosystem disruption, population growth beyond the carrying capacity of resources, and depletion of the natural resources of soil, air, water, and biota.[7] In many areas a critical loss of wilderness has resulted through following the growthmania model with its relegation of wilderness values to the unimportant status of "externalities." By destroying these ecosystems, these natural laboratories of organic evolution, mankind loses the valuable gene pool contained in the diversity of their species.

The fourth deficiency is that, despite the promises of economic growth, the gap between the standard of living of the developed nations and the masses of the underdeveloped countries is increasing. The annual growth rate in per capita GNP for eighty-five developing countries over the period 1960–1972 was 2.3 percent, while that for the twenty-five industrialized countries was 4.2 percent. In 1972, the per capita income for the 1,570 million people in those eighty-five developing countries was still only $279 (U.S.), while for the 662 million in the twenty-five industrialized nations income had risen to $3,670 (U.S.).[8] Ironically enough, it is often argued in these industrialized countries that only by perpetuating such "healthy" rates of economic growth can society afford to carry out the necessary task of cleaning up the ugliness and pollution that this rapid growth has produced.

Although certainly revealing, these mean growth rates still gloss over the real picture of the distribution of the GNP. While the industrialized nations are getting richer than the developing nations, there is also an increasing polarity of income distribution and power *within* the poorer countries. Virtually all developing countries are now plagued to varying degrees by this "dual economy" phenomenon of a rich, usually urban, elite and the poor rural masses, and by the associated twin evils of unemployment and mass migration to the cities.[9] The dual economy is part of a broader phenomenon that has split both developed and developing, international and domestic societies into "centers" and "peripheries,"[10] the center being composed of those regions, nations, groups, and individuals who are in a position to substantially influence or control the progress of the periphery. The nations and groups that make up the periphery, on the other hand, have no such influence on the center or on the ultimate determination of the distribution of benefits. These crucial problems of inequity will be discussed in more detail in chapter 4.

The deficiencies and serious negative consequences that are inherent in this growthmania model lead us to reject its suitability as a paradigm for development. For, as will be shown throughout the following chapters, uncontrolled, undifferentiated, quantitatively oriented growth logically leads to an eventual decline in the benefits of growth—the decline in "quality of life," shown in figure 1.2. It is a fundamental thesis of this book that the point of decline in quality of life has now been reached in many of the highly industrialized, highly populated countries in the developed world. Data will be presented in chapters 3, 4, and 5 showing how these countries and regions are beginning to experience problems of decreasing ecosystem and economic system balance, increasing inflation and unemployment, increasing inequity, and decreasing satisfaction of basic physical and social needs.

Although we reject the growthmania model, we do not reject growth, for we believe that economic development does indeed offer societies the potential for improving their quality of life. But the critical error that we urge the world to avoid is the assumption that the conventional pattern of undifferentiated growth now followed by the industrial societies is the only appropriate development strategy. It must be realized that each society has its own needs, priorities, and carrying capacity, all of which must be carefully studied before setting the targets and selecting the methods for achieving

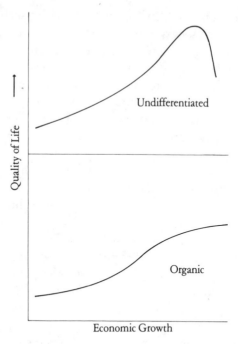

Figure 1.2. Projection of Quality of Life
with Type of Economic Growth

development goals. The task before contemporary societies, therefore, is to identify those components that constitute an improved quality of life for the people of their own societies, without jeopardizing the interests of other societies or preempting the choice of options for future generations. Once the relative importance of the components of quality of life is determined, then growth policies aimed at providing and sustaining these components can be developed. Thus an *optimum*, *sustainable* quality of life, existing within the carrying capacity set by the milieu of local, regional, and even international resources, is the goal of organic growth.

Naturally enough, it is easier to point to the absence of this steady-state condition of homeostasis from the present order than it is to outline a plan for the achievement of a new world model. There is, nevertheless, a growing literature describing the economic, social, environmental, political, and moral dimensions of such a steady-state economic model.[11] Although a full treatment of this complex subject is beyond the scope of this book, in our concluding chapter we outline our ideas on a variety of strategies that might promote the modification of the growthmania model and, ultimately, provide an orderly transition to a steady-state economy.

ENVIRONMENTAL PROBLEMS AND QUALITY OF LIFE

If quality of life is to be a sustainable optimum, it follows that environmental problems will be kept at a minimum. In recent years "quality of life" has become a popular term for a concept that is rarely defined rigorously. Every culture will probably place a different emphasis upon the many dimensions of an optimum quality of life, just as each culture varies in its perception of environmental problems. However, we believe that there are three major dimensions of this quality of life concept which must ultimately be met if environmental problems are to be avoided. They are:

(a) Maintenance of ecosystem and economic system balance.
(b) Satisfaction of basic physical needs for human development.
(c) Satisfaction of basic social needs for human development.

The main data chapters of this book (chapters 3 to 5) are structured around these quality of life dimensions. They demonstrate the degree to which the components of quality of life are being satisfied in different regions of the world. However, it must be emphasized that an optimum quality of life is not provided solely by a condition of stability and the satisfaction of material needs; on the contrary, these chapters show that environmental problems can arise through the denial of man's fundamental sociopolitical rights such as equality of opportunity, access to knowledge and information, and participation in planning in bringing about national development. Furthermore, even though we have repeatedly acknowledged that the relative weight attributed to each quality of life component will vary from society to society, we contend that excessive emphasis given to any one component at the expense or neglect of others will most probably limit the ability of a society to achieve an optimum and sustainable quality of life.

ENVIRONMENTAL PROBLEMS: A SUMMARY

It is our belief that the major environmental problems facing human society today stem directly from a model of world development that has paid little heed to the universal achievement and maintenance of an adequate quality of human life. The instabilities and disruptions evident in the environment result from man's failure to recognize the necessity of maintaining ecosystem balance and to plan effectively toward that end. The poverty, inequality, and dependency so apparent in periphery societies have their roots in the failure of the growthmania model to provide a condition of equity. The unrealistic perceptions and inadequate knowledge evident in large numbers of people are perpetuated by the limitations of educational opportunities and by the manipulation of information built into most contemporary societies. The lack of participation in those crucial decisions that affect one's own life is the logical product of systems that monopolize power. And the unemployment and poor conditions of work increasingly plaguing societies are inseparably intertwined with the instabilities created by undifferentiated growth.

These major problems that are the antithesis of an improved quality of life affect the physical and social environment of people all over the world. It is to an analysis of these problems and their relationship to growth and culture that the following chapters are directed.

Notes to Chapter 1

1. The concepts of "undifferentiated" and "organic" growth have been introduced and discussed more fully in Mihajlo Mesarovic and Edward Pestel, *Mankind at the Turning Point*, pp. 1–9.

2. Herman E. Daly, "The Steady-State Economy: Toward a Political Economy of Biophysical Equilibrium and Moral Growth," pp. 149–150.

3. Negative feedback is the impulse fed back from the output of a self-regulatory system to the control center, when the output is too far on one side of a preset equilibrium point. "Negative" refers to the fact that the sign is changed in the control device to bring the output back to equilibrium. In simpler terms, in a negative feedback loop a change in one element is transmitted around the loop until it comes back to change that element in a direction *opposite* to the original change. A fuller description of both *negative* and *positive* feedback loops is given in Donella H. Meadows et al., *The Limits to Growth*, pp. 38–45.

4. W. W. Rostow, *The Stages of Economic Growth: A Non-Communist Manifesto*, p. 58.

5. John M. Culbertson, *Economic Development: An Ecological Approach*. Harry T. Oshima, "Development and Mass Communication: A Re-examination."

6. Oshima, "Development and Mass Communication."

7. Raymond F. Dasmann, John P. Milton, and Peter H. Freeman, *Ecological Principles for Economic Development*.

8. These figures are calculated from data given in *World Bank Atlas: Population Per Capita Product and Growth Rates, 1974*. The 110 countries analyzed exclude the centrally planned economies and the 11 listed petroleum-exporting countries (Algeria, Ecuador, Gabon, Indonesia, Iran, Iraq, Kuwait, Libyan Arab Republic, Nigeria, Saudi Arabia, and Venezuela). While most of the latter are poor developing countries (their mean 1972 GNP per capita was only U.S.$280), they have been excluded, since their growth rates are much higher because of the rapid increase in the export prices for their petroleum. This rapid economic development does not conform to the classical, urban-based, capital-intensive model of industrial development.

9. E. F. Schumacher, *Small Is Beautiful: Economics as if People Mattered*, pp. 154–160.

10. The terms *center* and *periphery* refer to the comparative access to and control over power and benefits which various individuals, societies, and socioeconomic groups enjoy both in inter- and intra-national contexts. The center-periphery terminology is increasingly replacing phrases such as elites-masses, rich-poor, and developed-developing in social science literature. (For an excellent treatment of the center-periphery concept see Johan Galtung, "A Structural Theory of Imperialism.")

11. The dimensions of the steady-state have been treated in the writing of many scholars, ranging from that of John Stuart Mill over a century ago to the modern works of, among others: Kenneth E. Boulding, Daniel Burhans, Herman E. Daly, Jay Forrester, John Kenneth Galbraith, Johan Galtung, Garrett Hardin, Robert Heilbronner, Donella H. and Dennis L. Meadows, Howard T. Odum, Jørgen Randers, and Robert Theobald. An important collection of writings on the subject has been edited by Herman E. Daly in *Toward a Steady-State Economy*.

2
Cultural Dimensions
of Environmental Problems

The major environmental problems briefly discussed in the preceding chapter have their roots in a complex array of forces. One of the most important of these forces is culture, or more specifically, the cultural belief-systems that provide so many of the characteristics of social behavior. It seems logical, therefore, that our analysis of the major environmental problems confronting mankind begin with an investigation into several key categories of cultural beliefs that have direct relevance to environmental questions.

These categories are as follows:
Man and the environment
The nature of society
The growth and development of society
The socioeconomic system
The role and potential of technology

Since it has already been suggested that today's dominant development model, the quantitative growthmania approach, has contributed significantly to environmental problems, it becomes important that the belief systems underlying this influential model be identified. To facilitate this identification, we will first describe in broad terms the elements of the dominant technological culture's belief system (hereafter, the "technoculture"[1]), and then offer a few explanations of how and why the system has developed. Following these introductory remarks, we will explore some eighteen beliefs we identify as critical to the technoculture and contrast each with other beliefs that constitute alternative paradigms.

In attempting to understand the characteristics of the dominant technological culture, it is helpful to realize that a culture and a nation are not necessarily one and the same entity. That is, when we speak of a technoculture we are not referring to any one nation or set of nations but rather to a paradigm that transcends national identity and political ideology. Furthermore, the technoculture does not necessarily conform to any one economic system. Instead, it combines a wide range of beliefs and priorities into a loosely organized system in which quantitative growth and dependence on technology are the dominant concerns.

Further insight into the technoculture belief system can, of course, be gained through a study of the numerous writings that deal with the origins of cultures. However, since an exhaustive historical study is beyond the scope of this book, we will merely focus on several recent phenomena that can help accentuate the importance of understanding the historical roots of the technoculture.

The first of these historical phenomena is urbanization. As Spengler and Ortega y Gasset point out,[2] urbanization has helped to deemphasize the role resources and the natural world play in human affairs. And although big cities have existed in many earlier cultures and civilizations, never before have so many people lived in a world where they were so completely cut off from any understanding of the fragility and finiteness of resources and of the effort required to develop these resources. One of the results of this separation from reality perception is a widespread assumption that resources are virtually limitless, a basic assumption of the technoculture.

Another factor that has contributed to the notion of resource limitlessness can be found in Western history. European man has just come through four centuries of the most incredibly lucky salvations imaginable. The run of luck has come to be interpreted as a product of man's genius. By the time European populations were becoming large enough to put pressure on resources, large land areas in what are now North America, Africa, India, Australia, and Latin America became available to accommodate the overflow. In many of these regions the Europeans found resources in great abundance. In North America, for example, good agricultural land; trees for building and for fuel; herds of buffalo for meat, hides, leather, and fertilizer; and the sperm whale for illuminant, lubricants, bones, and meat, were all plentiful. Three of these resources were used in such large quantities that, by 1885, buffalo had been reduced from 75 million animals to under 200, and sperm whales and trees were also significantly reduced. But just as resource depletion was becoming serious, two more resources were discovered to replace the trees and sperm whale: coal and oil. Still later, gas was developed and used commercially at a rapidly increasing rate. Then, by the middle of the twentieth century, atomic energy was discovered.

But now as we enter the fourth quarter of the twentieth century the string of luck has run out. There is no more land to be discovered, the supply of fossil fuels is running out, and nuclear energy is highly suspect as a viable substitute, considering its great expense, inconvenience, and, most of all, its potential danger. And yet, ten to fifteen generations of Westerners have internalized an incorrect lesson; namely, that it is possible to make profligately irresponsible and wasteful use of natural resources without facing major tragedy. This belief is an important characteristic of the technoculture.

Another important factor in the development of the technoculture's belief system is that few humans ever get a chance to develop a mature sense of "before" and "after" that would enable them to see the extent to which the world has been ruined and the speed with which the destruction has occurred. Thus, for example, few people have any real appreciation of the change in stocks in whales, because they rarely see whales, and few understand the wholesale destruction of the Indian lion, the Tasmanian devil, or the North American bison. One of the problems is that few records of animal abundance have been kept.[3] One of the best insights into the explanation as to why few people have this historical sense of resource depletion is found in the idea that, because historians are social scientists or humanists, they usually write about relations of human beings with each other, not their relations to resources.[4] Historians are seldom people who have to wrest resources from worn-out stocks or land. They usually live in cities and get their food from markets. By the time a civilization has wiped out its resource base and is on the decline, few historians have compiled any records. And those people doing the depleting, the ones in the best position to know most about the depletion, have little motive to record events accurately.

The development of a sense of before and after is also obstructed because civilizations shift sites after they disintegrate. Thus those citizens of Manhattan, São Paulo, Berlin, Tokyo, Moscow, or Sydney, who have little sense of how civilization can destroy its resource base, have few if any examples, such as Palmyra, Persepolis, Babylon, or Carthage, to visit and observe the consequences of resource destruction.

Still more troublesome is the evidence that civilizations have failed to see the value of setting aside and protecting representative natural areas or check plots that could serve as a benchmark against which the effects of civilization could be evaluated. Without these protected areas to use as comparisons, it is extremely difficult to understand the specifics of why and how a country has been devastated. It can always be argued later that the devastation resulted from a climatic change or drought and not from human misuse; for most people are reluctant to face the fact that a once splendid land, now barren, has been totally ruined by civilization. In a very few places where a check plot, wildlife refuge, or national park has been set aside and totally protected, the contrast between it and surrounding areas is overwhelming and revealing.

The tendency of people to accept as perfectly normal the limited experiences to which they have been exposed can further obstruct a sense of before and after. Not many people will speculate, for example, that the ruined landscape they have seen all their lives is the result of excessive human population pressure, and that a reduction of the population to a quarter its present level might create an impressive improvement in the situation. Also, the effects of such a reduction would show up so long after it began that few people would understand the cause-effect relationship. But even if given a choice, most people might well prefer to stay with the status quo, rather than do anything so drastic as agreeing to a rigidly enforced, population-wide reduction in the birth rate. Indeed, present educational systems do not train people to think in terms of the evaluation of options. Thus it simply does not occur to many people that there might well be a trade-off between very large numbers of people living very badly, and a smaller population living very well, even though such clear examples as the relationship between urban land prices and income are numerous.

Finally, the development of the technoculture has been greatly influenced by propaganda and advertising. Most large, powerful organizations put great resources into extolling the merits of expanded markets and increased resource consumption. They never mention that the benefits will accrue largely to a few people, and they certainly never mention the frequent cost: higher prices relative to income, pollution, resource depletion, a ruined landscape, terrible congestion, and problems of food supply, health, and mental disorder.

Although purposely limited, the above discussion of several recent influences on the development of technoculture beliefs helps show the depth and complexity of belief-formation processes. The belief system of the dominant technological culture that has emerged from these processes has many priority tenets. We have identified some of the ones we feel are pertinent to an understanding of environmental problems. A description of each of those beliefs now follows, and, for purposes of contrast, alternative belief paradigms are also discussed.

BELIEFS CONCERNING MAN AND THE ENVIRONMENT

1. *Technoculture belief*: Man exists separately from the natural world and is superior to it, having a right and responsibility to dominate it and use it in the interests of his own development (Dualism).

Dualism considers all phenomena in two separate categories: the human being and the nonhuman environment. The human being is treated as a separate entity who confronts the cosmos as an object and a challenge. New discoveries, new theories to conquer the universe, technology, science, and industry all become the thrust of man's response to nature. Thus, within this conceptualization, it becomes man's right, and sometimes even his duty, to dominate, conquer, and exploit resources for the benefit of mankind. This outlook has led to a series of "unbroken successes" in terms of technology and exploitation of resources, and has encouraged people to act and work on a rational base that frees man from theology and finds meaning in secularism. The ethical values under dualism emphasize the personal intent and objectives of a certain act. All actions are primarily subject to personal responsibility, not to considerations of a communal nature. Out of dualism have grown three dominant schools of thought: rationalism, empiricism, and materialism.

A contrary position: Man is a part of nature and should learn to live in harmony with it (Monism).

Monism relates the origin of the world's diversity to a single and unified source ("tout système philosophique qui considère l'ensemble des choses comme réductible à l'unité").[5] Under monism, a human being is considered as only one phenomenon among the diversified phenomena of the cosmos, with no special status among the phenomena. Being qualitatively equal to the rest of the universe, a human being has no mandate to confront or conquer the cosmos.

A cultural implication of this attitude is manifested in the form of the unbroken continuity. Under this cultural setting all living creatures will act in accordance with traditional behavior. Tradition, therefore, is seen as one of the fundamental foundations of life. Everything should follow the existing order and be bound to rules and regulations that are fixed and dramatized in the form of rites and myths.

This emphasis on the traditional way of life often creates a dependence on nature, although the extent of dependency may not necessarily be absolute. Thus, under monism, man and society must adjust to the environment rather than try to dominate or conquer it. In some respect, the environment under monism is perceived as a macrocosmos which constitutes a sacred totality. Indeed, environmental elements such as big trees, certain animals, fire, and water are sometimes even treated as sacred phenomena.

Another important belief of monism is communalism, a concept in which common interests are of first importance. This belief stands in complete contradiction to individualism, a primary tenet of dualism and the technoculture. A very common example of communalism can be found in the communal ownership of land in many parts of the developing nations. Typically a village, not an individual, owns land or forests. Only the community is permitted to cultivate the land. Aliens can use the land only with the consent of the community, generally upon payment of a certain amount of rent or royalty to the entire village. The community, not individual members, thus supervises utilization of the land.

Another good example of monism is found in the Indonesian *gotong royong*, a communal principle based on the attitude that common interests come first, and that individual interests should be sacrificed if they go against the common good. The human being is not primarily an individual, but merely one part of the total community.

It is thus obvious that monism may be somewhat resistant to an economic growth model that stresses individual accumulation and often deemphasizes communal needs. For under monism, possessions should rightly have more social than economic significance. It is not utility to the possessor which is most important but rather the good for society. Under such a belief system any attempt to rationalize the utilization of goods and services on grounds of giving advantage to certain individuals will have very little appeal. In such a social setting people do not work primarily for profit, but for satisfying needs. Work schedules and other endeavors are therefore often shaped according to customs and natural events rather than to rigid schedules based on efficiency goals.

Dualism, on the other hand, often leads to individualism and secularism, and as such is undergoing extensive questioning, even in the West. The persistent question is whether dualism's cultural attitudes can be justified under conditions of resource depletion, individual monopolization of power, and increasing inequality.

The crucial task of the modern world is to discover how we might take advantage of the valuable beliefs found in monism and those in dualism to develop a concept of man and nature that is appropriate to the contemporary world.

2. *Technoculture belief*: For the forseeable future, there are no limits on the number of humans this planet can support at a high standard of living. Technological innovation will be able to deal with any foreseeable problems. Indeed, the modern economy *makes* resources. (Petroleum was not a resource until the economy figured out what to do with it. In the same way, the economy will gradually make resources out of everything.) Once civilization rises to a high enough level, people can determine what they will do and, through exercise of will and ingenuity, do it. High civilizations are not limited, directed, or shaped by external factors.

A contrary position: All civilizations are limited, directed, and shaped by an extensive list of factors, including climate, space, the availability of energy, soil, forests, the amount of time available to solve critical problems, diversity, food availability, capital, technological know-how, and the like, all of which may be inadequate for the solution of critical problems. It is entirely possible for the population in any civilization to grow to a quantity that overwhelms the resource base. Malfunctions in government institutions, the inadequacy of Adam Smith's "invisible hand" in maintaining homeostasis, and numerous other factors, are involved.

There is an enormous amount of literature on this point, ranging from general treatments of cultural history that explain changes in attitudes, to highly technical controversies concerning a specific type of resource, such as trees or petroleum. From among this literature we cite two general interpretations.

> For the "common" man of all periods "life" had principally meant limitation, obligation, dependence; in a word, pressure. . . .

> The world which surrounds the new man from his birth does not compel him to limit himself in any fashion . . . ; on the contrary, it incites his appetite, which in principle can increase indefinitely.[6]

In short, in the past, a sense of being limited was a primary characteristic of most people's lives. Now, a primary characteristic is that some people feel unlimited, in spite of the fact that a massive amount of evidence indicates that a variety of limits are about to become very important. One of the most obvious of these limits is land shortage, a limitation that is inimical to the future growth of civilization in several ways. It means that urban land prices move so high that few people can earn enough to afford decent living quarters. Literally, the only solution is to lower the population so that demand drops relative to the supply of land. Also, no matter how much fertilizer is applied, there are limits to the amount of food that can be produced on one hectare of land. Thus, when all arable land has been converted to crop growing, a limit has been reached in the ability of a country to grow food. Finally, a new type of trap is showing up with respect to national economic development. In much of the world, most of the potentially productive land is already in cultivation, and anywhere from 26 to 60 percent of the rural population of developing countries has no land.[7] This land shortage contributes greatly to a mass migration to urban centers which, in many countries, simply overwhelms all urban services. The problem is further compounded because jobs cannot be created fast enough to absorb the rural unemployed.

As more and more land is converted from forest or wilderness to agriculture, and as more and more of that land is excessively used or mismanaged, a number of difficulties occur. Removal of forests causes a marked change in local microclimate, and can decrease precipitation and increase flooding downstream from the denuded watersheds.[8] As if this were not enough, there is a large, impressively documented literature arguing that the mismanagement of forests, soil, and irrigation has been a major determinant of the rise and fall of civilizations.[9] We have been surprised to discover that this body of literature appears to be almost totally unknown to most historians, who make almost no reference to forests, trees, soil management, or irrigation, in treatises on the rise and fall of ancient civilizations.

But land is only one of the significant limitations on mankind. The fact is well documented that at recent rates of increase in world energy consumption, all world supplies of oil and gas will be depleted within a few decades.[10] Time is also limited in the sense that there simply may not be enough time available to get a new energy technology in effect to replace an old one.

Or, mankind might also be limited by a lack of diversity. Competition may have so reduced the number of species or the number of corporations left on earth that the entire sociopolitical-economic-environmental system becomes wildly unstable. The availability of capital is also limited, not just in the developing countries where there is an inadequate supply to provide enough jobs for the labor force,[11] but in the developed countries as well, where capital is scarce for the many new ventures required (mass transit, urban renewal, new energy technologies, a revival of intercity trains, and others). And, of course, shortages of food might be the most critical limit of all.

Thus, the technoculture's belief system discourages a sobering acknowledgment of the finiteness of both man and the earth's resources.

BELIEFS CONCERNING THE NATURE OF SOCIETY

3. *Technoculture belief*: Society is an arrangement of numerous components, each with a rather specialized role to play. Society functions best when the expertise of each of the specialized components is improved. If problems arise in the system, the causes can be traced to one or several malfunctioning components. When the malfunction is cured, the problem will, most probably, be solved.

A *contrary position*: Society is primarily a systemic phenomenon, or expressed in more specific terms,

> Society is a whole system of integrated behaviors and patterns that cannot be effectively understood, acted upon, or predicted by dealing with any one or several of

the system's component parts. For society is indeed "greater" than the sum of its parts. More precisely, society creates new properties, propensities, and capabilities for its component parts that make their behavior within the interconnected system take on characteristics not necessarily existent in their individual behavior apart from the total system.[12]

Thus when a problem arises, the entire integrated system may have to be investigated. In many problems it well may be that without a wide-ranging systemic change the negative effects of the problem will, at best, merely be postponed.

Nowhere is the technoculture's compartmentalized view of society more evident than in its embrace of specialization as a priority value. Buckminster Fuller comments at length on the evils of specialization in the following passages.

We are in an age that assumes the narrowing trends of specialization to be logical, natural, and desirable . . . [However,] advancing science has now discovered that all the known cases of biological extinction have been caused by overspecialization, whose concentration of only selected genes sacrifices general adaptability. . . . Specialization has bred feelings of isolation, futility, and confusion in individuals. It has also resulted in the individual's leaving responsibility for thinking and social action to others. Specialization breeds biases that ultimately aggregate as international and ideological discord, which, in turn, leads to war.[13]

We are so specialized that one man discovers empirically how to release the energy of the atom, while another, unbeknownst to him, is ordered by his political factotum to make an atomic bomb by use of the secretly and anonymously published data. That gives much more expedient employment, which solves the politician's momentary problem, but requires that the politicians keep on preparing for further warring with other political states to keep their respective peoples employed. . . .[14]

The technoculture's obsession with parts rather than the systemic whole thus obstructs a realistic identification of the causes of problems, and greatly reduces society's ability to solve system-wide problems. Perceiving man as a potentially independent component of the total life system of the planet can lead to the wholesale disruption of the ecosystem. Viewing change as a phenomenon of parts within a system rather than as a systemically integrated phenomenon can lead to severe disruptions and alienations as various parts struggle for self-interested changes (or suppressions of change), many of which can ultimately cause devastation to the whole system, whether it be the ecosystem, species "system," or political-socioeconomic system.

4. *Technoculture belief*: Society evolves primarily in response to the ag-

gregate will of the populace. This aggregate will is reflected through the policy decisions of government leaders.

A contrary position: Society is largely influenced by dominant individuals, groups, and institutions, powerfully aided by clever propaganda.

The technoculture's assumption that the aggregate will is the guiding hand of social evolution shows up perhaps most clearly in the theory of the market system and in a leave-it-to-the-experts type of apathy that keeps public participation in decision-making to a minimum. This assumption is being strongly contested by numerous citizens groups who are finding that more and more policies are being made without the "aggregate will of the populace" ever having an opportunity to be expressed. Consequently, the public's interest is frequently damaged as food shortages, spoilage of the environment, economic chaos, and social alienation increasingly become the spin-off effects of policy programs.

It is through propaganda, the contrary position argues, that the public is led to *think* its will is being served. Or as some writers argue,[15] the public will is even created and manipulated, especially through the advertising media. The power of information manipulation is evident not only in blatant acts of censorship but in more subtle and sophisticated ways as well.

> . . . today we recognize that techniques go further. Psycho-analysis and sociology have passed into the sphere of technical application; one example of this is propaganda. Here the operation is of a moral, psychic, and spiritual character.[16]

5. *Technoculture belief*: It is important to stress an optimistic view of life. Life is not basically tragic. Life is, and of course *should* be, very easy and pleasant. Problems that occur can be overcome by expending more capital, using more technology, adding more profit incentives—and the good life goes on and on. Accordingly, good news should be emphasized, because if people *believe* the system is running well, there is a greater likelihood that the system *will* run well.

A contrary position: It is good to think positively but not to the point of twisting reality just to justify a policy or keep the populace believing in a particular system. The truth is that large-scale tragedies are facing humanity, and to suppress this reality will only make it more difficult for man to devise ways of forestalling tragedy.

As mentioned, an optimistic outlook on life bordering on the unrealistic has many of its roots in the Western historical experience. Good fortune and decisive action combined to create a rapid process of success that has led Western man to expect more of the same "good life." As Fennelly expresses it,

. . . Western man remains congenitally optimistic, and such an attitude is probably essential for his survival. If all of us despaired of the future, we would certainly lose our will to live, and there would cease to be a future. . . .[17]

Although Fennelly goes on to point out that ". . . it is equally important that we become fully aware of the hard realities of the contemporary world and of the dangers which threaten our society. . . ,"[18] the hard realities are often lost in the race for success. One of the reasons may be a dread of reality.

Added to all this is the universal *dread of reality*. We "pale-faces" have it, all of us, although we are seldom, and most of us never, conscious of it. It is the spiritual weakness of the "Late" man of the higher civilizations, who lives in his cities cut off from the peasant and the soil and thereby from the *natural* experiencing of destiny, time, and death.[19]

In earlier periods of civilization widespread epidemics and other tragedies gave no firm grounds for unbounded optimism. And as chapter 4 reveals, in many cultures today conditions of life are such that a sense of tragedy and hopelessness often overwhelms whatever feelings of optimism may be present. But for the modern technological culture to assume that the eradication of epidemics, the wizardry of machines, and the enormous power of the new technology ensure man a glorious future may be the height of folly. For the very power of which the technoculture is so proud is creating unforeseen and complex phenomena that make past dangers seem minuscule. As Ortega y Gasset expresses it,

Every destiny is dramatic, tragic in its deepest meaning. Whoever has not felt the danger of our times palpitating under his hand, has not really penetrated to the vitals of destiny, he has merely pricked its surface.[20]

BELIEFS CONCERNING THE GROWTH AND DEVELOPMENT OF SOCIETY

6. *Technoculture belief*: The aim of society should be to maximize gross output from all processes.

A *contrary position*: Maximizing *net* output should be the desideratum, and this may lead to very different strategies than those which maximize gross output.

This contrary point of view requires explanation, because most people assume that net output is the current target of society. But it is net output measured in *money* and *profit*, not in other variables. This profit maximization ethos guarantees very high rates of flow through the system of all other variables, such as matter and energy (and profligately wasteful use of space, human time, and diversity). Three excerpts from Odum[21] point to a very different perspective.

> The biosphere with industrial man suddenly added is like a balanced aquarium into which large animals are introduced. Consumption temporarily exceeds production, the balance is upset, the products of respiration accumulate, and the fuels for consumption become scarcer and scarcer until production is sufficiently accelerated and respiration is balanced. In some experimental systems balance is achieved only after the large consumers which originally started the imbalance are dead. Will this happen to man?[22]

> A very cruel illusion was generated because the citizen, his teachers, and his leaders did not understand the energetics involved and the various means by which the energies entering a complex system are fed back as subsidies indirectly into all parts of the network. The great conceit of industrial man imagined that his progress in agricultural yields was due to new know-how in the use of the sun. A whole generation of citizens thought that the carrying capacity of the earth was proportional to the amount of land under cultivation and that higher efficiencies in using the energy of the sun had arrived. This is a sad hoax, for industrial man no longer eats potatoes made from solar energy; now he eats potatoes partly made of oil.[23]

> Much of the power flow that supports the agriculture is not spent on the farm but is spent in the cities to manufacture chemicals, build tractors, develop varieties, make fertilizers, and provide input and output marketing systems which in turn maintain mobs of administrators and clerks who hold the system together. As we stand on the edge of the vast fields of grain with tractors and production as far as the eye can see, we are tempted to think man has mastered nature, but the plain truth is that he is overcoming bottlenecks and providing subsidy from fossil fuel.[24]

Thus, while most people think that net output is being optimized, it is gross output with respect to energy (and matter) that is being optimized, making the true efficiency of the system quite low. This problem runs all through modern society. Pimentel and John and Carol Steinhart[25] have shown that agriculture now produces as little as 10 percent of the energy it consumes; and in atomic energy there is a lively debate over the net energy output, partly because of the enormous energy cost of nuclear fuel enrichment. Only recently has research begun to determine the real net efficiency of various processes in terms of variables other than money.

7. *Technoculture belief*: Exponential economic growth is inevitable, desirable, and necessary in order to solve social and economic problems. The most vigorous and progressive nations are those which have maintained high rates of growth in energy consumption and the use of natural resources.

Contrary positions: (1) Cyclical behavior is inevitable. (2) Culture and economy flourish best in a stable state and it is desirable, and possible, to convert our present growthmania civilization to a viable steady state.

The cyclical theory holds that economic and population growth are not inevitable. Rather, modern civilization, like all others, will complete a cycle of birth, growth, decay, and disintegration. This cycle is difficult to resist because it is strongly influenced by dynamic changes in people's value systems, resulting in part from excessive urbanization. Urban population masses increasingly lose a realistic concept of the dependence of civilization on wise use of resources. Further, as civilizations become more complex, it takes a very high level of sophistication to ensure that human beings will gain mastery over, rather than become slaves to, human institutions and techniques.

Toynbee[26] has popularized the notion that civilizations go through a historical pattern of genesis, growth, breakdown, and disintegration. However, he believes that a possible scenario for the future of mankind is evolution into a universal state, which might be permanent. Sorokin[27] has assembled a massive amount of statistical evidence showing that, over the long term, the affairs of man have a strong tendency to fluctuate or cycle, rather than remain in a steady state, or grow indefinitely. And as we have mentioned, Spengler and Ortega y Gasset have both presented a convincing hypothesis to the effect that urbanization is the key to the disintegration of civilization, because it promotes an unrealistic view of the world amongst great masses of people.

> . . . the Megalopolis . . . is found arising in the Late period of all Cultures. Into this world of stone and petrifaction flock ever-growing crowds of peasant folk uprooted from the land, the "masses" in the terrifying sense, formless human sand from which artificial and therefore fleeting figures can be kneaded: parties, organizations modelled on program and ideal, but in which that inherent power of growth that the course of the generations had saturated with tradition, and that most of all expresses itself in the fruitfulness of all life—the instinct for the permanence of family and race—is extinct.[28]

> How is this possible? How can man withdraw himself from the fields? Where will he go, since the earth is one huge, unbounded field? Quite simple; he will mark off a portion of this field by means of walls . . . . Here you have the public square. It is not, like the house, an "interior" shut in from above, . . . it is purely and simply the negation of the fields. The square, thanks to the walls which enclose it, is a portion of the countryside which turns its back on the rest, eliminates the rest and sets up in opposition to it.[29]

The significance this belief of the technoculture holds for environmental problems is found in the disturbing fact that a large number of people do not acknowledge the need for civilization to operate within certain limits. Recognition of these limits is increasing, however, and is leading to a growing acceptance of the concept of a steady state, which Herman Daly defines as

> . . . a constant stock of *physical* wealth (capital), and a constant stock of people (population). Naturally these stocks do not remain constant by themselves. People die, and wealth is physically consumed—that is, worn out, depreciated. Therefore the stocks must be maintained by a rate of inflow (birth, production) equal to the rate of outflow (death, consumption).[30]

This constant balance of stocks can be accomplished by maintaining a low birth rate and an equally low death rate, and a low production level and an equally low consumption level. High life expectancy, greater durability of goods, and less time sacrificed to production are all benefits accruing from a condition of steady state.

Lest anyone think this emphasis on a low profile is tantamount to nongrowth, let us go back to one of the first proponents of a "stationary state" concept, John Stuart Mill.

> It is scarcely necessary to remark that a stationary condition of capital and population implies no stationary state of human improvement. There would be as much scope as ever for all kinds of mental culture, and moral and social progress; as much room for improving the Art of Living and much more likelihood of its being improved when minds cease to be engrossed by the art of getting on.[31]

Daly further accentuates the value of a steady state by discussing the consequences of policies obsessed with growth of GNP.

> At some point . . . an extra unit of GNP costs more than it is worth. Technological advances can put off this point, but not forever. Indeed it may bring it to pass sooner because more powerful technologies tend to provoke more powerful ecological backlashes and to be more disruptive of habits and emotions.[32]

The technoculture also frequently infers that high population growth leads to progress and vigor. This inference is opposed just as strongly as is the exponential economic growth belief. It is not at all clear that culture flourishes best in states with high rates of population growth. In one possible area of "progress and vigor," book production, the opposite seems true. Countries with the highest rates of book production (new titles published per capita per year) have had some of the lowest population growth rates of all countries. Indeed high rates of population growth may be inimical to development and transmission of culture between generations. Ortega y Gasset has made this same point, emphasizing that high rates of population increase mean that "heap after heap of human beings have been dumped on to the historic scene at such an accelerated rate, that it has been difficult to saturate them with traditional culture."[33]

8. *Technoculture belief*: The socioeconomic system of modern society has certain built-in forces (such as the economic "invisible hand" of Adam Smith) which are innately adequate to maintain stability of the socio-economic system. There is little if any danger that the system could suddenly go into relaxation oscillations (fluctuations of ever-increasing amplitude).

A contrary position: Stability and resilience of complex systems can be endangered if the complexity becomes excessive, or if there is excessive homogeneity, or a loss of homeostasis (self-regulatory ability). (See chapter 3.)

This subject can be approached on two levels: the empirical and the theoretical. Agricultural experts have empirically discovered that continued intensive cropping increases the possibility of instability in food supply, largely by endangering the soil structure.[34] Many other writers note the possibility of great instability introduced into society by scientific and technological "solutions" which actually do great harm to society and man.[35]

As will be discussed in chapter 3, a whole new perspective has recently emerged suggesting that stability theories may have parallel applications in both ecological and socioeconomic systems. Using general mathematical models, R. M. May has shown that increasing complexity leads to decreasing stability.[36] However, if a system has gone through a long process of evolution, it will likely evolve strategies that work against this general principle. The problem is, of course, that man-made socioeconomic systems rarely evolve in response to any rational plan and have neither stability nor resiliency mechanisms built into the system. Holling and Fiering[37] point out that in these complex times of flux, socioeconomic systems desperately need to be resilient enough to recover from numerous shocks, and that man's mismanagement of the economy could destroy this vital resilience.

9. *Technoculture belief*: Looking far into the future is a low priority. The fast-moving times necessitate making decisions from a short-term point of view; and short-term, observable successes will all add up to long-term successes. Besides, a society can always lengthen its perceptions if needed.

A contrary position: A long look ahead is mandatory, and may lead to a very different sequence of policies than will short-term vision. Further, it may not be true that society can increase the span of its perception. Certain beliefs can entrap a culture within an increasingly closed pattern of short-term vision, decisions, and commitments.

In understanding this debate on long-term versus short-term, it is helpful to explore the significance of multistage decision processes. Suppose we have a phenomenon or system which is being managed at each time-point within a series of times, 1, 2, 3, . . . n, with actions being taken at each of these times so as to optimize the performance of the system. One way of doing this is to take the policy which produces the best result over the following time interval and make it the policy for the present time interval. But this policy might be suboptimal over the whole lifetime of the system. A more sophisticated procedure is to pick for the present time periods that policy which produces the optimal result over the *entire* sequence of time periods beginning with the following period and extending to the end of the lifetime of the system (n). A considerable theory of such methodology has been developed by Bellman.[38] While this type of methodology has been applied to subsystems, no attempt has been made to apply it to the entire economic or socioeconomic system. There may be a very deep explanation as to why there has not been more application.

> Technique demands the most rapid possible application; the problems of our day are evolving rapidly and require immediate solutions. . . . It would be foolish not to use the available means. But there is never time to estimate all the repercussions. And, in any case, they are most often unforeseeable. The more we understand the interrelation of all disciplines and the interaction of the instruments, the less time there is to measure these effects accurately.
>
> Moreover, technique demands the most immediate application because it is so expensive. It must "pay off," in money, prestige, or force. . . . There is no time for precautions when the distribution of dividends or the salvation of the proletariat is at stake.[39]

Georgescu-Roegen[40] speaks of the very long view:

> Yet no population expert seems to have raised the far more vital question for mankind's future: How long can a given world population—be it of one billion or of forty-five billion—be maintained? Only if we raise this question can we see how complicated the population problem is. Even the analytical concept of optimum population, on which many population studies have been erected, emerges as an inept fiction.

Society does not now perceive the future as a sequence of times at which optimal policies must be selected, each of which is optimal with respect to the remainder of the sequence. Yet there is a definite need for this perceptual approach. In numerous fields the short view has made problems worse, or made a temporary problem into a permanent one (freeways, pesticides, the Green Revolution). But now we are facing more and more situations, like the energy crisis, in which the short view will have calamitous effects. It will take thirty years at least to get new energy technologies in place to replace oil and gas when, shortly after the turn of the century, they have become largely depleted. This means, of course, that we should begin to plan for that day. But the short-term view inhibits this essential task.

10. *Technoculture belief*: Material affluence is a priority goal that, when achieved, can bring happiness. The path of growth that leads to material affluence winds onward and upward through industrialization and automation and the high production levels they bring. Man must be free to release his enterprise along this path. The "simple life" of yesteryear was an underutilization of the best of man's potential. Now man has advanced to a stage where his system of technology and the institutions it has created can carry humanity to even greater heights.

A contrary position: Some of the best ideas underlying a position contrary to this technoculture belief come from the writings of Mahatma Gandhi.[41] Inspired in several conceptual areas by Henry Thoreau, Gandhi emphasized that an increase in material affluence was positive only if it helped the moral and spiritual advancement of the individual and society. The growth that mattered to Gandhi was the "growth of the soul." Thus man and society will be best served by a curtailment of demand and material desires. It is in this curtailment that man finds true freedom, the freedom from wants, passion, and greed that leads to a fuller life.

As one of the major threats to a healthy, fuller life, Gandhi focused on industrialization.

> Industrialism is, I am afraid, going to be a curse for mankind. Industrialism depends entirely on your capacity to exploit, on foreign markets being open to you, and on the absence of competitors. . . . The future of industrialism is dark. . . . And my fundamental objection to machinery rests on the fact that it is machinery that has enabled these [industrialized] nations to exploit others. . . . Today machinery merely helps a few to ride on the back of millions. The impetus behind it all is not the philanthropy to save labour, but greed.

Although opposed to exploitive industrialization, Gandhi was not against the judicious application of science and technology. Explaining the practical side of the question, he said,

> Machinery has its place; it has come to stay. . . . I am not against machinery as such. The Charkha (hand spinning wheel) itself, for that matter, is machinery. But I am a determined foe of all machinery that is designed for exploitation of people.

Akin to the exploitation of people is the exploitation of natural resources. For to Gandhi and other Eastern thinkers, the continuum and harmony linking man and nature must be respected, and the assets of nature, being near-sacred entities, must be preserved.

Another great resource of priority concern to Gandhi was human labor. Indeed, it represented to him the greatest potential capital, and as such must be utilized to its fullest (jobs for *all* people) if society were to realize its greatest potential. Security against unemployment thus should be the first criterion of every healthy society. If this essential objective is sacrificed, then all other measures of economic development cannot bear fruit. Accordingly, the use of machines must be secondary to the gainful employment of man. Or, as Thoreau expressed it, "We do not ride upon the railroads; but the railroads ride upon us." By using this priority arrangement to guide policy, the potential environmental and social costs caused by the indiscriminate adoption of technology can be minimized.

But the control of ever-growing industrialization, automation, and material desires cannot be achieved in isolation. Our values and attitude toward life have to be carefully examined and redefined. We cannot afford to control industrial-consumerism without reducing our wants and limiting luxuries. Gandhi believed in "plain living and high thinking" and emphasized that "man's happiness really lies in contentment. He who is discontented, however much he possesses, becomes a slave to his desires."

Thus, Gandhi's message to the problem-ridden modern society is that every human being should lead a simple, austere life, reduce his needs to the minimum, and avoid wastage of finite resources. Unless this is practiced widely, all that is done at the higher intellectual and political levels will have little perceptible effect. For Gandhi was convinced that man is superior to the systems and institutions he has created. If these systems, institutions, and technologies are allowed to gain control over man, the self-reliant community that should be the ultimate goal of society will be buried under a deluge of exploitation, totalitarianism, and environmental problems.

BELIEFS CONCERNING THE SOCIOECONOMIC SYSTEM

11. *Technoculture belief*: Only monetary measures of the functioning of society are required, because all important social parameters can ultimately be expressed in monetary terms. The main "efficiency" which needs to be discussed and sought is *economic* efficiency, or profitability. It is quite appropriate and desirable to use benefit/cost ratios as the criterion for evaluating the performance of all social systems, including government, education, research, and the arts.

A contrary position: Environmental quality, aesthetic measures, and many other important aspects of society (including some economic variables) cannot be adequately expressed in purely monetary terms. Many other measures of "efficiency" are highly important and should be major inputs to the policy-making process. If only economic efficiency is pursued as a goal, it may ultimately have a negative effect on society as a whole.

A remarkable number of economists are becoming extremely critical of the focus by economics on purely monetary measures. The following quotations, by *economists*, are illustrative.

> The judgement of economics . . . is an extremely fragmentary judgement; out of the large number of aspects which in real life have to be seen and judged together before a decision can be taken, economics supplies only one—whether a thing yields a money profit to those who undertake it or not.[42]

> The economist forgot about physical dimensions long ago and centered his attention on value. But the fact that wealth is measured in value units does not annihilate its physical dimensions. Economists may continue to maximize value, and value could conceivably grow forever, but the physical mass in which value inheres must conform to a steady state, and the constraints of physical constancy on value growth will be severe and must be respected.[43]

> Nothing could, therefore, be further from the truth than the notion that the economic process is an isolated, circular affair—as Marxist and standard analysis represent it. The economic process is solidly anchored to a material base which is subject to definite constraints. It is because of these constraints that the economic process has a unidirectional irrevocable evolution. In the economic world only money circulates back and forth between one economic sector and another. . . . In retrospect it appears that the economists of both persuasions have succumbed to the worst economic fetishism—money fetishism.[44]

Given these criticisms by economists, it is interesting to see what specialists in other fields say about the implications of using "efficiency" as a desideratum.

> . . . "economically efficient" farming, in a cash-crop economy, is far more liable than "inefficient" subsistence farming to destroy soil fertility. That this should be so is not surprising: the advantage of subsistence farming in terms of soil fertility inheres in the relationship between the soil, and the needs and interests of the men who work it.[45]

> In liberating the city from the car we will make the city efficient, ironically, just as Henry Ford made his auto factory efficient with the assembly line. But our efficiency will be organized for people—their behavior, their bodies, their senses, their associations, and even their casual inclinations. It will not accelerate the incestuous cycle of runaway production and compulsive consumption. The environment will be made free for men, not wild machines.[46]

While experts press home the argument that freeways are three to five times more efficient per lane for moving vehicles than ordinary thoroughfares, they rarely point out that rapid transit can be twenty to thirty times more efficient than a freeway for moving persons. Automobiles are thus terribly extravagant brokers between man and free mobility.[47]

The preceding quotations lead us to suggest that if efficiency measures other than purely economic ones are used (for example, people moved per hour/foot width of right of way), the shape and direction of policies will be changed for the overall benefit of society. Thus the world can be seen through new glasses when space and the use of human time are regarded as important priorities to optimize, not just as means to profit.

> Man will truly prosper only when the dollar is no longer the fundamental measure of human progress. . . . Two cars in every garage simply destroys real prosperity. The organized waste now employed by the economy to maintain its phenomenal output—to make the city grossly inefficient and therefore more consumptive—will be cut out like a malignant tumor.[48]

The preoccupation with money as a universal measure is perceived as being a symptom of the decline of civilizations by numerous scholars. Spengler[49] postulates that with the rising importance of urbanization in any culture, money replaces goods as the system of value. This money value system works not for needs, but for sales and profit. Terms like *speculation*, *gain*, and *acquisition* come to be important descriptors of social functioning. Thinking in terms of money becomes the enemy of conservation of resources, since resources exist purely to be converted into financial energy. Spengler's hypothesis is arresting, given the typical modern observation that "Everywhere we turn we see the consequence of an economic policy that does not recognize as the number one priority the production of crops on crop lands. . . . there are thousands of acres of non-agricultural or marginal land suitable for homesites and industry. The only consideration now seems to be the easiest profit to the developer."[50]

12. *Technoculture belief*: "Bigness" should be a desideratum in all types of activities due to the principle of economies of scale (decline in the cost per unit as the number of units produced increases).

A contrary position: Bigness can become excessive and harmful.

Four basically different types of arguments have been advanced in opposition to bigness: it ultimately becomes uneconomic; it is destructive to the environment and dehumanizing to man; it decreases the degree of organization of matter and energy on the planet until ultimately the process approaches irreversibility; and it is inimical to diversity, thus increasing instability. (See chapter 3.)

One author notes that there may now be evidence showing decreasing returns from science and technology because of diseconomies of scale occasioned by the very large size of the operation.[51] Another points out that small operations, and small communities, are less likely to be environmentally destructive (including, of course, irreversible soil destruction).[52] And yet a third observes that "better and bigger" implies more pollution, and that recycling, or waste disposal, involves additional low entropy.[53]

The sharpness of the contrast between conflicting points of view about the value of economies of scale is astonishing. One of the best-known proponents of further population growth as a means of achieving economies of scale is Colin Clark, from whom the following is a typical statement.

> A number of economists have shown the factors which cause population growth usually have a beneficial and not adverse effect upon economic growth. By increasing the proportion of young men in the population compared with old, it raises the rate of savings (as has been seen in India). It also reduces per head capital requirements by spreading the cost of large "economic indivisibilities," such as the transport system, over greater numbers . . . a large and growing population gives the industrialist great opportunities for what are known as economies of scale.[54]

At the opposite pole, we have statements such as those of Schumacher: "In places like London, or Tokyo, or New York, the millions do not add to the city's real value but merely create enormous problems and produce human degradation."[55]

Hutchinson is even more explicit.

> The conurbation is a bad habit, not an economic necessity. It is inconvenient, inefficient, and expensive. It aggravates the problems of supply and transport, and of disposal . . . the supply of an adequate quantity of pure water . . . is a major, and costly, engineering enterprise. So also is the transport, both of work people and of supplies of food and raw materials. Further, the disposal of effluent and waste presents problems that have yet to be solved. The results of continuing uncontrolled growth are not to be contemplated. Yet in none of the great states has any system of control been devised. If this is development, the people of the small states may well conclude that they are fortunate to be excluded from it.
> This, though the most recent, is not the only form of development, and it is well to remember that most of man's great achievements were accomplished by small communities living in small independent states.[56]

The problem is that both points of view have merit. Whereas one social group, the industrialists and businessmen, benefits from scale, everyone else shares the cost. The economist would say that there is inequitable internalization of costs and benefits. Even though there has been a great deal of writing about this issue in the last decade, none of the actual or proposed mechanisms to deal with the problem has been effectively administered; and none will be until fundamental reforms (such as the means by which politicians raise money to pay for terribly expensive election campaigns) are accomplished. For it is unlikely that government will apply rigorous control against the hand that feeds it. As Earl Finbar Murphy[57] has noted, the problem in preventing pollution is not in getting effective laws on the books; the problem is in administering existing laws effectively.

13. *Technoculture belief*: Work is understood as being an activity for which one receives monetary payment; and the amount of pay greatly determines the respect awarded the worker.

A contrary position: Work should be understood as an activity whose purpose is to contribute to basic human fulfillment and the social welfare.

If work is perceived primarily as a commodity that is exchanged for wages, it is not surprising that human labor is reduced to economic values. But the ramifications of evaluating work in monetary terms go much deeper. Marx dealt with this issue in his writings on alienation.

> The alienation of the worker in his product means not only that his labor becomes an object, assumes an external existence, but that it exists independently, outside himself, and alien to him, and that it stands opposed to him as an autonomous power.[58]

The argument of the contrary position sees numerous other negative effects arising from the technoculture's attitude toward work. Inferior products, corruption, deemphasis on service jobs, excessive wages—all are prevalent outcomes of this work ethic.

14. *Technoculture belief*: Full employment (0-1 percent unemployment) is desirable, but highly improbable and not a major priority.

A contrary position: Full employment is a major priority.

Many writers are discussing various aspects of full employment now that the phenomenal productivity potential of modern industrial organization and science has made man seem obsolete to many growthmania advocates.[59]

> . . . machinery has not only been keeping prices down by replacing expensive labour—but also by replacing older and more expensive machinery and saving on capital costs as well as labour costs. . . . one cannot argue that we are yet close to the all-mechanised end of the machines-versus-labour continuum: globally, there is still ample scope for replacing labour. . . .[60]

There is clearly a logical inconsistency in the technoculture's belief system regarding the use of labor, an inconsistency that has implications for environmental problems. On the one hand, there is pressure to dispense with labor in many individual industries in order to increase "efficiency." Yet on the other hand, in the total of all industries, labor must be fully employed in order for society to achieve its economic goals. The way out of this dilemma is to keep starting up new enterprises fast enough to absorb the labor displaced by the increased efficiency of old enterprises. What if that isn't possible? Clearly, the value of "economic efficiency" is being pushed too hard: it not only is leading to wasteful use of matter and energy but also is putting people out of work. As Hutchinson, Yudelman,[61] and others have noted, this is a particularly serious problem in the developing countries. As Schumacher puts it:

> The system of mass production, based on sophisticated, highly capital-intensive, high energy-input dependent and human labour-saving technology, presupposes that you are already rich, for a great deal of capital investment is needed to establish one single workplace. The system of production by the masses mobilises the priceless resources which are possessed by all human beings, their clever brains and skillful hands, and supports them with first-class tools.[62]

15. *Technoculture belief*: Wage rates should be high and should continue to rise.

A contrary position: High wage rates can lead to a wasteful use of resources and unemployment.

Beliefs in opposition to the technoculture's attitude contend that when wage rates become very high relative to the value of resources, several undesirable things happen: service personnel become so expensive that services decline; people are replaced by machines because people become too expensive; and pollution and resource depletion increase as matter and energy become so cheap that few people have any motive to use them wisely. Some writers have noted other difficulties associated with very high wage rates.

> . . . British labor unions have become fully as powerful as those of the United States and equally unwilling to accept any control over wage rates. The result, of course, has been continuing inflation accompanied by a series of devaluations of the pound, and the end of the process does not appear to be in sight. . . .[63]

Schneider[64] notes that the seeds of civic tyranny represented by the automobile were sown, in part, through the high wages initiated by Henry Ford. The argument was, of course, that high wages would translate into higher quality of life. This is simply not true if, for example, the higher wages go to buy cars which then create traffic jams, increased pollution, and more displacement of people and land by highways.

Statistical analysis shows that increased wage rates also translate into more displacement of workers by automation (that is, the increased per-worker "productivity"). This displacement may not be a major problem if there are alternate jobs available. But when employers throughout a society are replacing workers by machines, the result is mass unemployment. There is considerable evidence that this is now happening in many countries. (See chapter 5.)

16. *Technoculture belief*: A person's objects or material possessions are extremely important. The private ownership of these objects is a vital right that must be protected.

A contrary position: Object-orientation should not be given such emphasis that people-orientation is neglected or taken for granted. Private ownership is highly conducive to utilization patterns that favor the special interests of the owner, interests which are often in conflict with the welfare of the society as a whole. Communal ownership, on the other hand, often avoids the social and environmental problems resulting from self-interested property utilization patterns.

The notion of private property is so basic to many cultures that not only are alternative types of ownership often ignored, but the negative consequences of private ownership are conveniently sublimated. To learn about the nature and implications of alternative patterns of ownership it might be helpful to look briefly at the culture of North American Indians.

> The Indians . . . had no conception of soil as property. Such an idea must have seemed to them immoral and irreligious; land tenure among them was not several but tribal, not personal but communal. There is no clearer nor more final answer to those who still believe that there is something "natural" about the idea of each man as a freehold smallholder, than the persistent, obstinate and despairing resistance offered by the Indians to the . . . suggestion . . . that land should be distributed among them in severalty, that every adult Indian should receive 160 acres of good land. . . .[65]

Placing great importance on private ownership of material objects may also have an effect on the much more basic problem of *object*-orientation becoming more important than *people*-orientation. A clue to this phenomenon is provided by modern sociological research on subcultures that have not yet been fully assimilated into the dominant culture. Herbert J. Gans, in a well-known study of native-born Americans of Italian parentage living in a Boston slum, noted that the group he studied was more person-oriented, and less object-oriented, than is the case in the dominant American culture. He defined these terms as follows.

> The difference between object-orientation and person-orientation is that whereas the former exists prior to and apart from a group, the latter is intrinsically tied to,

and is itself a product of, participation in the group. Object-oriented people may enter secondary groups or reshape primary ones in order to achieve their object goals; person-oriented ones develop their aspirations within a primary group in which they are members, and which they are not interested in leaving. Without such a group they have no aspirations, and for them, being alone is undesirable precisely because aspirations are so closely tied to the group.[66]

This example suggests that there may indeed be a linkage between person-orientation and emphasis on collective orientation. Numerous contemporary examples of collective or communal ownership could also be discussed, but all would merely add up to the same major point: communal ownership has a better chance of serving the needs of the community than does private ownership. Private ownership provides a structure that legitimizes self-interested policies that may, as in the case of corporate land ownership in Oklahoma's dustbowl, adversely affect the human and natural environment.

BELIEFS CONCERNING THE ROLE AND POTENTIAL OF TECHNOLOGY

17. *Technoculture belief*: Technology is good and provides the means of solving man's problems.

A contrary position: Technology cannot solve *all* problems and indeed often creates problems, some of which are quite severe.

It is surprising how vast and diverse the literature on this theme has become. Yet the contrary position has not really had a strong influence on most societies. The first response to a problem is invariably to seek more technology as the solution. The numerous alternatives are often ignored, and the possiblity that it might be technology itself that is *causing* a particular problem is rarely, if ever, considered. Three particularly well-documented areas in which technology may be counterproductive are the use of pesticides to control destructive insects, the use of freeways to relieve congestion, and the use of atomic power to relieve energy shortages.

In the first instance, it is now quite clear why there has been so little objective evaluation of pesticides. Alexander notes:

> There is no way the influence of chemical pesticide companies on entomology departments during my graduate-student days can be overemphasized. National entomology meetings sometimes seemed like one long series of hospitality suites rented by the pesticide people. . . . More insidious, perhaps, were the votes cast by hordes of direct and indirect representatives of the pesticide companies who filled the meeting halls.[67]

The result is that remarkably little experimentation has been done to determine if pests could be diminished in numbers by *removing* pesticides. In fact, the spruce budworm, a well-known and important pest of north-eastern U.S. and eastern Canada, only became a persistent pest after 1945 when pesticide spraying over large areas was conducted almost every year. Prior to that time, the species had attained importance in white spruce–balsam fir forests only for the last eight out of every thirty-two years in the forest cycle, at a time when the trees were overmature, near death, and ready to be replaced by a new generation of seedlings.

Hard evidence of the consequences of stopping spraying has come from obscure places not well penetrated by the influence of the chemical companies. Conway[68] and Wood[69] present startling reviews of experience in developing countries. The following excerpts from Wood are illustrative:

> As leaf-eating caterpillars became injurious consequently, more spraying was undertaken with a range of materials, inducing more pests of various groups to appear, and yet more insecticides to be used, until psychid bagworms caused total defoliation. Spraying stopped, after which several pests diminished rapidly in abundance.[70]

> Another instance of DDT-induced outbreak in a potential pest species was recorded for the leaf-roller. . . . The outbreak ended after the spraying ceased. The role of broad-spectrum insecticides in causing the original outbreaks was demonstrated experimentally. . . . A block of about 2 acres was sprayed recurrently with a small quantity of dieldrin, while periodic counts were made of the main bagworm . . . along three transects through the study area. . . . The pest gradually increased in, and spread from, the sprayed block, forming an infestation gradient.[71]

Technoculture beliefs also hold that freeways and other limited-access rights-of-way for cars relieve congestion. But the fact is that they create congestion. Increased freeway construction increases both city size and the proclivity to drive long distances within cities. In turn, these increase the requirement for foot-width of right of way per person, thereby creating the need for construction of more freeways. Critical experiments have shown that when a roadway is closed, congestion vanishes rather than worsens because *traffic* "vanishes."[72]

Atomic energy technology raises problems that may be much more serious than pesticides or freeways. Plutonium, the essential ingredient of breeder reactors, is not only the material out of which guerrilla groups could make atomic bombs, but is also one of the most toxic poisons known. Plutonium toxins are considered so likely to cause lung cancer that concentrations of one part per million billion is the permissible concentration in air. The release of this dangerous poison through weapons testing and possible breeder-reactor malfunction points to the need for highly dependable institutional and technological safeguards that could function perfectly for thousands of years, since the half-life of plutonium is 24,000 years. But no technology has ever worked perfectly, no matter how great the input from engineering man-power has been. Among the most carefully designed apparatus on earth have been the Russian and U.S. manned space-capsules, the Fermi breeder reactor, and the Boeing, Lockheed, and McDonnell-Douglas jumbo jets. All have failed at least once.

The number of instances in which technology has turned out badly has led some people to ask if this is an accident, or if there is some underlying feature inherent in all technology which commits it to turn out badly. In fact, this is the major thesis of alarming books by Ellul, Schwartz, and Vacca.

The conventional wisdom is that technology evolves in response to direction by mankind, so as to advance the public good. Ellul develops an elaborate and convincing hypothesis to the effect that once technology really begins developing, it evolves in accord with a causally directed system that is internal to technology, not imposed on it from the outside, by man. "There is no purpose or plan that is being progressively realized. There is not even a tendency toward human ends."[73]

Schwartz[74] presents a very interesting and comprehensively documented treatise on the functioning of technology. He argues that technology characteristically provides quasi-solutions to problems. These "solutions" in turn have three important sets of "residue" problems: the solutions are incomplete, they augment the original problem, and they give rise to secondary effects. The secondary effects, in turn, are treated with quasi-solutions, and they, in turn, are incomplete, augment the problems they were "solving," generate tertiary effects, and so on, ad infinitum.

Vacca[75] argues that for each of the various types of technology, be it traffic systems, communication, electrical power generation and distribution, waste disposal, or others, "saturation effects" show up as demands on the system increase exponentially. Further, because all such systems become more and more interactive, a systems failure in one becomes progressively more likely to generate a sequence of failures in the others, as in a sequence of falling dominoes.

The analyses of Schwartz and Vacca are particularly interesting because of who they are. Neither is a nature-lover living in the wilderness, angry about all technological advances of the last several centuries. Both are senior systems scientists with backgrounds in computers, and information and electronic systems.

Thus the contrary position holds that the more society becomes dependent on a very high level of technological sophistication, the more vulnerable it is to total systems breakdown. As Ortega y Gasset says,

. . . the common man, finding himself in a world so excellent, technically and socially, believes that it has been produced by nature, and never thinks of the personal efforts of highly-endowed individuals which the creation of this new world presupposed. Still less will he admit the notion that all these facilities still require the support of certain difficult human virtues, the least failure of which would cause the rapid disappearance of the whole magnificent edifice.[76]

So it need not be an economic catastrophe that brings the whole system crashing down. A large-scale *social* disruption could also cause a major fall. And technology's impact on this social dimension should not be underestimated. As Schumacher expresses it:

. . . modern technology has deprived man of the type of work that he enjoys most, creative, useful work with hands and brains, and given him plenty of work of a fragmented kind, most of which he does not enjoy at all. It has multiplied the number of people who are exceedingly busy doing kinds of work which, if it is productive at all, is so only in an indirect or "roundabout" way, and much of which would not be necessary at all if technology were rather less modern.[77]

18. *Technoculture belief*: Technology transfer from more "technologically sophisticated" to less sophisticated nations is all to the good.

A contrary position: The transfer should be mutual.

A rather startling contrast to the technoculture belief can be seen in the following quotation from Odum.

What a sad joke that a man from an industrial-agricultural region goes to an underdeveloped country to advise on improving agriculture. The only possible advice he is capable of giving from his experience is to tell the underdeveloped country to tap the nearest industrialized culture and set up another zone of fossil-fuel agriculture. As long as that country does not have the industrial fuel input, the advice should come the other way.[78]

The theme that there are horrendous defects in technology transfer between countries is also well developed in the writings of Yudelman, Butler, and Banerji.

It is a common observation that the ratio of labour to capital employed in the secondary industries being established in developing countries is as low—or almost as low—as it is in the labour-scarce economies of the developed countries. Either the relative market prices of labour and capital do not reflect the true relative social costs of the resources, or the imported technology of manufacturing does not permit a substitution of labour for capital.[79]

. . . there is cause for concern if technological changes that have begun in developing countries are replicating the Western structure of agriculture. Not the least reason for this is that the Western structure of agriculture has been shaped by notions of efficiency involving the assumption that displaced labour can always find alternative forms of remunerative employment.[80]

. . . in the absence of certain controls, the distribution of income and wealth among agricultural households will become increasingly skewed as the scope of technological change expands.[81]

In the preceding pages we have attempted to identify, however briefly, some of the most important beliefs of the dominant technological culture. Although a satisfactory summary of these beliefs might well be impossible, the following critical description adequately highlights the major themes characterizing the technoculture.

> Rooted in a network of exploitation, the technoculture begins with Man, the con-
> sumer, standing front and center in the universe. Man's planet and its resources
> exist to be used by Man in meeting his needs and satisfying his drive for consump-
> tion. It is in trying to satisfy this drive for material consumption that Man
> develops. Increased material production and consumption feed each other, with
> advances in technology aiding the process. Motivated by profit maximization and
> higher levels of consumption, the leading sectors of human society show the way
> toward "progress," the benefits of which then spread throughout society. Man's
> growth quantity can continue to increase in all aspects of life, and whatever prob-
> lems may arise can be solved by quickly repairing the faulty part and putting it
> back on the ascending track toward more and more progress.[82]

The cultural dimensions of environmental problems need to be examined thoroughly. Unless contemporary humanity comes to an understanding of the beliefs and attitudes that underlie many of the destructive policies and behaviors threatening us, the identification and implementation of alter-native paradigms and structures will at best be superficial. In the following chapters we will attempt to test these major technoculture beliefs against data gathered from a wide range of domestic and international scenes.

Notes to Chapter 2

1. We use the term *technoculture* as employed by Dudley Weeks ("The Dominant Network of Exploitation: A Technoculture in the Making") to describe "an interrelated set of values and perceptions of identity that when translated into socioeconomic and political policies becomes a complex network of exploitive interaction patterns in which environmental equilibrium and basic human needs are relegated to subordinate importance."

2. Oswald Spengler, *The Decline of the West*, vol. 2, *Perspectives of World History*; José Ortega y Gasset, *The Revolt of the Masses*.

3. Dary points out that the buffalo was so abundant that plainsmen may have felt that no one would have believed their estimates, even if they *had* kept records. D. A. Dary, *The Buffalo Book: The Full Saga of the American Animal*.

4. Vernon Gill Carter and Tom Dale, *Topsoil and Civilization*, pp. 89–91.

5. H. Lalande, as cited in O. Notohamidjojo, "On the Social and Cultural Aspects of Indonesian Development," *Warta Bksaksi*, Jakarta, 1974.

6. Ortega y Gasset, *Revolt of the Masses*, pp. 62–63.

7. David B. Grigg, *The Harsh Lands: A Study in Agricultural Development*, p. 111.

8. See Raphael Zon, *Forests and Water in the Light of Scientific Investigation*. In his work Zon cited several large studies as bases for his assertion. Further, the notion that trees have an effect on local climate persists today, as evidenced by Jen-hu Chang, *Climate and Agriculture: An Ecological Survey*.

9. George Perkins Marsh, *Man and Nature*; Graham V. Jacks and Robert O. Whyte, *Vanishing Lands: A World Survey of Soil Erosion*; Carter and Dale, *Topsoil and Civilization*; Edward Hyams, *Soil and Civilization*.

10. M. King Hubbert, "Energy Resources," pp. 157–242.

11. E. F. Schumacher, *Small Is Beautiful*, pp. 197–198.

12. Weeks, "Dominant Network of Exploitation," p. 1.

13. R. Buckminster Fuller, *Synergetics*, p. xxv.

14. Ibid., p. xxvii.

15. See the writings of Vance Packard, John Kenneth Galbraith, Kenneth B. Schneider, Ivan Illich, and numerous others.

16. Jacques Ellul, *The Technological Society*, pp. 14–15.

17. J. F. Fennelly, *Twilight of the Evening Lands*, pp. 173–174.

18. Ibid.

19. Oswald Spengler, *The Hour of Decision*, p. 7.

20. Ortega y Gasset, *Revolt of the Masses*, p. 23.

21. Howard T. Odum, *Environment, Power, and Society*.

22. Ibid., p. 18.

23. Ibid., pp. 115–116.

24. Ibid., p. 118.

25. David Pimentel et al., "Food Production and the Energy Crisis"; John S. Steinhart and Carol E. Steinhart, "Energy Use in the U.S. Food System."

26. Arnold Toynbee, *A Study of History*.

27. Pitirim A. Sorokin, *Social and Cultural Dynamics*, tables 1, 14, 15.

28. Spengler, *Hour of Decision*, pp. 87–88.

29. Ortega y Gasset, *Revolt of the Masses*, p. 165.

30. Herman E. Daly, *Steady-State Economy*, p. 14.

31. John Stuart Mill, *Principles of Political Economy*, as cited in Daly, *Steady-State Economy*, p. 13.

32. Daly, *Steady-State Economy*, p. 11.

33. Ortega y Gasset, *Revolt of the Masses*, p. 51.

34. From Joseph B. Hutchinson, *Farming and Food Supply: The Interdependence of Countryside and Town* (© 1972 Cambridge Univ. Press. Reprinted by permission), p. 11; Hyams, *Soil and Civilization*, p. 149.

35. Schumacher, *Small Is Beautiful*, p. 31; Alvin Toffler, *The Eco-Spasm Report: Why Our*

Economy Is Running Out of Control; Eugene S. Schwartz, *Overskill: Technology and the Myth of Efficiency;* Roberto Vacca, *The Coming Dark Age.*

36. Robert M. May, *Stability and Complexity in Model Ecosystems.*

37. C. S. Holling, "Resilience and Stability of Ecological Systems"; M. B. Fiering and C. S. Holling, *Management and Standards for Perturbed Ecosystems.*

38. Richard E. Bellman, *Dynamic Programming;* idem., *Adaptive Control Processes: A Guided Tour;* Richard E. Bellman and S. E. Dreyfus, *Applied Dynamic Programming.*

39. Ellul, *Technological Society*, pp. 105–106.

40. Nicholas Georgescu-Roegen, "The Entropy Law and the Economic Problem," p. 45.

41. The paragraphs on Gandhian philosophy are a compilation and condensation of ideas expressed in several of Gandhi's works, the most notable of which are *Man v. Machine* and *Modern v. Ancient Civilization.* "Man and His Environment," an address by Indira Gandhi at the Plenary Session of the United Nations Conference on Human Environment, Stockholm, 14 June 1972, also proved helpful.

42. Schumacher, *Small Is Beautiful*, p. 40.

43. Daly, *Steady-State Economy*, p. 7.

44. Georgescu-Roegen, "The Entropy Law," p. 43.

45. Hyams, *Soil and Civilization*, p. 117.

46. Kenneth R. Schneider, *Autokind vs. Mankind*, p. 23.

47. Ibid., p. 75.

48. Ibid., p. 261.

49. Spengler, *Decline of the West*, vol. 2, *Perspectives of World History*, chap. 8, "Money."

50. I. M. Cowan, "Ecology and Discretion," p. 147.

51. Christopher Freeman, "Malthus with a Computer," p. 11.

52. Schumacher, *Small Is Beautiful*, p. 33.

53. Georgescu-Roegen, "The Entropy Law," p. 44.

54. Colin Clark, "Economics and Population Growth" pp. 116–117.

55. Schumacher, *Small Is Beautiful*, p. 63.

56. Hutchinson, *Farming and Food Supply*, pp. 121–122.

57. Earl F. Murphy, *On Governing Nature.*

58. Karl Marx, "Alienated Labor," as cited in *The Capitalist System*, p. 254.

59. Schneider, *Autokind vs. Mankind*, p. 75.

60. R. W. Page, "The Non-renewable Resources Sub-system."

61. Hutchinson, *Farming and Food Supply;* Montague Yudelman, Gavan Butler, and Ranadev Banerji, *Technological Change in Agriculture and Employment in Developing Countries.*

62. Schumacher, *Small Is Beautiful*, p. 145.

63. Fennelly, *Twilight of the Evening Lands*, p. 121.

64. Schneider, *Autokind vs. Mankind*, p. 26.

65. Hyams, *Soil and Civilization*, p. 143.

66. Herbert J. Gans, *The Urban Villagers: Group and Class in the Life of Italian Americans*, p. 90.

67. Richard D. Alexander, "Natural Enemies in Place of Poisons," p. 92.

68. Gordon R. Conway, "Ecological Aspects of Pest Control in Malaysia," pp. 467–488.

69. B. J. Wood, "Integrated Control: Critical Assessment of Case Histories in Developing Economies," pp. 196–220.

70. Ibid., p. 198.

71. Ibid., p. 201.

72. Schneider, *Autokind vs. Mankind*, pp. 219–220.

73. Ellul, *Technological Society*, p. 97.

74. Schwartz, *Overskill*.

75. Vacca, *The Coming Dark Age*. Also see Schumacher, *Small Is Beautiful*; Toffler, *Eco-Spasm Report*.

76. Ortega y Gasset, *Revolt of the Masses*, p. 63.

77. Schumacher, *Small Is Beautiful*, p. 142.

78. Odum, *Environment, Power, and Society*, pp. 119–120.

79. Yudelman, Butler, and Banerji, *Technological Change*, p. 7.

80. Ibid., p. 10.

81. Ibid., p. 47.

82. Weeks, "Dominant Network of Exploitation," p. 2.

3
Ecosystem and Economic System Balance

Regardless of the particular cultural belief-system a society may follow, the one inescapable requisite for all human societies is the maintenance of ecosystem balance. Of the numerous factors related to this vital concern, one of the most important is the balance within a society's economic system. An understanding of these two conditions, ecosystem and economic system balance, thus becomes a necessary next step in our analysis of growth, culture, and environmental problems.

In essence, ecosystem and economic system balance exist when a relationship between man and his natural, social, and economic environment is maintained in which:

(1) Human survival is protected and conserved.

(2) The delicate and interdependent equilibrium of the rest of the ecosystem is protected and conserved.

(3) Any departures from conditions of equilibrium are kept within manageable limits so that amplitudes in fluctuations with respect to the physical-biological environment, resource availability, food supply, prices and wages, unemployment rates, and others, can be quickly reduced or, at worst, contained in a constant condition.

Ecosystem and economic system balance are integral parts of a much broader phenomenon known as systems stability. Defined in its two most appropriate contexts, stability refers to (1) "the property of a body that causes it, when disturbed from a condition of equilibrium or steady motion, to develop forces or moments that restore the original condition," and (2) a condition that shows "resistance to decomposition or disintegration."[1]

We accept and make use of this definition of stability, with one important alteration: the restoration of the *original* condition is neither essential nor always desirable. It is a restoration of the equilibrium, the balance, that is crucial to systems stability. With this conceptualization in mind, we now turn to a discussion of stability in complex systems.

THE THEORY OF STABILITY IN COMPLEX SYSTEMS

Many works of research have devoted attention to theories of stability in complex systems and, more specifically, to causes of systems instability.[2] These theories have identified two general reasons why instability occurs in systems: (1) the lack of adequate protection against the risk of a systems component failure and (2) the lack of homeostatic mechanisms. After identifying these two general areas, it is then possible to discover more specific causes for systems instability. We have elected to focus on three of these specific causes.

The first is what can be termed the "all the eggs in one basket" phenomenon: because a system has limited diversity it becomes highly vulnerable to a systems component failure. If a society depends primarily on one crop for its food, then that society is likely to suffer a terrible calamity if a plant disease reduces the availability of that food—an event that happened in Ireland at the time of the potato famine. Likewise, if a country depends for its economic health on sales of one product (sugar, coffee, bananas, cotton, anchovies, petroleum, rubber), and serious problems such as lower world prices or depletion occur, then the entire country may face an economic disaster. And in urban areas if one industry or one corporation is primarily responsible for a city's economic health, as in the case of Detroit (automobiles) or Seattle (aircraft), then that city is very vulnerable.

Thus increased diversity or variety within a system can be a blessing that helps promote systems stability. An increase in the number of items which can independently support a system decreases the probability that all will fail simultaneously. Suppose, for example, that a city depends for its economic livelihood on N industries, and over a 50-year period there is a probability of exactly .5 that any one of the industries will fail. Then what is the probability that all N industries fail over the 50 years? Chart one indicates how rapidly the risk of simultaneous failure drops with increasing N.

So a lack of diversity is the first specific cause of systems instability, an instability that may manifest itself in wide-amplitude fluctuations in basic need resources, unemployment, and numerous other dislocations. The second major cause—increased complexity—is sometimes confused with diversity. When examined, however, the two phenomena are shown to be quite different. *Complexity*, in a systems context, refers not only to size but also to a high degree of interconnection among components of the system that ties

CHART ONE

N The number of components which each, independently of the others, could support a system	The probability that all N components will fail together
1	.5
2	.25
4	.0625
8	.0039
16	.000015

them together into a somewhat interdependent web of causal pathways. A perturbation or shock applied from the outside to one component can ultimately travel the interconnected pathways and affect a large number of components. Consequently, the total system becomes more vulnerable and fragile as it becomes more complex. The only devices capable of protecting the system from this vulnerability are homeostatic negative feedback mechanisms with short response times. These mechanisms control a system by negating or counterbalancing a particular occurrence with the introduction of another occurrence. A theoretical example can be found in the following sequence: prices rise so high that consumption decreases; but the increase in prices is counterbalanced by the decrease in demand, which then brings prices down, which in turn increases demand and thus increases consumption.

But modern society is increasingly developing mechanisms which have the opposite effect of these balancing, stabilizing controls. For example, as more gasoline is used to drive on freeways, more gas tax revenues are generated. These revenues are then used to pay for the construction of still more freeways, which in turn means that more gas will be used, more tax revenues created, and still more freeways built. Few people seem to have noticed that there is literally no check on such a process. Indeed, it is designed to grow forever, faster and faster.

Even though numerous other examples can be cited in which increased complexity leads to instability, this need not always be the case. Systems can be made more stable as they become more complex. For example, mechanisms can be developed that decrease the vulnerability of transportation systems to the diminishing availability of petroleum. Diverting a proportion of gasoline taxes to the development of public transportation facilities would be one such mechanism, especially if the proportion of revenues allocated to bus and rail systems would be increased as freeway congestion increased. Or an even more direct homeostatic control, a negative feedback mechanism, would be provided by increasing the proportion of gasoline taxes going into mass transportation facilities, as gasoline prices increased.

Another brief example of potential control mechanisms illustrates that although increased complexity does tend to increase the likelihood of instability, this tendency can be regulated. For example, larger companies are often able to buy raw materials in vast quantities, thereby enjoying reduced prices. This encourages both a trend to monopoly and an excessive use of raw materials. But the opposite effect can be achieved by instituting higher unit costs as the quantities purchased increase. For instance, in the case of electricity, the consumer could be charged a higher rate per unit whenever he used excessive amounts of electricity.

A third specific cause of instability in complex systems is actually a set of factors which can, to varying degrees, operate independently of the size of the system. These factors are the numerous shocks that affect systems, shocks such as drought, flood, depletion of resources, significant climate alteration because of pollution, and/or a population increase that overwhelms the capacity of the available soil to meet the demand for food. Although some of these shocks are beyond human control, many are the direct result of man's destructive policies and lack of far-sighted planning. Thus, as is true with the other two major causes of instability, man can contribute greatly to stability maintenance by designing and implementing homeostatic control mechanisms.

Building on these various theoretical approaches to systems stability, we now return to the two major dimensions of stability in contemporary society: ecosystem and economic system balance.

ECOSYSTEM BALANCE

One of the most far-reaching effects of modern man's technological growth is the potential disruption of the earth's ecosystem. Nowhere is this destructive potential more apparent than in the worldwide pollution of our environment. Even though in many cases the effects of pollution have been largely localized, the disturbances they cause present a sad commentary on human disregard of natural laws and ecosystem balance. The wastes dumped into Lake Erie, the Thames and Rhine rivers; the eutrophication of numerous bodies of water throughout the world; Minamata and Itai-itai diseases in Japan; the air pollution disasters in the Meuse Valley, Belgium (1930), Donora, Pennsylvania (1948), and London (1952, 1956 and 1962)—these are only a few of the well-known local or regional examples of the negative effects of rampant, dangerous industrial growth. Although there are many local, national, and international improvement projects, such as the cleaning of the Thames and the restoration of many freshwater lakes in Sweden, the overall pollution problem is quite serious and goes well beyond the local or regional level. Increasingly, we are finding that pollutants have cumulative and far-reaching global implications, not only for man but for all other living organisms. These harmful effects are often irreversible, and damage the basic life-support systems by altering natural cycles and ultimately destroying ecosystem balance. Chlorofluoromethane, a gas used both as a refrigerant and a propellant in cosmetic sprays, is one such pollutant. This relatively inert compound ultimately finds its way into the stratosphere, where it is broken apart by the sun's ultraviolet radiation. Free chlorine atoms are then released, which decompose atmospheric ozone into oxygen through a self-sustaining chemical reaction. The available evidence indicates that current usage levels can lead to an ozone decomposition that could exceed natural sinks of ozone from all sources by 1985 or 1990.[3] The worldwide consequence of the destruction of the ozone layer will be extremely grave, because it is the ozone layer in the upper atmosphere that effectively absorbs the highly mutagenic ultraviolet radiations from the sun and thus acts as an effective barrier that safeguards all living organisms. With no ozone layer, overexposure to ultraviolet radiation will result, causing widespread skin cancer in man and genetic mutations in other organisms. And although it is the highly industrialized societies that produce the overwhelming bulk of fluorocarbon pollution, the potentially fatal effects will extend throughout the globe.

The effect of pollution on the atmosphere is, of course, not limited to the ozone layer. The numerous gases that compose the earth's atmosphere play an important part in the functioning of the biosphere. The natural cycles of important gases like carbon dioxide and oxygen developed throughout a long process of evolution. They are now maintained in a constant concentration in the atmosphere because the quantities of these gases utilized by living organisms remain equal to the amounts released back into the atmosphere through certain other activities. For example, the concentration of carbon dioxide (CO_2) in the atmosphere is a little over 0.03 percent by volume, or about 320 ppm. In spite of its relatively small proportion, it plays a very important role in the life of the biosphere. It acts as a heat insulator and produces the so-called greenhouse effect by trapping the heat waves radiating from the earth's surface. Green plants utilize this gas from the atmosphere for food production through the process of photosynthesis, while respiratory activities of living organisms and decomposition of organic matter release it back into the atmosphere. Thus this perfect balance between utilization and production maintains a uniform concentration of CO_2 in the atmosphere. Recently, however, as a result of the burning of fossil fuels, the carbon dioxide level in the biosphere has steadily increased. It is estimated that from 1860 to 1950 the concentration of carbon dioxide in the atmosphere has increased at about 0.2 percent per year, or 0.7 ppm out of 320 ppm. Given the increase in industrialization that is characterizing the last half of the twentieth century, the rate of increase in CO_2 concentration will likely grow. The implications of such a rise are still not fully clear, but the best model made so far suggests that an increase in CO_2 concentration from present levels up to 600 ppm (an increase that could take at the most only a few hundred years) would lead to an increase of 2° C in temperature at the surface of the earth.[4] Such a rise in temperature would not only have extremely harmful effects on crop productivity but could also alter the entire life system of the planet through the eventual melting of the earth's ice caps.

Other pollutants are also having a destructive effect on the earth's climate. The increasing quantity of man-induced aerosols (fine suspensions of solids or liquids in air) being released into the atmosphere can change the reflectivity, or albedo, of the earth's surface by the back-scattering of incoming solar radiation in space. These aerosols can also change the pattern of cloud formation by serving as condensation nuclei. Although it is difficult to predict precisely the impact of man-made aerosols, certain observations are indeed disturbing. For example, recent data show that the dust particle content of glaciers on the high Caucasus has increased twentyfold (from 10 mg to 235 mg per liter) from 1920 to 1950,[5] an increase that, unless halted, will most certainly melt the Caucasus glaciers.

A more publicized case of modern technology's role in pollution is the supersonic transport (SST) which flies at altitudes so high it reaches into the stratosphere. Because it is a very rarefied region with little vertical mixing, the stratosphere can be seriously polluted by jet exhaust and can consequently affect the climate of the entire globe.[6]

Man-made radioactivity is yet another problem, one that is made even more serious by the proliferation of nuclear power plants. All nuclear plants produce large quantities of nuclear wastes, which remain radioactive for very long periods of time. These wastes need to be stored and disposed of in a manner that prevents the contamination of the environment with radioactive pollution; but no satisfactory way has yet been developed to store the radioactive waste material over long periods without running the risk of leakage. In spite of this fact, plans for building new nuclear plants continue.

Indeed, in the U.S., even the fact that as many as ten existing plants may have to be shut down because there is no place to send their spent fuel for reprocessing and no room for storing it has failed to slow plans for new plant construction.[7] Even if techniques are rapidly improved, the transportation, storage, and reprocessing of lethal radioactive material will still involve great risks. As more and more disturbing examples become known (such as that of the plutonium that is now believed to be *missing* from the West Valley plant in the U.S.,[8] or the evidence of the continued construction and stockpiling of nuclear weapons), the serious threat of radioactive pollution both to man and the total biosphere will increasingly call into question present attitudes and policies.

But the pollution of the atmosphere and its direct effect on man is only one of the contemporary threats to ecosystem balance. A less sensational yet more immediate and crucial environmental problem is the continued destruction of *natural* ecosystems and the wealth of plant and animal communities contained therein; for it is upon these natural systems that humans have always depended for their food, water, shelter, clothing, medicines, recreation, and the myriad needs essential to full development. History is full of examples that reveal what can happen when man overexploits these life-support systems, often to such a degree that humans, crops, and herds can no longer be supported. The ruins of hundreds of cities such as Palmyra, Kish, Ctesiphon, and Thumgadi throughout Mesopotamia, North Africa, and Mediterranean Europe bear witness to the presence of earlier civilizations which flourished until their resource base was exhausted.[9] And in both the old and the new world, man has, throughout history, destroyed his agroecosystems by engaging in bad cultivation practices, devegetation, and overgrazing, all of which contribute to the devastating erosion of soil.[10]

Yet modern man rarely acknowledges these past ecological and human disasters, except, perhaps, as irrelevant and temporary setbacks to the progressive development of mankind. Indeed, few people today realize that there are only four pathetic forest remnants remaining of the famous Cedars of Lebanon; even fewer relate this despoliation to the exploitive practices of the merchants of Phoenicia and of King Solomon of Israel. Similarly, ecosystem disruption and human tragedy on such a massive scale as that of the American Great Plains Dust Bowl of the 1930s is remembered more through the fiction of a John Steinbeck novel than the stark reality of history. Thus, while it must be acknowledged that climatic change has had a historical role in ecosystem modification, the overwhelming role in changing the face of the earth has been played by man.[11]

The effect this modification of the earth's ecosystems has on the quality of life of modern man is twofold. First, to achieve and maintain ecosystem balance it is imperative that those natural ecosystems modified for agricultural production (agroecosystems) be managed in such a manner that their productivity is sustained without detrimental effect upon the rest of the environment. Second, it is essential that efforts be made to conserve the remaining unmodified natural ecosystems, not only as insurance against the destruction of genetic diversity but also because of the importance of retaining benchmarks which future societies can use to evaluate the quality of their management policies.

The Stability of Agroecosystems

Tribal or village agriculture. Since Neolithic times, man has gradually refined his agriculture—from fire, to basic tools for tillage, to the domestication of plants and animals, to the development of systems of crop rotation and herd management. Although chapter 2 mentioned the role resource destruction plays in the decline of nations, it must be stressed that many of the agricultural practices of earlier cultures did not lead to ecosystem imbalance or destruction. The contrast between the pastoral husbandry of temperate northern Europe and the herding and cultivation of arid Mediterranean Europe is a case in point. In the one case, even though forests were removed, there was an emphasis upon their replacement with grasses and legumes to provide food for stock. In the other case, the vegetation and soil resources were gradually depleted to the point where no natural balance between plants and animals could be restored.

Again, much recent investigation has shown that, contrary to the popular wisdom, the shifting cultivation[12] traditionally practiced by the cultures of the tropics has evolved as an attempt to maintain the long-term stability and productivity of their land.[13] Indeed, the ethnocentricity of Western, temperate-zone observers has led them to label this shifting tropical cultivation with the derogatory phrase "slash and burn" agriculture. Yet there is ample evidence that these techniques are a highly rational use of the fragile, tropical ecosystem with its limited nutrient resource. Basically, these traditional farming methods minimized risk, and the subsistence farmer's resistance to exhortations for a change to more "advanced" technological innovation was often soundly based on the fear that such changes would increase the vulnerability of his agroecosystem.[14] In their cultural ignorance, many Western observers considered this resistance as "backwardness." Yet in reality this shifting cultivation promoted stability in many ways: *local* knowledge of soils, climate, and pests was accumulated and used; generally, only second-growth forest was cleared on a rotational basis; soil erosion was limited through the use of a close cover of crops; diversity was maintained through the use of several plant species; management flexibility was ensured through mixed plantings that minimized pests, through multiple harvesting (including weeds for cattle forage), and through periodic intensive labor for weeding; and the institution of a judicious use of firebreaks.[15] When it became necessary to move on after several years of farming, it was usually because of lowered crop yields. But the cause of the lowered yields was not soil nutrient depletion, as the conventional view often suggests, but rather the increase in pest and weed competition.[16] Consequently, these agroecosystems of shifting cultivation did not irreversibly overtax the resource base of the fragile tropical environment, provided, of course, the population did not increase too rapidly.

Most of the more permanent forms of agriculture among tribal or village cultures also developed while maintaining the long-term stability of the agroecosystem. This agriculture was generally of two types: a sustained pastoralism, or a permanent cultivation. The role of exploitive pastoralism in bringing about the destruction of ecosystem stability in semiarid regions has already been referred to—through fire and overstocking man has converted much of the forest of these regions into grassland and, in many places, into actual desert.[17] However, some pastoralist cultures, such as the North American Plains Indian,[18] did maintain the stability of the grasslands prior to European colonization, generally because the temperate climate was conducive to the development of deep soils and sod-forming grasses.

The permanent cultivation by these tribal cultures involved either irrigation (usually with a complex terrace network for rice-growing) or the development of "village gardens."[19] In the most stable of these cultures, the system was highly integrated, often containing a mixture of hunting and gathering, shifting dryland cultivation, permanent wetland cultivation, and village orchards or gardens. Well-known examples are the *sawah/ladang* system of the Malay-speaking countries and the *ahupua'a* system of the Hawaiians and other Polynesians.[20] The stability of such cultures lay in the social flexibility and insurance against natural disasters that these diverse agroecosystems provided. Such a village retained surrounding forest to regulate rainfall runoff, to provide materials for shelter, and to protect useful wild fruits and animals; to protect these valuable forest sanctuaries strict taboos forbidding entry or misuse were often instituted. Limited areas of pasturage were also maintained near the village for grazing animals, and the animal wastes were used as fertilizer for the orchards and gardens. The water resources were conserved by the retention of the forest and used for a variety of purposes, such as drinking, washing, irrigating, and fishing. Overall, the community was self-sufficient, with no real production surplus and no need to trade or engage in warfare. Moreover, this stable society generated an aesthetically pleasing landscape and an opportunity for artistic self-expression.

Modern technological agriculture. Unlike these tribal/village agricultural systems, the modern technological agriculture is causing serious disruption to the balance of the ecosystem, particularly in the industrial nations. Whereas the traditional systems predominantly used animal and human labor and organic manures, the modern agricultural system depends for its high gross productivity on mechanization, scientific skills, and a large energy subsidy in the form of fuel, fertilizer, and pesticides. The two agricultural systems are contrasted in a highly simplified manner in figure 3.1. Just as the permanent cultivation of a tribal society was structured around a village, the technological agriculture is interwoven with the whole modern urban/industrial ecosystem. But now the agroecosystem must be pushed to its productivity limits to support rapidly increasing urban populations that rarely understand or care about its long-term stability.

Farm mechanization, population increase, and the pressure to feed this growing urban population have resulted in the removal of most of the checks and balances which maintained the stability of the tribal/village agroecosystem. Where agricultural products were once consumed locally, they now must be transported large distances, involving energy, labor, and large marketing networks; local knowledge of soils, plants, and climate has largely been replaced by a cost-saving standardization in management; where wastes were once recycled as manure or fuel, they now accumulate as pollutants in cities, processing factories, or on the farm; where a diversity of crops and land use was once encouraged, monocultures are now maintained by the use of fertilizers and pesticides; where nutrients were once largely retained within the ecosystem, they now "leak" from this high energy-throughput soil/plant/animal system, giving rise to air pollution and eutrophication of waterways; where the less intensive production systems conserved soil structure, many mechanized systems of continuous cultivation now promote the breakdown of soil structure and consequent accelerated soil erosion.

While the technological agroecosystem is less efficient at converting the sun's energy into total organic matter per unit area, its success lies in the much greater yield of utilizable food or product. In providing this increased yield, however, the homeostatic functions of the natural ecosystem are sacrificed and are not fulfilled by the various forms of energy subsidy offered by technology as replacements.[21] Simplicity rather than stability becomes the main priority.

Commercial preparation and mechanized planting replace natural methods of seed dispersal; chemical pesticides replace natural controls on population numbers in an attempt to remove unwanted plants (weeds) and to reduce direct competitors among the insect and vertebrate populations (pests); and genetic manipulation replaces natural processes of plant evolution and selection. Even the decomposer element is altered since plant growth is harvested and soil fertility maintained not through the natural recycling of nutrients but through the application of fertilizers. By and large, such artificial systems have proved capable of supporting a growing population, but there is considerable evidence that the equilibrium in such highly specialized systems is much more delicately poised.[22]

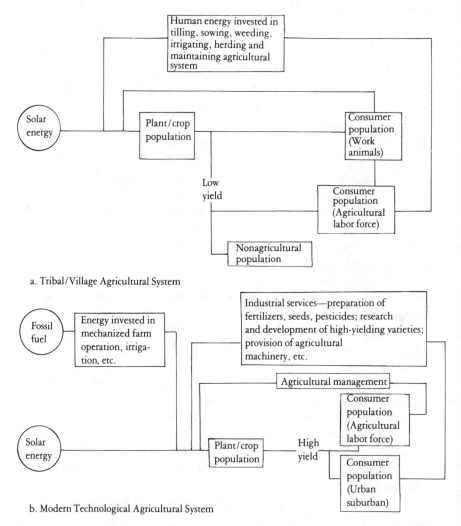

a. Tribal/Village Agricultural System

b. Modern Technological Agricultural System

Figure 3.1. Tribal/Village and Modern Technological Systems

Modified from Ian R. Manners, "The Environmental Impact of Modern Agricultural Technologies," in *Perspectives on Environment*, 1974. Ian R. Manners and Marvin W. Mikesell, eds., pp. 184–185, as adapted by Manners from Howard T. Odum, *Environment, Power, and Society*. Reproduced by permission of the Association of American Geographers.

In its pattern of energy flow and nutrient cycling, modern technological agriculture is basically the equivalent of an immature natural ecosystem. An analogy can be drawn using the processes of *undifferentiated* and *organic* growth discussed in chapter 1. In the early stages of ecological succession a small number of species grows rapidly to cover the soil and minimize nutrient loss. Since gross primary production exceeds the respiration of the plant community at this stage, the rate of net production of biomass is quite high. But as the community evolves toward maturity, production and respiration become more balanced. This natural process of organic growth thus moves a plant community toward a climax condition of homeostasis in which production of biomass is close to zero, nutrients are tightly cycled within the ecosystem, and there is a highly complex diversity of structure and function as the number of different plants and animals tends to reach a maximum.[23] This diversity is most pronounced in tropical rain forests, such as those on Mount Makiling in the Philippines, on which more woody plants have been recorded than in the entire United States of America.[24] It is precisely this species diversity that makes the forest so resilient, and thus highly resistant to man's attempts to develop a permanent technological agriculture in the tropics.[25]

It is clear, then, that the modern technological agriculture is man's attempt to reverse nature's successional sequence by artificially maintaining a highly producing, early-successional ecosystem, be it grain crops of corn, wheat or rice, herbage such as ryegrasses and clover, or plantation forests of pines. To sustain this high level of production without detrimentally affecting the rest of the environment is a heavy responsibility, one that requires a full knowledge of the ecological consequences of technological input. Whether we have this adequate knowledge of ecosystem function has been hotly debated in public since Rachel Carson's *Silent Spring*, and has been a matter of concern in scientific circles since the early days of the soil conservation movement in the 1930s.[26] While it is not possible to devote a significant section of this book to the detailed impact of modern agricultural technology, it is advisable, nevertheless, to highlight four aspects of this technology that are crucial to the proper balance of the agroecosystem. They are: the inducement of erosion; the role of "cultural energy" inputs; the impact of fertilizers; and the impact of pesticides.

Erosion. Accelerated soil erosion is a problem that has always been a part of man's agricultural environment. We have already discussed its role in the destruction of early civilizations and their agroecosystems. Virtually all the ancient agricultural lands of the world have suffered severe erosion, as evidenced by the depleted landscapes of Mediterranean Europe, Africa, and the Near East, the gullying in India and in the volcanic soils of Southeast Asia, and the denuded uplands of China.[27]

Yet the most spectacular erosion in modern times has been through the impact of man's agriculture in the New World—the U.S., Canada, Central Mexico, Chile and other regions of Latin America, South Africa, Australia and New Zealand.

> In about 150 years the agricultural soil resources of the United States have been cut by perhaps a half, and in some areas such as Oklahoma, a single generation sufficed to destroy almost 30 percent of the soil mantle. Such a systematic if unconscious rape of the land has had an impact that rivals or exceeds that of 6 to 10 millennia of cultivation in the Mediterranean world.[28]

Not all of this erosion, however, was through the impact of the horse- or tractor-drawn plough, which more than any other factor, destroyed the structure, organic matter, and biota of the topsoils of the New World. In many areas the introduction of traditional grazing patterns and exotic browsing mammals destroyed vegetation and gave rise to spectacular erosion. An outstanding example is New Zealand where rabbits, deer, goats, pigs, opossums, and chamois were systematically introduced throughout one hundred years of European settlement and sentiment. These animals destroyed native flora that had evolved in complete isolation from browsing mammals, and, with the help of the burning and overgrazing practices of numerous sheep farmers, gave rise to some of the worst mountain erosion in the world.[29] There, as in Oklahoma and most other agricultural regions, many farmers were unwilling, or unable, to recognize that they were destroying those resources essential to their own livelihood. The myopia of the 1949 Royal Commission on the sheep-farming industry in New Zealand typifies the problem that vested interests have in perceiving how they are destroying the balance of their agroecosystem:

> If one looks at the basic problems as we have examined them, one is forced to the conclusion that the root causes are lack of fertility and rabbit infestation. . . . Raise the fertility and exterminate the rabbits and with few exceptions you will end the causes of erosion. . . . We are concerned about the bulletins on soil erosion which have appeared and which we can only describe as propaganda rather than scientific fact.[30]

The attempts of the commission to have the offending scientific bulletins[31] on the human causes of erosion withdrawn from print is an example of the political opposition that has faced most national soil conservation services throughout their turbulent history.[32]

The problem with soil erosion is that it is not just a simple matter of understanding the interaction of climate, slope, soil, and vegetation; it also involves a major cultural input.[33] These cultural factors influence (1) the nature of forest or scrub clearance (clear-felling or retention of windbreaks and riparian strips), (2) the method of soil cultivation (digging-stick or deep-furrowing steel plough), (3) planting techniques (row planting or broadcasting, monocultures or intercropping), (4) landscaping (contour-plowing, strip-cropping, or terracing), (5) harvesting (clear-felling or selective logging in forests), and (6) pastoral activities (burning, overgrazing, lea farming, or permanent pasture). The best of these practices have been developed by different cultures to maintain the stability and productivity of the soil resource of their agroecosystem. As such, these practices constitute an important step toward a desirable steady-state modern agriculture.

The role of cultural energy. The various energy inputs into agriculture made by man, his animals and materials (as distinct from the 1 to 3 percent incident solar energy harnessed during photosynthesis) have been described by the term *cultural energy*. The role of cultural energy in *modern* agriculture deserves attention; for, whereas in a village garden agroecosystem the cultural-energy input would have been almost entirely from human labor, plus some organic manure, in modern crop-agriculture human labor is often an insignificant input since fuel, fertilizer, pesticides, processing, and depreciation of equipment and buildings constitute 80 to 90 percent of the cultural energy required.[34] For instance, it has been estimated that for modern rice production in the U.S., ". . . fuel consumption contributes about 41%, depreciation of machines and buildings contributes about 33%, fertilizer and pesticides each contribute about 5%, and labor only contributes 0.05% of the cultural energy used."[35]

The recent sharp increases in the cost of fossil fuel have highlighted the fact that the impressive crop production achieved through technological agriculture, especially in the U.S., has been gained through very large inputs of fossil energy.[36] Were this energy subsidy to be removed or become prohibitively expensive (as is currently occurring), the agricultural output of modern agroecosystems would decrease drastically, and possibilities for recovery would be minimized since work animals, genetic varieties, and other potential aids are no longer available. Therein lies a major source of instability in the modern technological agriculture.

The concept of "net caloric gain," a concept akin to the net energy idea used in industrial contexts (and discussed later in this chapter) is another factor that illustrates the effects modern cultural energy inputs have on both agroecosystem stability and society as a whole. Net caloric gain refers to the number of calories of digestible plant energy yielded for one calorie of cultural energy input.[37] Figure 3.2(a) and (b), illustrating the comparative caloric efficiency of fifteen various cropping systems (all classified as either "primitive," "traditional," or "modern"), reveals that while the yield of digestible energy per acre was low in the primitive agricultural systems, their "caloric gain" was as high as sixteen. Transitional systems (with a low technological input of both animal labor and metal implements) had a caloric gain of only three to six, somewhat higher than that for many crops such as oats, soybeans, and sugarcane (caloric gain, two to three) produced by the modern agriculture with its high energy input. Corn as grain and silage did give a higher gain of approximately five, but crops demanding high cultural energy inputs, such as sugar beets, peanuts, and rice, had a very low gain of close to, or less than, one.

However, an even more disturbing picture of decreasing caloric efficiency is given by other recent authors:

> . . . the yield [U.S.] in corn calories decreased from 3.7 kcal per one fuel kilocalorie input in 1945 to a yield of about 2.8 kcal from the period of 1954 to 1970, a 24 percent decrease.[38]

> In "primitive" cultures, 5 to 50 food calories were obtained for each calorie of energy invested. . . . In sharp contrast, industrialized food systems require 5 to 10 calories of fuel to obtain 1 food calorie.[39]

Like the net energy controversy in nuclear power generation discussed elsewhere in this volume, the net caloric efficiency of modern agriculture is of vital importance to the stability of modern society and the agroecosystem. The concept clearly requires considerable further research. One specific area where research might prove especially valuable is noncropping agriculture methods, such as pastoral farming, where lower fuel inputs would seem adequate. For example, the use of legumes in pastoral farming, as practiced in Australia and New Zealand, would be expected to bring about considerable savings in the cultural energy associated with nitrogenous fertilizers, especially when alternative crops and utilization practices are examined. Perhaps the most glaring comparison is with the corn, barley, oats, and soybean production in the U.S., where as much as 90 percent of these crops is fed directly to animals,[40] with a conversion efficiency of as low as 14 percent for beef. The pitifully low caloric gain generated by such a policy clearly argues for experimentation with a system from which greater benefits to society can be realized.

Fertilizers and wastes. More has been written in recent years about the roles of fertilizers and nutrients from wastes in ecosystem degradation than about most other dimensions of the environmental problem. Terms such as *eutrophication, algal blooms, nitrate poisoning,* and *biodegradable* are

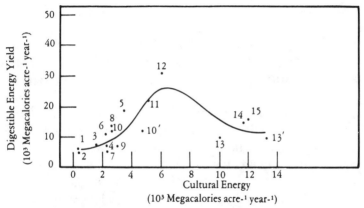

(a) Expenditure of cultural energy and yield of digestible energy in 15 agricultural systems.

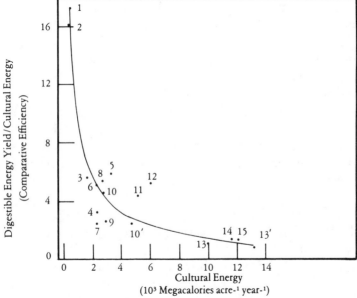

(b) The caloric gain, or ratio of the yield of digestible energy to the investment of cultural energy, of 15 agricultural systems. This ratio is used as a measure of the efficiency of energy use.

Figure 3.2. Cultural Energy

The following code applies to the 15 agricultural systems shown in this figure: 1. Paddy rice, Philippines, 1970; 2. Vegetable garden, New Guinea, 1962; 3. Corn for grain, Iowa, circa 1915; 4. Corn for grain, Pennsylvania, circa 1915; 5. Corn silage, Iowa, circa 1915; 6. Alfalfa-brome hay, Missouri, 1970; 7. Oats, Minnesota, 1970; 8. Sorghum for grain, Kansas, 1970; 9. Soybeans, Missouri, 1970; 10. Sugarcane, Hawaii, 1970, cultural energy excludes processing; 10'. Sugarcane, Hawaii, 1970, cultural energy includes processing; 11. Corn for grain, Illinois, 1970; 12. Corn silage, Iowa, 1970; 13. Sugarbeets, California 1970, cultural energy excludes processing; 13'. Sugarbeets, California, 1970, cultural energy includes processing; 14. Peanuts, North Carolina, 1970; 15. Irrigated rice, Louisiana, 1970.

Adapted from G. H. Heichel, *Comparative Efficiency of Energy Use in Crop Production*, Connecticut Agricultural Experiment Station, Bulletin 739 B (November 1973), pp. 10, 13.

becoming increasingly familiar; and the cycling of nitrogen and phosphorus in agricultural and urban ecosystems has been intensively studied to better understand their role in ecosystem degradation. This attention is appropriate because artificial fertilizers have come to play a pivotal role in modern agriculture. Their unavailability due to high prices or genuine shortages is among the major constraints on development. At the same time, only a part of the total fertilizer production is often effectively utilized. Plant nutrients are lost in storage and transportation, particularly in the case of urea in humid tropical conditions. Once applied to soil, up to 50 percent of the nitrogen can be lost through leaching, gasification, or biological transformation. Under certain other conditions plant nutrients are transformed into insoluble forms and are not available for the growing crop.

The fertilizer problem is a complex one because judicious use of synthetic fertilizers has a vital role to play in restoring nutrients taken from the agroecosystem as food products or in establishing vegetation to heal the scars of erosion. The causes of accelerated eutrophication are also complex and cannot always be blamed solely on poor agricultural management.[41]

The overriding problem is to plug up the "breach in the flow of mineral nutrients" in the urban/agroecosystem complex.[42] To do this, the absurd levels of fertilization employed in many industrialized countries will have to be lowered, since such excessive use is simply self-defeating. For instance, one of the world's most intensive agricultural users of superphosphate is New Zealand, with its high producing ryegrass/clover permanent pastures. Yet recent work there indicates that root nematode infestation has reached such a level in this duoculture that up to five times the level of superphosphate may have to be applied to the infected clover plants to achieve the same level of production as noninfected plants.[43]

It will also be necessary to make better use of natural manures and organic wastes. A case in point is the Netherlands. While the greater proportion of the world's population is deficient in protein, the Netherlands has based its animal production largely on massive importation of protein feeds such as fish meal, feed grains, and soybeans. Not only is there a net loss in the output of protein from these animals, but they are now producing more manure than is required to fertilize all the farmlands of the Netherlands.[44]

Pesticides. The increasing use of pesticides by modern agricultural technology is another major contributor to agroecosystem instability.[45] Perhaps more than any other practice, the use of these powerful chemicals characterizes the "more is better" syndrome in the technological society—"If the pest is not controlled by one application, then surely two applications will suffice!'' And therein lies the tragedy of the ecosystem disruption wrought in the past thirty years by the indiscriminate use of such wide-spectrum pesticides as DDT, which have not only eliminated certain pests[46] but have also destroyed many of the natural predators that aid in pest control.

The pesticide problem is further compounded by the fact that some pests have developed a resistance to certain chemicals, such as the organochlorine group, thereby prompting modern farmers to switch to a wide range of organophosphorus compounds, which are significantly more toxic but less persistent in the ecosystem. The resiliency and adaptiveness of pests, the potential dangers to humans these toxic chemicals represent, and the millions of dollars that have been wasted on fruitless pest elimination campaigns are increasingly demonstrating that pesticides offer no real long-term, safe solution for the control of agricultural pests.

One of the most controversial programs in recent years has been the $115 million effort to eliminate the stinging fire ant *(Solenopsis richteri)* from nine of the southern states of the U.S.[47] While only 2,000 acres were infested in 1932, the ants had spread across 2 million acres by 1959. Federal and state attempts at eradication began in 1957, and, in response, the ants spread across 126 million acres between 1959 and 1969. When the highly unsuccessful attempt at eradication was stopped on June 20, 1975, a welter of accusation and counter-accusation began, marking a fitting end to the most expensive single pest-control effort ever carried out in the United States.

As mentioned earlier, not only have many of the target organisms successfully developed a resistance to pesticides (or have simply been replaced by different pests at population levels much higher than prepesticide levels), but important species of wildlife, such as birds of prey, have been destroyed.[48] This situation is analogous to the Kuznets cycles or Kondratieff waves discussed elsewhere in this chapter. As in those economic-demographic cycles, a reduction in system diversity leads to a shortage of fast-acting feedback control loops. The result is a tendency to instability, with resulting wide-amplitude cycles or waves. Indeed, the schematic representation adapted from Manners (figure 3.3) explains not only pest outbreaks but is the type of explanation that would help explain economic long waves. Manners' solution for restoring some stability to agroecosystems, also proposed by other researchers,[49] focuses on integrated pest control through a combination of biological predators or pathogens, sterilization, and the breeding of disease- and pest-resistant varieties of plants.

Thus it would seem that only by understanding numerous complex ecological situations can a balance be achieved. The war against pests has many

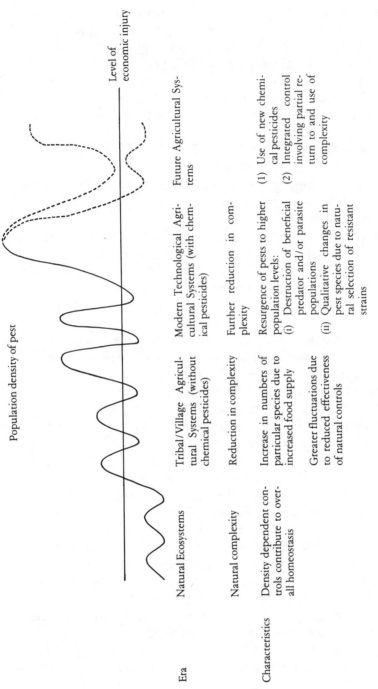

Figure 3.3. The Historical Development of Pest Control and Pest Fluctuations

From Ian R. Manners, "The Environmental Impact of Modern Agricultural Technologies," in *Perspectives on Environment*, 1974, Ian R. Manners and Marvin W. Mikesell, eds., p. 201, as adapted by Manners from Norman W. Moore, "A Synopsis of the Pesticide Problem," in *Advances in Ecological Research*, J. B. Cragg, ed. Reproduced by permission of the Association of American Geographers.

parallels with the past decade of American military involvement in Southeast Asia; both involved the "we had to destroy them to save them" mentality, and both campaigns ended in failure. As Kenneth Boulding has appropriately pointed out:

> . . . the ecological point of view is profoundly antithetical towards war on anything, whether insects or poverty. You see the War on Poverty means eliminating the poor.[50]

The Impact of Modern Technological Agriculture on Developing Countries

One of the many tragedies resulting from Western colonialism has been the substitution of temperate zone agriculture and technology for traditional tropical village agriculture. The numerous environmental problems that have grown out of this substitution process—low soil fertility, soil erosion and the formation of lateritic crusts, pest infestation, and weed competition—generally stem from temperate man's lack of understanding of tropical ecosystems. Basically, most of the lowland tropics are marginal for farmland use except the limited areas of fertile river valleys and recent volcanic soils. Most of the nutrients in the tropical ecosystem are contained in the living biomass of the forest; when this is cleared through burning, these nutrients are easily leached and lost. Any intensive agriculture then has to compete against a vigorous natural succession.

This transference of energy-intensive, reductionist techniques of temperate zone agriculture has been widely criticized,[51] primarily because of the instability it has caused in tropical agroecosystems. But this technology has also contributed greatly to an even deeper problem: the breakdown of traditional cultural values. In its arrogance and ethnocentricity, Western science has pushed aside the wealth of folk knowledge and experience that is embodied in the tribal/village agroecosystem.[52] The resistance to the adoption of Western technology has often been soundly rooted in fear of the destructive consequences it might have for the continued stability of the tribal/village society.[53] The breakdown of cultural values and the disruption of the agroecosystem are thus two of the major reasons why many of the attempts to bring about the rapid economic development of the poorer societies in the world have failed miserably. It seems that only through the recognition of these two interrelated aspects of the problem will stable agroecosystems be developed:

> When examining the problems that confront the development of a sustained-yield tropical agroecosystem . . , it is impossible to separate the biological problems of

practicing agriculture in the tropics from those of inadequate education, public facilities, administration, and social aspirations.[54]

Perhaps the best-known example of the application of modern technological agriculture in the tropics is the Green Revolution. Although this revolution has given impressive yields of grains in many areas, its overall performance has not matched the promise that heralded its implementation. The high-yielding varieties of wheat and rice introduced were bred specifically to respond to an increase in cultural energy inputs such as fertilizers, pest control, and improved irrigation, inputs that are key parts of the modern technological agriculture of the Temperate Zone.[55] The maintenance of these high-yield grain varieties can thus lead to an overdependence on inorganic fertilizers, pesticides, and water control technology, most of which will bring about increasing dependence upon the foreign sources of supply in the industrial nations.

Furthermore, the risk of biological instability is built into the Green Revolution, since the high-yielding varieties have replaced the genetically diverse traditional plants. Once again, the vulnerability of monocultures to disease and pest applies; in fact, the likelihood of introducing genes susceptible to some pathogen (through the universal incorporation of the dwarfing gene) has been pointed out.

> That this should be so is fairly improbable, except that it has already happened once. The epidemic of southern corn blight that destroyed a fifth of the U.S. crop in 1970 was caused by a genetic linkage of this type.[56]

It should also be realized that the Green Revolution became possible only through the use of gene material drawn from wild varieties of plants. This fact should make even more apparent the necessity of preserving adequate reserves of wild plants, even if they seem to some technology advocates to be "out of place" in the high-yield, rapid-production scheme.

The socioeconomic impact of the Green Revolution is also significant. Although the effects vary from region to region, there are reports that in many areas the impact is leading to a breakdown in the stable traditional patterns of ownership and distribution of wealth. This problem will be given additional attention in chapter 4.

The Role of Natural Ecosystems in Maintaining Ecosystem Balance

Throughout recent history, man has modified most of the world's biota for his own purposes. Indeed, there are very few habitable areas left in the world that have not been modified to some degree.[57] Those natural areas that remain deserve preservation not only in their own right as wild places, but also because they can provide a role in the maintenance of ecosystem balance. As we have already discussed, to maintain environmental balance with modern technological agriculture requires a fundamental understanding of the functioning of the urban/agroecosystem. Yet, so many agroecosystems have undergone such extensive cultural modification that it becomes necessary to compare them with an undisturbed ecosystem to fully evaluate their stability. This benchmark or baseline function is only one of several rationales for the preservation of natural ecosystems. For these natural areas can also:

(1) provide scientific knowledge of the structure and function of natural ecosystems as stable communities which are evolving as the result of complex environmental forces;

(2) preserve gene pools of natural organisms, including those that are rare or endangered; and

(3) play a role in educational and training programs.[58]

While the need for the preservation of some natural areas (usually for aesthetic or historical/cultural reasons) has been recognized in most countries of the world, this concern is often superficial.

> In most countries people are scarcely aware that such areas exist, and in many countries the areas are viewed by local residents as land taken away from their legitimate use for the benefit of city folk or foreigners.[59]

National Parks and Research Natural Areas— a Network of Ecosystem Preservation

Historically, the need for the preservation of natural areas has been realized through the world's national park system, a system that has grown to more than twelve hundred parks since the establishment of Yellowstone in 1872. The concept and definition of national parks has evolved until now there is general agreement that a national park is an area where

> . . . one or several ecosystems are not materially altered by human exploitation and occupation, where plant and animal species, geomorphological sites and habitats are of special scientific, educative and recreative interest or which contains a natural landscape of great beauty . . .

and where steps have been taken by governments to

> . . . eliminate as soon as possible exploitation or occupation in the whole area and to enforce effectively the respect of ecological, geomorphological or aesthetic

features which have led to its establishment and . . . [to permit] visitors . . . to enter, under special conditions, for inspirational, educative, cultural and recreative purposes.[60]

This definition clearly acknowledges public use of parks; but it also emphasizes the preservation function of parks. Herein lies the fundamental management paradox of the national park system: the reconciliation of *preservation* with *public use*. To deal with this paradox, zoning schemes have been developed in the national park system[61] to provide a graded system of protection, ranging from a "facilities" area of full public access, to the "strict natural area or nature reserve" where access is allowed only by permit. This zoning system has worked moderately well in parks where management supervision is of a high standard, but the increasing number of public visitors is placing such pressures on the park systems that it is becoming difficult to maintain the scientifically important natural areas in an unmodified state. This has often been called the syndrome of "loving the parks to death."

Gradually, the need for a complementary system of natural areas for research has been realized.

Some natural areas were held and managed primarily for scientific research, others for conservation of game or wildlife, others because of special geological, archeological or historical interest. Some others were mainly attractive for recreation of various kinds, and others for viewing scenery. Some were even underground or under water. These distinctions involved vast differences in size, in access, in facilities, in management, and in public control, and raised the question whether the upholding of a clear standard and image for national parks did not demand the recognition of a whole series of related distinct categories of protected natural or seminatural areas, which could not be lumped in with national parks if credibility and essential character of the latter were to be maintained.[62]

Quantitatively, the most important of the world's landscapes and biota will probably be preserved eventually in the national park system and the associated categories of reservation such as national monuments, national wildlife refuges and ranges, wilderness areas, recreational areas, scenic reserves, and national forests. Many of these latter areas can be devoted to multiple use functions such as recreation, mining, a variety of outdoor recreation, tourism, and commercial hunting. But perhaps most important, they all fulfill one extremely valuable function: the maintenance of ecosystem stability through water and soil conservation in primarily mountainous areas.

One possible crude measurement of the relative importance that a country places upon the national park or natural area reserve concept is provided by the percentage of its nonagricultural land that is protected as national park or equivalent reserve.[63] Naturally, it would be expected that the less densely populated countries would face fewer difficulties in creating such reserves; but the data presented in figure 3.4 show that this is certainly not the case. Many densely populated countries such as Israel, the Netherlands, Japan, and Sri Lanka have made a significant attempt to preserve some of their nonagricultural land in its natural state. On the other hand, two of the most sparsely populated developed nations, Canada and Australia, have set aside a very low percentage of their nonagricultural land for national parks or reserve areas. Even though this admittedly is a very crude quantitative model, it is clear that the countries of the world fall into three broad categories (low, intermediate, and high) in terms of the priority they attach to national parks. However, it must be stressed that this rating does *not* represent the priority that each country places upon natural area reservation for the purpose of ecosystem preservation. For instance, it is well known that the raison d'être for many of the great African national parks is tourism, which, in a country such as Kenya, provides 3 percent of the GNP and is the nation's fastest growing and most efficient earner of foreign exchange.[64] The important role the economic considerations of tourism play in the creation of African national parks is further illustrated in figure 3.5, which shows the relationship between GNP per capita and the percentage of nonagricultural land in parks. While the African nations are among the poorest, nevertheless, as a group, they stand out as having made the creation of national parks a high priority. Of the more affluent nations, New Zealand, and to a lesser extent Japan, Israel, and the Netherlands, have been the only ones who have preserved more than 1 to 2 percent of their nonagricultural land as national parks.

Shortcomings of National Parks in the Preservation of the World's Important Ecosystems

In a *qualitative* sense, however, these national parks and equivalent reserve areas do not adequately represent all the world's important ecosystems.[65] As can be seen in figure 3.4, the majority of reserved areas are concentrated in relatively few countries; and in many important regions, such as Asia, Central and South America, the Middle East, and the Sahara, there are few, if any, protected regions. In recognition of this need, several national and international cooperative efforts are being made to set up a worldwide system of natural terrestrial and aquatic ecosystems, primarily for conservation and scientific study. At the national level, many countries are setting up natural area systems like the Research Natural Area program of the U.S.[66]

International concern for the preservation of endangered plant and animal

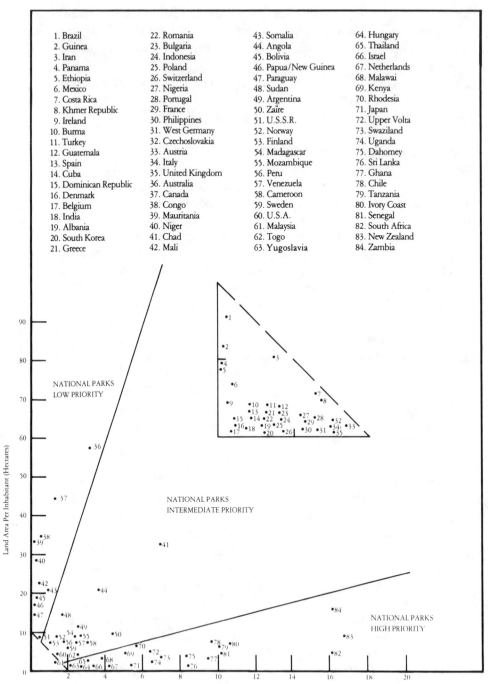

1. Brazil
2. Guinea
3. Iran
4. Panama
5. Ethiopia
6. Mexico
7. Costa Rica
8. Khmer Republic
9. Ireland
10. Burma
11. Turkey
12. Guatemala
13. Spain
14. Cuba
15. Dominican Republic
16. Denmark
17. Belgium
18. India
19. Albania
20. South Korea
21. Greece

22. Romania
23. Bulgaria
24. Indonesia
25. Poland
26. Switzerland
27. Nigeria
28. Portugal
29. France
30. Philippines
31. West Germany
32. Czechoslovakia
33. Austria
34. Italy
35. United Kingdom
36. Australia
37. Canada
38. Congo
39. Mauritania
40. Niger
41. Chad
42. Mali

43. Somalia
44. Angola
45. Bolivia
46. Papua/New Guinea
47. Paraguay
48. Sudan
49. Argentina
50. Zaïre
51. U.S.S.R.
52. Norway
53. Finland
54. Madagascar
55. Mozambique
56. Peru
57. Venezuela
58. Cameroon
59. Sweden
60. U.S.A.
61. Malaysia
62. Togo
63. Yugoslavia

64. Hungary
65. Thailand
66. Israel
67. Netherlands
68. Malawai
69. Kenya
70. Rhodesia
71. Japan
72. Upper Volta
73. Swaziland
74. Uganda
75. Dahomey
76. Sri Lanka
77. Ghana
78. Chile
79. Tanzania
80. Ivory Coast
81. Senegal
82. South Africa
83. New Zealand
84. Zambia

NATIONAL PARKS
LOW PRIORITY

NATIONAL PARKS
INTERMEDIATE PRIORITY

NATIONAL PARKS
HIGH PRIORITY

Land Area Per Inhabitant (Hectares)

Percentage of Nonagricultural Land in Parks

communities has long been channeled through the International Union for the Conservation of Nature and Natural Resources (IUCN) and the World Wildlife Fund. These two organizations have been working together toward the establishment of national parks and equivalent reserves to protect the endangered communities. Since 1962, further emphasis has been given to such a network by the Conservation of Terrestrial Communities section of the ten-year International Biological Program (IBP).[67]

Although efforts to establish an adequate network of reserves were successful in some countries, the global result was disappointing. The major problem seemed to be lack of coordination and government commitment. Recognizing this problem, UNESCO has developed its Man and the Biosphere (MAB) Program, an international project aimed specifically at the creation of a comprehensive network of biosphere reserves through the cooperation of member governments.

> It is intended that biosphere reserves should comprise not only completely natural ecosystems but also semi-natural ecosytems, including those maintained by long-established land-use practices. Among the proposed reserves there should also be areas that have outstanding potential for restoration to near natural conditions.

> The concept of biosphere reserves involves a broad philosophy of conservation which recognizes that successful stewardship will depend on adequate control of the use of land and water in surrounding areas. It may be viewed as an approach to maintaining the integrity of biological support systems for man and nature throughout the whole biosphere. As such it involves conservation, restoration and the acquisition of knowledge for improving man's stewardship of the domesticated and wild countryside.

> The programme to establish biosphere reserves is not meant as a substitute for programmes to establish national parks and equivalent reserves. Biosphere reserves may often coincide partly with or incorporate national parks or equivalent reserves but they may include areas which do not conform to the IUCN definition of na-

---

Figure 3.4. Relationship between Land Available to Population and Percentage of Nonagricultural Land in National Parks and Reserves

"Land area per inhabitant" is calculated from areas given in *WHO Statistics Annual*, vol. 1 (1971) and 1974 population figures given in *1974 World Population Estimates*, The Environmental Fund, Washington, D.C. The percentage of "nonagricultural land in parks" is calculated as follows: total park area has been calculated from the data in the 1974 *United Nations List of National Parks and Equivalent Reserves* (Morges, Switzerland: IUCN, 1974). The "tentative areas," in countries such as India and Indonesia have been included. (For explanation of "tentative areas" see p. 7 of 1974 *List*.) Only countries with one million or more population have been included. Norway data do not include those parks on the islands of Spitzbergen within the Arctic Circle. "Nonagricultural land," according to *FAO Production Yearbook 1972*, includes alpine regions, forests and woodlands, urban areas, wasteland, and water surfaces.

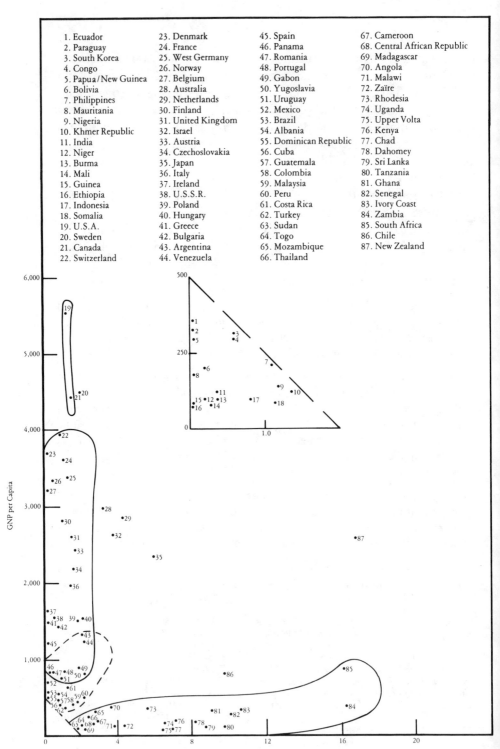

tional parks. They may also include buffer zone areas where manipulative research may take place. The most significant and distinct characteristic of biosphere reserves, however, will be their links by international understanding on purposes, standards and exchange of information and personnel.

. . . the establishment of biosphere reserves in the biomes of the world is of world concern on behalf of this and future generations. It must be viewed not only as part of the overall use and development of the natural resources of a country, but as a part of the planned and conservative development of the resources of the biosphere. Accordingly, the biosphere reserves of the world require the close and active collaboration of all the international organizations concerned with the environment and the conservation of environmental quality, foremost among them UNESCO, FAO, UNEP, IUCN, and ICSU.

Great emphasis is placed on conservation of natural areas in the developing world, particularly in tropical forests, grasslands, coastal systems and islands.[68]

It would appear that the international scientific community fully realizes the need for the reservation of such ecosystems, but time is very short. With the pace of development and population growth accelerating throughout the world, the chances of creating new natural area reserves, and of protecting the existing ones, are rapidly diminishing.[69]

The Role of Ecosystems in Baseline Studies of Environmental Quality

As global pollution increases, natural ecosystems will become invaluable in providing a baseline to indicate background levels of changing environmental quality. Programs now monitoring atmospheric and water pollution, changes in soil fertility, and pollution of ecosystems from pesticides, heavy metals, pathogenic organisms, and radioactivity, all depend to some extent upon various evaluation procedures that use a natural ecosystem baseline.[70] These procedures vary from the use of unmodified control catchments to indicate nutrient loss during clear-felling forestry operations,[71] to the use of sensitive epiphytes and lichens in natural areas to indicate levels of atmospheric pollution from adjacent industrial areas.

The Gene Pool Function of Natural Ecosystems

A major function of these natural ecosystems is to preserve the gene pools of natural animal and plant organisms as well as the diversity found in wild

---

Figure 3.5. Relationship between GNP per Capita and Percentage of Nonagricultural Land in National Parks and Reserves

"Percentage of nonagricultural land in parks" is calculated as for figure 3.4. GNP per capita is that given in the *World Bank Atlas: Population, Per Capita Product and Growth Rates*, 1972.

strains of organisms. Since A.D. 1600, 36 of the 4,226 species of mammals then living have become extinct, and at least 120 more of them are presently in danger of extinction. In the same period, 94 of the 8,684 species of birds then living have become extinct, and at least 187 more are now endangered.[72] However, this is the estimate of *full species*; the number of threatened geographical races, or subspecies is even greater—223 for mammals and 287 for birds.[73] The distribution of these threatened animals is shown in figure 3.6, which is based on the latest data in the *Red Data Book* on rare, vulnerable, or endangered animals. Within recorded history man has exterminated at least 369 species and subspecies; and today some 1,054 vertebrate species and subspecies are threatened with extinction.[74]

The most threatened group of birds is the Oceanic group whose habitats are found on formerly isolated islands. It is in these limited, fragile ecosystems that modern man is having the greatest impact on the rates of bird extinction. This is particularly true of some of the larger islands (or groups of islands) such as New Zealand, Hawaii, and the West Indies, where extensive colonization threatened a natural avifauna that had been relatively free of predators for long periods. The reduction of mammals is closely related to destructive patterns of human settlement and agriculture. Predator species which have threatened man's domestic herds or flocks (such as the wolf and members of the cat family) have been universally hunted, often to the point of near extinction. The overwhelming role of man in this process of extinction, as opposed to extinction through natural causes, is illustrated in table 3.1. From 68 to 86 percent of the causes of extinction for birds or mammals can be traced to human activities such as hunting, the introduction of predators or competitors, and the destruction of habitat. Tragically, this elimination of rare wildlife is continuing today. Poachers kill rare animals in national parks and reserves and use the meat, fur, and skins for commercial purposes; the Russians and Japanese continue to deplete the whale population; and zoo and museum enterprises continue to capture wildlife to put on display. In 1971 alone it is estimated that 101 million live wild animals were exported to the U.S.,[75] many of them dying in transit. Similarly, in 1967, 22 million pounds of wild animal skins were imported into the U.S.[76]

However, the overwhelming impact today is probably through habitat destruction, as man clears forests, drains swamps, improves rangeland, pollutes estuaries, and drives roads through the heart of the remaining virgin lands. This rampant development poses serious threats to the last remaining undeveloped wild lands in Alaska, the Amazon basin, and the forests of Southeast Asia.[77] Recently, even the New Zealand government, with a

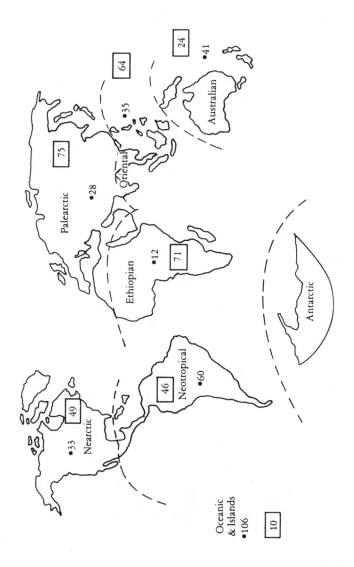

●Birds

☐ Mammals

Figure 3.6. Distribution of Birds and Mammals Threatened with Extinction

The numbers represent the total threatened races (species plus subspecies) in each zoogeographical region, as calculated from the most recent listings appearing in the IUCN *Red Data Book*.

TABLE 3.1   Causes of Extinction and Rarity for Birds and Mammals
Since 1600

		Birds (%)	Mammals (%)
Cause of Extinction	Natural	24	25
	Human		
	hunting	42	33
	introduced predators	15	17
	other introductions	4 ⎫ 76	6 ⎫ 75
	habitat disruption	15	19
	Total	100	100
Cause of Present Rarity	Natural	32	14
	Human		
	hunting	24	43
	introduced predators	11	8
	other introductions	3 ⎫ 68	6 ⎫ 86
	habitat disruption	30	29
	Total	100	100

reputation for sound nature conservation, has been severely criticized for its initial proposal to utilize nearly 300,000 hectares (ha) of South Island beech forests; for such a policy would have harmful effects on complex and diverse rare plant and animal communities not represented in existing national parks or reserves.[78] Scientific and official government opinion was sharply divided over the impact of the conversion (by clear-felling and burning) of 140,000 ha of these native forests to the fast-growing exotic pine, *Pinus radiata*. Many government officials publicly adopted the highly dubious position that this fauna could eventually exist in the exotic forests or move into adjacent biological reserves, riparian strips, or green belts.[79]

The threat of extinction is not the only impetus for the conservation of gene pools in natural areas. The other rationale is fundamental to the stability of modern technological agriculture: the conservation of genetic diversity that breeders can call upon to replenish their domestic stock. It must be stressed that no single plant or animal is without some importance to man, and the recent history of agriculture points to the need to maintain a wide genetic base as an insurance against the catastrophic losses that occasionally occur in agricultural monocultures with their narrow genetic base.[80] Indeed, it has already been discussed how the Green Revolution was dependent upon the selection of wild strains of wheat and rice to develop new high-yielding varieties, and how these high-yielding, dwarf varieties are genetically more uniform than the native strains they replace and, consequently, are more susceptible to epidemics.[81] There is a serious danger that, as these varieties are transplanted from one part of the world to another, they will become susceptible to pests and pathogens to which they have not adapted. Furthermore, there is considerable evidence that the establishment of these varieties is destroying the irreplaceable source of genetic diversity of local crop varieties whose germ plasm would be essential for future breeding programs.[82]

This trend is cause for concern, especially in those numerous areas where resources are inadequate to combat serious epidemics among crops. The race is clearly on between nature and the crop breeders, with the continued balance of agroecosystems at stake.

The Educational Function of Natural Areas

The effectiveness of any program aimed at ecosystem preservation for conservation or scientific purposes is clearly related to the degree of public support given to the program. And although it is true that the public often shows a lack of interest in preserving natural areas, it is important to realize that this is frequently the case because the resource managers of society often fail to inform, or are restricted from adequately informing, the public of the ecological reasons underlying the need for such conservation. Without this understanding industrial man may, in his growing use of nature as a periodic refuge from the squalor of the city, increasingly place these natural areas under intolerable ecological pressures. Education thus clearly has an important role to play in assisting the public to understand the ecological importance, and fragility, of natural ecosystems in addition to the recreational functions these natural areas provide. For, in the long run, the continued balance of our ecosystems will rest largely in the hands of a dedicated citizenry. Acting as watchdogs in the restraint of government and corporate abuses, and providing valuable information and knowledge to the general public, concerned citizens can help develop a public respect for natural areas.

ECONOMIC SYSTEM BALANCE AND STABILITY

A society embarked upon a steady, organic growth process will maintain not only ecosystem balance but economic system stability as well. As was pointed out earlier, stability in an economic context requires that amplitudes in fluctuations, whether they be in prices, wages, unemployment rates, and/or production-consumption levels, be contained within equilibrium limits.

When contemporary societies are examined closely, few cases of healthy economic stability appear. Rather, we find that the amplitude of fluctuation is increasing in many of the most important economic variables of global society.

Since the relationship between demographic and economic variables is of such fundamental importance, let us turn first to demographic factors. There is an important connection that links the birth rate and age structure of the population with the rate of unemployment, fluctuations in the economy, cycles of pessimism and optimism, political fluctuations, and unmanageable fluctuations in resource demand. Various aspects of this system of interacting cycles have been studied by Kuznets (Kuznets cycles), Kondratieff (Kondratieff waves), Easterlin and Schumpeter,[83] and several interesting features have become apparent. In figure 3.7, the bottom panel shows that the net addition of people to the U.S. population has occurred in two large waves over the last century, with the amplitude of the second wave being much greater than the amplitude of the first. The top panel, depicting GNP per capita in 1929 dollars, shows a pronounced break between 1925 and 1940. We know that such breaks in the economy are characterized by a very high percentage of unemployment, which is most severe in the younger age groups of the labor force. One of the reasons for the high unemployment (and hence one of the main driving forces in the creation of depressions) is the addition of a greater number of new recruits to the labor force than the tempo of economic activity can utilize. We note further that the peak in the curve for additions to the population occurs about twenty years prior to the nadir in the GNP per capita curve. This is understandable, since approximately twenty years elapse from the time a year class is born until the time it tries to break into the labor force for the first time. Unfortunately, GNP computations are not available before 1869 in the United States, so we cannot study the behavior of long-term waves back more than two wavelengths. Thus, it appears that there may be very important relationships between the birth rate and the behavior of an economy, even though the lack of reliable time-series data over long periods involving large numbers of countries makes it difficult to understand fully the dynamics of this process. If the postulated relationship exists, however, it would appear to be most important to attempt to dampen the amplitude of the waves, or cycles. The motive, of course, would be to suppress unmanageable fluctuations both in the economy and in the rate of demand for resources. The way to dampen the fluctuations would be to discourage periods of excessive reproduction and speculative frenzy in economic affairs.

As this book goes to press, startling evidence is becoming available that

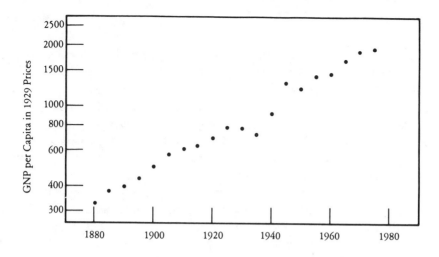

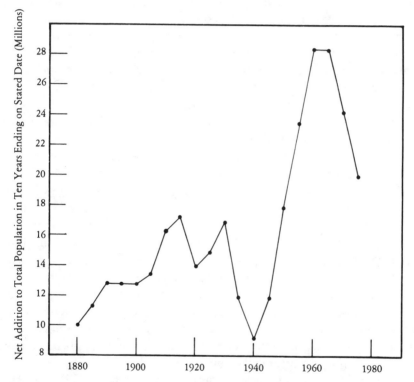

Figure 3.7. The Kuznets Cycle, or Kondratieff Wave, Applied to the
United States, 1880–1973

Data on GNP per capita from *Historical Statistics of the United States* and *Statistical Abstracts of the United States* (both produced by the U.S. Dept. of Commerce, Bureau of the Census). Data on population additions from Simon Kuznets, *Economic Growth and Structure* and *Statistical Abstracts of the United States*.

the Kondratieff wave still operates in some economies. By 1930 GNP per capita in constant dollars showed a very sharp decline, just 15 years after the peak in rate of population increase in 1915. In 1975, it appears that there will again be a very sharp decline in GNP per capita in constant dollars, just 15 years after the last peak in rate of population increase in 1960. If the amplitude in constant dollars per capita GNP increases as the rate of population increase has increased in amplitude, then we should expect a very low nadir indeed by 1980. If this happens, then it will appear that there has been massive resource wastage in the last two decades on such things as luxury housing, condominiums, hotels, resorts, jet planes, and other durable items for which economic demand could not be sustained over the long term.

The trends of net yearly increase in population from 1960 to 1985 for India, mainland China, and Japan, based on the United Nation's population projections, are given in figure 3.8. Populations of India and Japan do not show any evidence of wave phenomena. In the case of Japan a mild wave pattern resembling the Kuznets cycle can be recognized. It would be interesting to investigate the factors and their mode of action in producing the characteristic Kuznets cycles. One of the likely reasons for the difference between behavior patterns of population dynamics in various societies appears to be the level of economic development, and, in particular, the degree of concentration of economic activity in the hands of a few large enterprises.

Several other data series show similiar evidence of developing instability. Figure 3.9 shows that when industrial production for the twenty-four OECD countries is plotted as deviations about a long-term 5.5 percent growth line, the magnitude of the deviation about the trend line has increased sharply in the last year. Figure 3.10 shows how the wholesale price index in India, Indonesia, and the U.S. has increased up to mid-1975. Clearly the rate of increase is itself increasing, and this is, of course, one of the principal reasons for the present economic crisis. The Indonesian data provide an example of a severely distorted economy, for which the index was 1,750 times greater in 1972 than it was in 1958. This spectacular increase forced the government of Indonesia to devalue the currency by a thousand times in 1966. Figure 3.11 illustrates developing instability in quite a different type of phenomenon: world production of agricultural commodities, in this case cigarets, rice, and meat. Amazingly, when we hear so much about imminent mass starvation, it is only in rice production that we notice a recent downward production trend developing. In the other two series, which we would normally think of as luxury items relative to rice, production is increasing at an increasing rate.

The United States automobile industry provides an interesting example

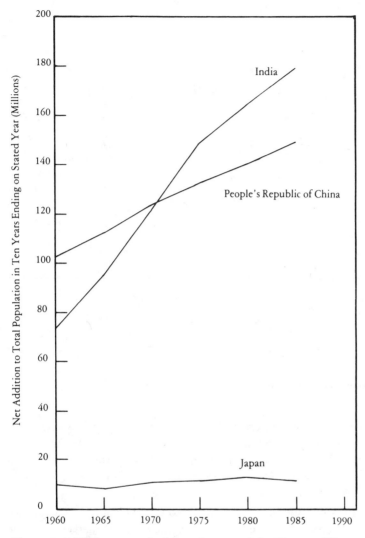

Figure 3.8. Evidence on the Nonexistence of the Kuznets Wave
in Certain Asian Countries, 1950–1985

Net population additions computed from population estimates in *Total Population Estimates for World, Regions, and Countries Each Year*, 1950–1985, UN
Secretariat.

of market conditions after years and years of growing production of cars.
Figure 3.12, a plot of sales of cars made each year in the U.S., reveals that
there has been wide fluctuation in sale rates in recent years, a factor related to
overproduction and market saturation. The amplitude and speed of fluctua-

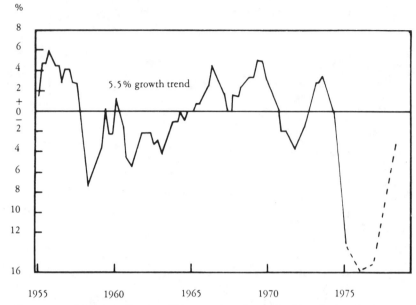

Figure 3.9. The Amplitude of Fluctuation about the Trend Line for 5.5 Percent per Annum Growth in Industrial Production in the Twenty-four Countries of the Organization for Economic Cooperation
and Development, 1955–1978

Graph from *The Economist* (London), 12–18 April 1975, p. 79. Reprinted by permission.

tions in sales has increased steadily to unprecedented levels, such as the drop
of 3.5 million sales within a short period of two years, 1973 to 1975. Even
during the Great Depression that began in 1929, a similiar drop in sales was
spread over four years. The market is now so saturated that slight increases in
price relative to average wages produce quite sharp reductions in sales. The
sales rate has become highly vulnerable to very wide amplitude fluctuations
because the economic system is trying aggressively to market a product for
which demand is waning.

Finally, in figures 3.13 and 3.14 we see still other instability phenomena
operating. In figure 3.13 it is clear that meat consumption is increasing at a
higher rate than GNP in several industrialized countries, a fact that we suggest may contribute to instability in the world food situation. And in figure
3.14, the amplitude of fluctuation in unemployment rate appears to be
related to the degree of concentration of the industrial base in U.S. cities in a
small number of large companies.

The diverse examples of instability depicted in the data just discussed

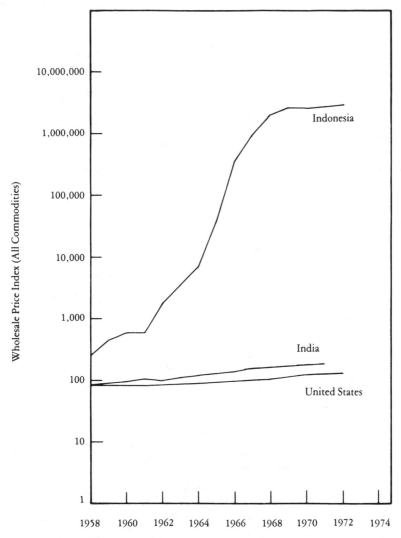

Figure 3.10. The Trend of Increasing Instability in the Wholesale Price Indices of India, Indonesia, and the United States, 1958–1972

Data on India from *India Pocket Book of Economic Information*, p. 119; on Indonesia from *Statistical Pocketbook Indonesia, 1972/1973*; on U.S. up to 1973 from *Statistical Abstract of the United States, 1974*, more recent data from newspaper stories based on news releases on the rate of changes of index.

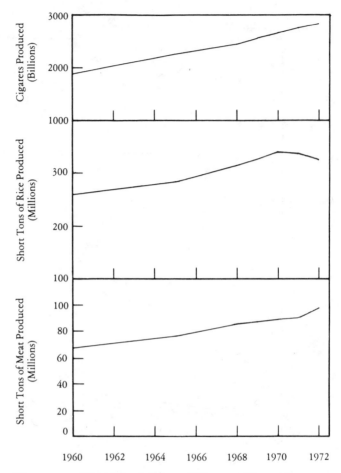

Figure 3.11. World Production of Cigarets, Rice and
Meat, 1960–1972

Data from *Statistical Abstract of the United States 1974*, table 1354, based
in turn on data from *United Nations Statistical Yearbook*.

serve as a foundation upon which to build an explanation of how the instabilities confronting contemporary society have developed. It is to that explanation that we now turn.

AN EXPLANATION FOR THE INSTABILITY IN PRESENT SOCIETY
At the beginning of this chapter we identified two general reasons for
systems instability: inadequate protection against the risk of a systems component failure (often manifested in a lack of diversity), and a lack of

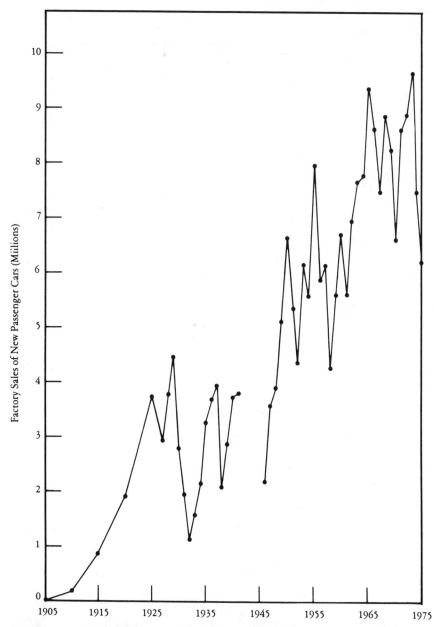

Figure 3.12. Annual Factory Sales of New Passenger Cars in the United States, 1905–1975

Data from *Statistical Abstracts of the United States*: table 644, 1954 volume; table 928, 1974 volume; and corresponding tables for intervening years. These data in turn from Motor Vehicle Manufacturers Association of the United States, Inc., Detroit, Michigan, originally published in *Automobile Facts and Figures* issued annually. Data for 1974 from the U.S. Department of Commerce, and for 1975 from the *Wall Street Journal*.

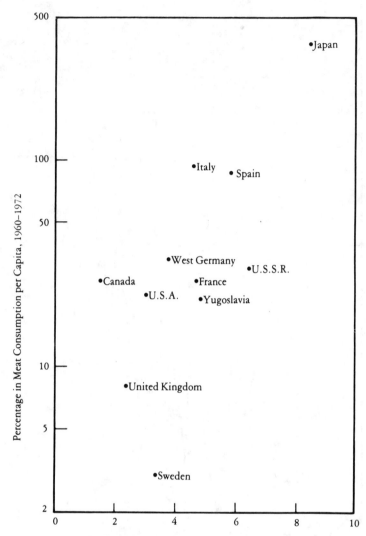

Figure 3.13. Relationship between Annual Meat Consumption
and GNP Increase per Capita

GNP data compiled from *World Bank Atlas: Population, Per Capita Product
and Growth Rates,* 1974. Meat consumption data from *United Nations
Statistical Yearbook,* 1972, table 162.

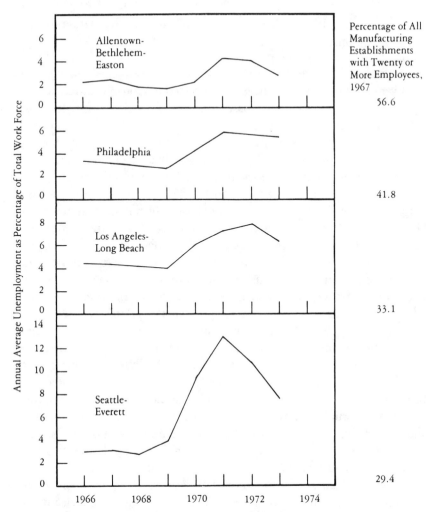

Figure 3.14. The Relation between the Degree of Concentration of the
Industrial Base in U.S. Cities and the Amplitude of
Fluctuation in Unemployment Rate

The smaller the percentage of all manufacturing establishments with 20 or more employees, the
greater the degree of concentration of large-scale manufacturing activity in a small number of
companies (as in the case of Boeing in Seattle). Data from Section 34, Metropolitan Area
Statistics, *Statistical Abstract of the United States*, 1974, 1972, and 1969 editions.

adequate homeostatic mechanisms that can contain fluctuations within manageable limits.

The first of these causes is perhaps best illustrated in figure 3.14. Four different "standard metropolitan statistical areas" (large urban centers), all with over 60,000 population, have been selected to represent different levels of diversity in their industrial base. The index of diversity used is the "percentage of all manufacturing establishments with 20 or more employees in 1967." It may be assumed that if this percentage is small, the economy of the city is probably dominated by a few extremely large enterprises (as in the case of Seattle, where Boeing is the major enterprise). On the other hand, if this percentage is high, then we assume that the economy of the city is based on many large enterprises, and thus there is less likelihood that any one of them can completely dominate the economic activity of the community. Thus, if the economic life of a city is too dependent on the success of one company, or a very small number of companies, there will be wide-amplitude fluctuations in the unemployment rate of the area. The Seattle-Everett area was strongly dependent on the success of one enterprise. When the market for aerospace products and jet aircraft approached worldwide saturation level, the problems of Boeing became an unemployment problem for the entire metropolitan area. The other three cities, with more diversified industrial bases, had lower amplitude of fluctuation in their unemployment rates. In general, then, the hypothesis can be drawn that the more diverse the economic activity of a city, the more chance there is that the risk of component failure will be diffused among many components. The probability of failure of the entire system is thus minimized. As pointed out earlier, this general principle of less diversity–greater instability is applicable to a wide variety of situations, whether in industrial or agricultural contexts.[84]

The second cause of instability—the lack of adequate homeostatic mechanisms—is illustrated in figure 3.12. The economic system clearly cannot serve as an adequate homeostatic mechanism, and, in the data shown here, the theoretical price mechanism is simply not working. In the face of a clear reduction in demand for automobiles, the manufacturing rate remains high, thus wasting valuable resources that could be diverted to sorely needed mass transit buses and trains.[85]

Furthermore, the failure of the price mechanism to regulate demand is encouraging the entire population to buy on credit. From 1950 to 1973 in the United States, average consumer credit outstanding, as a proportion of disposable personal income, doubled from .104 to .205.[86] The historical record indicates that although widespread and massive debt has served to stimulate an economy to grow rapidly (with the usual spin-offs of wasted resources and pollution), it has also served to set up an economy for a traumatic collapse.

This and other data suggest that the U.S. may be becoming more like Latin America,[87] even though the former's economy superficially appears to be less vulnerable to wide-amplitude instability. The lack of necessary homeostatic mechanisms in the economy and the monopolization of control by a few powerful organizations have given rise to a whole series of environmental and social problems: unnecessary resource depletion; pollution from industry; unemployment; and complex social ills, such as inequity and crime, that are related to these other problems.

Figures 3.7 (the Kuznets cycle-Kondratieff wave), 3.10 (the wholesale price index, or inflation), and 3.11 (world production of cigarets, rice, and meat) further illustrate the instability that can result when systems become complex without evolving balancing homeostatic mechanisms. One would expect that a rational society would deal with these phenomena at some of the more vulnerable points, such as pro- and antinationalist legislation or taxation of capital gains. But the massive, uncontrolled growth that is often the companion of these wide-amplitude fluctuations seems to blind many nations to reality. For although the upswings in these cycles or waves may be exhilarating, they cannot be justified when they are accompanied by widespread human suffering in the following decades. Moreover, these side-effects are becoming increasingly intolerable as industry continues to construct and manufacture highly resource-consumptive and polluting items (such as luxury residences and hotels, automobiles, oil tankers, and the like) for which the long-term demand is as illusory as a mirage.[88]

Figure 3.11, in a most interesting way, further reveals that much of the present worldwide instability is due to the absence of balancing or self-regulatory mechanisms operating at the international level. "Shortages" in one part of the world or in one commodity may in part be a reflection of weak or missing mechanisms for allocating resources on the basis of *needs* rather than on the basis of *wants* that are often manipulated through media channels. The world food problem provides an excellent example of this phenomenon. Many developing countries are suffering food shortages and are unable to provide even a modest diet to their people, while in the developed world, particularly in the U.S., Canada, and Australia, food is abundant and consumed in a most lavish style. Thus it can be argued that the world food shortage has developed not only because of the rampant population growth in many regions, but also because of irrational patterns of demand and consumption, patterns that provide very few if any homeostatic mechanisms that might lead to an adequate degree of resource balance.

Finally, we turn to one more example of data to substantiate our explanation of instability in the present system. The very recent and large worldwide drop in industrial production depicted by figure 3.9 is partially the result of the large-scale resource depletion that has now reached unprecedented levels. As pointed out earlier in this chapter, ancient civilizations isolated in time and space have met their downfall largely because of widespread destruction of resource bases, particularly agricultural topsoil and forests. The growing crisis in the industrialized world now involves the availability of another primary resource—crude oil. Although numerous complex economic factors are also involved, the current economic instability is in part a product of several of the causes we have discussed: excessive dependence on one energy source (lack of diversity); inadequate development of other energy sources and energy conservation (lack of homeostatic mechanisms); and the effects of price fluctuations on the system (externally applied perturbations). More specifically, there are two important phenomena at work in this case; one being the net energy problem,[89] and the other the failure of the price mechanism to respond rapidly enough to alert the market to the need for alternative resources. The net energy concept (see chapter 2 and also earlier in this chapter for a discussion of the companion concept of "net caloric gain") basically points out that no source of energy is of net value if more energy is required to obtain the resource than is derived from using the resource. For example, before we contemplate using inch-thick coal seams that are found several thousand feet below the surface of the ground, we must consider the energy cost of growing the wood beams to support the tunnels, the energy cost of drilling the tunnels and shafts, lighting the mines, and running the elevators. This must all be added to the energy cost of transporting the coal, of building the vehicles which transport it, and so on. When we adopt this "net energy" type of reasoning about energy resources, it becomes apparent that the attractiveness of many energy resources has been based on the large hidden energy subsidy (in the form of cheap, readily accessible fossil fuels, particularly crude oil) that has made these resources available. Atomic power, particularly, has appeared feasible only because of enormous, hidden, fossil-fuel energy subsidies that can be used in building, operating and protecting atomic energy plants, enriching nuclear fuel, mining, transporting fuels and wastes, and disposing of wastes. Because this net energy concept has not been used in energy policy, homeostatic mechanisms have not been developed that can increase resource-base diversity and can adjust to sudden increases in the price of the previously cheap fossil fuel "energy subsidy."

PROBABLE CAUSES OF FUTURE INSTABILITY

We have attempted to provide an explanation as to why the world is experiencing rather serious instability. Unless institutional devices are conceived, implemented, and properly administered, it is logical to argue that instability will continue, and perhaps even increase, in the coming decades. To facilitate debate and action on new policy directions, we now identify several key factors which we suggest will be fundamental causes of instability in the future.

1. The price mechanism is failing as an effective means for regulating society. The conventional wisdom holds that this mechanism can and will protect the system against various kinds of disasters. For example, it is believed that as a resource approaches depletion, the price will rise, resulting in three consequences: a decrease in the rate of resource use, the promotion of an active search for new reserves of the same resource, and the stimulation of research in the development of suitable substitutes. Unfortunately, things have rarely worked out this way. All through history, all types of justifications have been advanced as to why there should be no economic penalty for depleting a particular resource. This occurred in the case of buffalo in North America and the sperm whale, and is presently occurring in the case of coal, oil, and gas, tropical hardwood forests, and other natural resources. Prices in many countries are too low to prevent depletion of these resources or to stimulate a sufficiently rapid search for substitutes.

Thus the question arises as to whether the price mechanism is really effective in dampening demand. Some people seem to think that the demand for certain products is so strong that their consumption is independent of, or unaffected by, price. One way to illustrate the actual situation is to explore the relationship between use rate per capita and price, where price has been adjusted for ability to pay. Figure 3.15 is a plot of gasoline use per capita against price relative to GNP per capita for thirty-five countries in 1972. The relationship is quite striking between the two variables—price accounts for over 94 percent of the variance between countries in use per capita. Thus it would seem that any government really serious about conserving gasoline could do so by increasing its price significantly, and that one form of instability in the future can be dealt with if governments take the unpopular step of allowing prices to rise to a level capable of conserving resources.

2. While many people still argue the point, there is a genuine energy crisis, leading to instability in the world industrial system. Part of the crisis

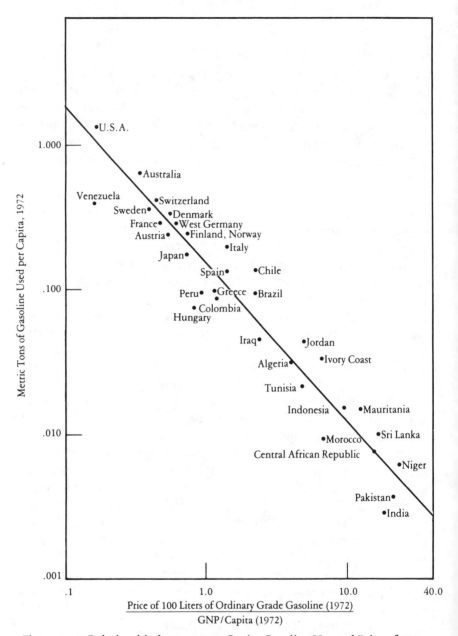

Figure 3.15. Relationship between per Capita Gasoline Use and Price of 100
Liters Relative to GNP per Capita

GNP per capita has been used as a surrogate variable for mean per capita spendable income. The
line was fitted statistically, and accounts for 94.2 percent of the variance in per capita use. The data
on 1972 population and GNP per Capita were obtained from *World Bank Atlas: Population, Per
Capita Product and Growth Rates,* 1974, The figures on petrol consumption and price were taken
from the 1973 edition of *World Road Statistics*, published by the International Road Federation.

stems from the inability, or unwillingness, of people to recognize and admit that the world is rapidly running out of fossil fuel energy sources. The true nature of the situation can be revealed in the starkest terms by determining the "lifetime of proven reserves." For crude oil this figure can be obtained by dividing proven reserves by the annual input to refineries. The calculations show that the estimated lifetime of proven oil reserves in the U.S. dropped at a rate of only .7 percent per year from 1955 to 1960, but dropped 8.98 percent from 1971 to 1972, and 7.89 percent in the following year.[90] There is simply no satisfactory argument to counter the contention that we are running out of fossil fuel energy. The fact that huge new reserves have not been discovered in the face of continued high consumption and new high prices indicates that there may no longer be any sufficiently large reserves waiting to be found. We can only conclude that a massive worldwide drop in availability of oil (and gas) will likely be upon us in the not too distant future, and that this will be a major cause of instability. It will be necessary to have a substitute source of energy developed and deployed on a worldwide scale to replace fossil fuels as a major source of energy, a feat that will probably take anywhere from twenty to sixty years. Still, governments continue to move at a glacial rate to deal with the problem. The most likely prospect is that the necessary alternate energy sources will not be in place in time.

For developing countries energy is a terrible problem. It is not widely recognized that energy actually costs much more in most poor countries than in rich countries. For example, suppose we compute the price of 100 liters of ordinary grade gasoline as a percentage of GNP per capita in various regions of the world. In 1970, those 100 liters cost two-tenths of 1 percent of GNP per capita in North America, 1 percent in Europe, but 19 percent in South Asia and 11 percent in Africa. Even though they are staggering, these facts show only the beginning of the problem; for now that energy prices have risen sharply, it means that, if poor countries are to continue to import fossil fuels, they will totally destroy their international balance of trade and, consequently, their economies. Logic dictates that they must seek some other solution to energy problems than continue to depend on importing more and more fossil fuel each year. (See chapter 7.)

3. The uncontrolled size of population and its age distribution is another important threat to future stability. Huge shifts through time in the age structure can create massive economic stresses. If there are too many young people relative to the number of older people, they cannot be educated properly or absorbed into the labor force satisfactorily. If there are too many older people relative to the number of young, they can destroy the ability of

society to provide adequate retirement benefits. Very large swings through time in the number of people born each year can set up economic perturbations of such wide amplitude as to create serious socioeconomic problems. At present the age structure of various populations is more distorted than at any prior time in history. Computer simulations have shown that the effect of such distortions can last for centuries.[91] To illustrate the magnitude of such age distribution problems, many countries now have 42 to 48 percent of their population under fifteen years of age. A much lower percentage of under-fifteens, 31 percent, in 1960 in the United States, will present massive unemployment problems as they reach the age for trying to break into the labor force, around 1980. Clearly, other countries will have enormous problems in accommodating their under-fifteens when they are under-thirty-fives, in 1990. Population policies must be so designed as to prevent such problems by giving detailed consideration to the long- term implications of the changing age structure.

Another major problem population planning must face is how to determine the number of people a country should have. Although there is no universal or simple answer, one way of beginning debate on this problem is to make calculations based only on the food produced in that country.[92] To illustrate, we compute the number of people that can live in the whole world, assuming that only grain is eaten, and that only the land most authorities classify as "arable" is used for growing grain. Under "worst case" assumptions, .786 hectares of land are lost to urbanization for each person added to the population, and .437 ha of land are required to grow the food to support one person. There is great disagreement amongst different authorities as to how much arable land there is in the world; but recent careful estimates, such as the one published in the Second Report to the Club of Rome,[93] seem to be converging at 2.3 to 2.5 billion hectares. Under these assumptions, the world could support only a little over 4.5 billion people, .5 billion more than the present number. The estimate of 4.5 billion is, of course, quite sensitive to changes made in the assumptions. If we assume that from all the arable land in the world we could increase production so that one person could be fed from .11 ha (with grain, only), and per capita losses to urbanization were only .2 ha, then the estimate of the world carrying capacity jumps to 10.4 billion people.

However, estimates this high may not be too reliable; for there are tricks in estimating the number of people that can be supported by the food from one hectare of grain. One gets entirely different figures depending on whether production estimates for grain come from carefully managed plots under ideal circumstances at agricultural research stations, from the best farms in a country, or from the national averages for all arable land. The national averages are much lower, because much of the land farmed in any nation is of such low fertility and in such a poor climatic zone that the farmer would be wealthier if he moved to another type of work.

Unquestionably, the population issue remains high on the list of major environmental problems. The complexities involved in the population problem include not only food and land availability but distribution policies as well. The agricultural production that feeds a population is highly dependent on the availability and price of energy; and the distribution patterns of food and other life-support needs are interwoven into the total political and socioeconomic structure of a society. Thus it is extremely difficult to make precise predictions about the maximum population the world can accommodate. But it seems glaringly obvious that the present structures of global resource development, distribution, and use are having a hard time meeting the basic needs of even the *present* population. To assume that the world can have a much larger population while still retaining present structures thus seems grossly unrealistic.

4. The destruction of species diversity in the ecosystem will be an important cause of future instability, unless measures are taken to halt this trend. The pressure of human populations on available land and other resources may become so intense that there is a strong temptation to stock most of the area now covered by wild plants and animals with domestic species. This is unwise for several reasons. Diversity of species ensures a reservoir of genetic material which can be used for outcrossing domestic species so as to maintain hybrid vigor. Also, we never know when a wild species will turn out to be of some totally unpredicted value in uses, such as in penicillin and other drugs. Further, reservoirs of native plants support insect-eating organisms that can be used in biological control of insect pests. Indeed, in some countries, it has turned out that no pest control is needed if luxuriant native vegetation surrounds orchards: if a pest breaks out in the orchard, its predators invade from the surrounding vegetation and prevent its numbers from becoming excessive. And, as we have mentioned, it is important to keep some areas in their pristine state as a benchmark (experimental control) to evaluate the impact of human activities. If, for example, check plots had been set aside in Phoenicia, Carthage, and Southern Greece and Rome, and had been fenced so as to exclude domestic animals, there would now be little argument as to whether the present ravaged condition of those areas was caused by climate or by man himself. In general, then, it provides a type of insurance for society to maintain a large number of species in the ecosystem; for this diversity

is accompanied by the evolution of feedback mechanisms which ensure great self-regulatory ability, and hence stability.

Several other likely causes of future instability deserve mention. *Capital shortages*, stemming in part from policies that waste huge amounts of capital on projects characterized by luxury, pollution, depletion, and low net energy yield, will make it difficult to fund those programs that maintain stability. *Capital- and energy-intensive programs*, already of highly dubious value to developed nations, will likely cause great instability if adopted by the developing nations where labor surplus, and energy and capital shortages, abound. *Alterations in the climate* of the earth caused by man's irresponsible industrialization, automation, and disregard for nature, can, in the long run, cause calamitous instability. And, finally, the inability of man to see stability as a priority goal is at the very heart of present and future problems. *Policies that sacrifice stability for quantitative growth* are as perilous as they are misguided.

The above discussion of future instability returns us once again to the major causes of instability with which we introduced this chapter. To counteract these causes it would thus seem essential for societies (1) to be on guard against reduction of diversity; (2) to ensure the existence of adequate homeostatic control mechanisms built into the fiber of the system; and (3) to take steps to anticipate, minimize, and contain perturbations to the system.

The more optimistic of the world's futurists like to argue that the momentous problems of instability we have discussed will ultimately be solved by major technological breakthroughs, such as the discovery of an unlimited source of energy. This argument that there is a "technological fix" that can solve the world's problems is indeed attractive, and has been debated at some length by the authors of this book. The conclusion we have reached is illustrated in the flowchart of figure 3.16. Very high flow rates of energy through any system confer a great competitive advantage to large corporations, or other institutions, which can so organize themselves as to capture an extremely high proportion of economic activity in the system. This is done by making rapid growth the desideratum for the corporation, and by maximizing economic efficiency through use of economies of scale. The rapid growth of the few dominant organizations creates a competitive environment which encourages near monopoly, or oligopoly, and is inimical to great diversity. Thus, this high rate of energy flow creates a system that is highly vulnerable to perturbations and, therefore, highly prone to instability. Although the nature of these perturbations has been discussed, it bears repeating. The pollution of the biosphere resulting from an increasing flow of

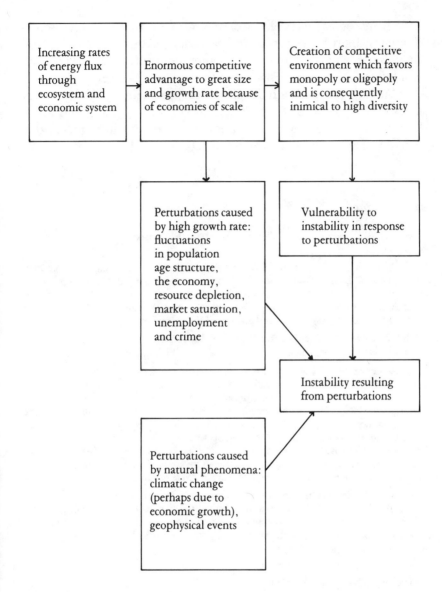

Figure 3.16. The "Technological Fix" Model, with No Resource Limitations

matter and energy; widespread outbreaks of pathogens, as monoculture favors outbreaks of epidemics; climatic changes influenced by high energy fluxes and the resultant pollution; changes in population age structure; and complex problems of market saturation, inflation, unemployment, and crime—all are consequences of a pattern of growth that, in the end, shocks itself into instability by the very perturbations it has caused.

Thus even in a situation where no resource limitations exist, serious problems of instability can occur. For even in the highly unlikely event that some technical miracle can, on this finite planet, provide an unrestricted supply of basic resources, present patterns of distribution, consumption, and more-and-more quantitative growth cannot ensure that needs will be met or that ecosystem and economic system stability will be maintained.

Notes to Chapter 3

1. *Webster's Third New International Dictionary* (Springfield, Mass.: G. & C. Merriam Co., 1964), p. 2217.

2. Robert MacArthur, "Fluctuations of Animal Populations, and a Measure of Community Stability"; Jane Jacobs, *The Death and Life of Great American Cities*; idem, *The Economy of Cities*; Robert M. May, *Stability and Complexity in Model Ecosystems*; Mark R. Gardner and W. Ross Ashby, "Connectance of Large Dynamic (Cybernetic) Systems: Critical Values for Stability"; C. S. Holling, "Resilience and Stability of Ecological Systems."

3. Ralph J. Cicerone, R. S. Stolarski, and Stacy Walters, "Stratospheric Ozone Destruction by Man-Made Chlorofluoromethanes."

4. *Man's Impact on the Global Environment: Assessment and Recommendations for Action*, pp. 46–47. Also, in a critique of an earlier version of this manuscript, Murray Ellis, an investigating officer of the New Zealand Ministry of Energy Resources, commented, "Your discussion of the effects of CO_2 enrichment of the atmosphere considerably understates the possible consequences of this badly understood phenomenon. You quote the effect of an overall 2° C warming, but it is quite possible that the warming would be confined to the tropics with the resultant increased evaporation producing increased cloud cover, and hence cooling of temperate and polar regions. This would generate an ice age while the increased temperature gradient would produce a much increased frequency of severe storms."

5. Helmut Landsberg, "Man-Made Climatic Changes," pp. 94–96. Kenneth E. F. Watt points out that it is believed by some authorities that the dust particle content of glaciers is directly proportional to the aerosol content of the atmosphere, and that the particle content of the glaciers has been increasing at the same rate as some measures of world industrialization, such as crude oil use (7 percent per year).

6. *Man's Impact on the Global Environment*.

7. Lee Hickling, "N-Plants Face a Shutdown."

8. Ibid. Several excellent sources on the nuclear power controversy are: John W. Gofman and Arthur R. Tamplin, *Poisoned Power: The Case Against Nuclear Power Plants*; the U.S. Atomic Energy Commission's 1957 *Brookhaven Report*; Kurt H. Hohenemser, "The Failsafe Risk"; and *Transition: A Report to the Oregon Energy Council*.

9. Vernon Gill Carter and Tom Dale, *Topsoil and Civilization*. In a personal communication Theodore Herman of Colgate University points out that this simple cause-effect explanation has long been debated, and that other causes of decline also need to be acknowledged. Herman also notes that some cities (old Venice, modern Monaco) can live largely by drawing on distant resources.

10. Karl W. Butzer, "Accelerated Soil Erosion: A Problem of Man-Land Relationships," pp. 57–78.

11. Many papers devoted to this theme can be found in *Man's Role in Changing the Face of the Earth*, William L. Thomas, Jr., ed.

12. "Shifting cultivation" or similar terms such as "swidden agriculture," and "slash and burn" have been defined by K. J. Pelzer, in *Pioneer Settlement in the Asiatic Tropics*, as involving rotation of fields rather than crops, clearing by means of fire, use of human labor only, lack of manuring, use of dibble or hoe, and use of short periods of cultivation alternating with long periods of fallow. See also: D. E. Dumond, "Swidden Agriculture and the Rise of Maya Civilization." A list of names for geographical variants of shifting cultivation in the tropics is given in: H. H. Bartlett, "Fire, Primitive Agriculture and Grazing in the Tropics," p. 693.

13. The conservation ethic involved in shifting cultivation has been discussed by many authors including: Harold C. Conklin, "An Ethnoecological Approach to Shifting Agriculture"; Carl O. Sauer, "The Agency of Man on Earth"; Daniel H. Janzen, "Tropical Agroecosystems."

14. C. Gregory Knight, "Ethnogeography and Change."

15. Conklin, "Ethnoecological Approach," pp. 140–141.

16. Janzen, "Tropical Agroecosystems," p. 1215.

17. See Carter and Dale, *Topsoil and Civilization*; Raymond F. Dasmann, John P. Milton, and Peter H. Freeman, "Development of Pastoral Lands in Semi-Arid and Sub-Humid Regions," chapter 4 in their book *Ecological Principles for Economic Development*, pp. 76–112; Bartlett, "Fire, Primitive Agriculture and Grazing," pp. 698–699.

18. Andrew H. Clark, "The Impact of Exotic Invasion on the Remaining New World Mid-Latitude Grasslands."

19. Bartlett, "Fire, Primitive Agriculture and Grazing," pp. 695–696.

20. An excellent description of the culture that developed the Hawaiian *ahupua'a* system which stretched from the mountain tops to the ocean is given in: *The Spirit of Kaloko-Honokohau* (a proposal for the establishment of a Kaloko-Honokohau National Cultural Park, Island of Hawaii, State of Hawaii), pp. 2–23.

21. Howard T. Odum, *Environment, Power, and Society*, pp. 116–117.

22. Ian R. Manners, "Environmental Impact of Modern Agricultural Technologies," p. 187. Reproduced by permission from the Commission on College Geography of the Assoc. of American Geographers.

23. The question of degree of diversity during ecological succession is a controversial one, for "diversity" has many aspects which change during the succession: species variety, equitability, stratification, and "biochemical diversity." For a discussion of diversity and stability during succession, see Eugene P. Odum, "The Strategy of Ecosystem Development."

24. Dasmann, Milton, and Freeman, *Ecological Principles*, p. 59.

25. A number of excellent case studies are given in: M. Taghi Farvar and John P. Milton, eds., *The Careless Technology: Ecology and International Development*. Also see Dasmann, Milton, and Freeman, "The Development of Humid Tropic Lands."

26. Hugh Hammond Bennett, *Soil Conservation*.

27. T. Min Tieh, "Soil Erosion in China."

28. Butzer, "Accelerated Soil Erosion'" p. 71.

29. H. S. Gibbs and J. D. Raeside, *Soil Erosion in the High Country of the South Island*. See also: L. W. McCaskill, *Hold This Land: A History of Soil Conservation in New Zealand*.

30. *Royal Commission to Enquire into and Report upon the Sheep Farming Industry in New Zealand*.

31. Gibbs and Raeside, "Soil Erosion."

32. R. Burnell Held and Marion Clawson, *Soil Conservation in Perspective*, pp. 41–56. See also: McCaskill, *Hold This Land*.

33. Butzer, "Accelerated Soil Erosion," pp. 63–65.

34. G. H. Heichel, *Comparative Efficiency of Energy Use in Crop Production*.

35. Ibid., p. 10.

36. David Pimentel et al., "Food Production and the Energy Crisis"; John S. Steinhart and Carol E. Steinhart, "Energy Use in the U.S. Food System"; Odum, *Environment, Power, and Society*, section titled "Potatoes Partly Made of Oil," pp. 115–121; Kenneth E. F. Watt, *The Titanic Effect*; Georg Borgstrom, "Food, Feed and Energy."

37. The concept of "caloric gain" has been used to evaluate the returns from expenditure of human labor in primitive agriculture by R. A. Rappaport in: *Pigs for the Ancestors: Ritual in the Ecology of a New Guinea People*.

38. Pimentel et al., "Food Production," p. 446.

39. Steinhart and Steinhart, "Energy Use," p. 313.

40. Frances M. Lappé, "Fantasies of Famine." The wasteful conversion of plant energy into animal foods has also been outlined in Borgstrom, "Food, Feed and Energy."

41. Manners, "Environmental Impact," p. 194.

42. Georg Borgstrom, "The Breach in the Flow of Mineral Nutrients."

43. J. P. Widdowson, G. W. Yeates, and W. B. Healy, "The Effect of Root Nematodes on the Utilisation of Phosphorus by White Clover on a Yellow-Brown Loam." Similar experiments in a field situation are described in: G. W. Yeates, W. B. Healy, and J. P. Widdowson, "The Influence of Nematodes on Growth of Plots of White Clover on a Yellow-Brown Loam."

44. Borgstrom, "Breach in the Flow," p. 134.

45. Manners, "Environmental Impact," section titled "The Impact of Chemical Pesticides on the Structure and Functioning of Ecosystems," pp. 194–202.

46. For instance, the World Health Organization has estimated that over 1,000 million people have been freed from the risk of malaria during the years 1959–1970. See: World Health Organization, *The Place of DDT in Operations against Malaria and Other Vector Borne Diseases*.

47. Colin Norman, "The Little Nipper Who Cost the South a Fortune."

48. Several papers deal with this problem in Farvar and Milton, *Careless Technology*, pp. 369–548.

49. Ray F. Smith and R. van den Bosch, "Integrated Control," pp. 295–340; Gordon R. Conway, "Better Methods of Pest Control," pp. 302–305.

50. Quoted from a discussion in Farvar and Milton, *Careless Technology*, p. 466.

51. F. R. Fosberg, "Temperate Zone Influence on Tropical Forest Land Use: A Plea for Sanity," pp. 119–120.

52. Knight, "Ethnogeography and Change," p. 49.

53. Margaret Mead, ed., *Cultural Patterns and Technical Change*, pp. 174–194. See also: Knight, "Ethnogeography and Change," pp. 47–50.

54. Janzen, "Tropical Agroecosystems," p. 1213.

55. Nicholas Wade, "Green Revolution (I): A Just Technology, Often Unjust in Use." See also: David Spurgeon, "Strategy for Survival: 2: The Green Revolution."

56. Nicholas Wade, "Green Revolution (II): Problems of Adapting a Western Technology."

57. Thomas, *Man's Role*.

58. Jerry F. Franklin, Robert E. Jenkins, and Robert M. Romancier, "Research Natural Areas: Contributors to Environmental Quality Programs."

59. Raymond F. Dasmann, "A Rationale for Preserving Natural Areas."

60. International Union for the Conservation of Nature and Natural Resources (IUCN), *United Nations List of National Parks and Equivalent Reserves*, p. 13.

61. Ibid., p. 26. See also 1974 edition, pp. 23–32.

62. E. Max Nicholson, "What Is Wrong with the National Park Movement?", p. 34.

63. An "equivalent reserve" has been defined in the 1974 *United Nations List of National Parks and Equivalent Reserves* as one in which the requirements of (a) status of general protection, (b) size in excess of a certain minimum, and (c) protected status adequately maintained are fulfilled but which can be either a strict nature reserve in which tourism is not permitted or a reserve with protection deriving from other than the central government authority (p. 11).

64. Norman Myers, "National Parks in Savannah Africa."

65. Raymond F. Dasmann, "Toward a System for Classifying Natural Regions of the World and Their Representation by National Parks and Reserves"; Nicholson, "What Is Wrong with the National Park Movement?" pp. 32–38.

66. Franklin, Jenkins, and Romancier, "Research Natural Areas," p. 135.

67. E. Max Nicholson, *Handbook to the Conservation Section of the International Biological Programme*.

68. UNESCO, *Criteria and Guidelines for the Choice and Establishment of Biosphere Reserves*, extract from Program on Man and the Biosphere, MAB Report Series, No. 22, 1974, reprinted by permission of UNESCO, pp. 6–7.

69. Kai Curry-Lindahl, "Projecting the Future in the Worldwide National Park Movement," pp. 82–94.

70. Franklin, Jenkins, and Romancier, "Research Natural Areas."

71. Gene E. Likens and F. Herbert Bormann, "Effects of Forest Clearing on the Northern Hardwood Forest Ecosystem and Its Biochemistry."

72. James Fisher, Noel Simon, and Jack Vincent, *Wildlife in Danger*, pp. 11–12.

73. Ibid.

74. United Nations Environment Program, *Fact Sheet* no. 4.

75. Ibid.

76. Ibid.

77. Robert Allen, "Woodman, Spare Those Trees."

78. An appraisal of the controversy is given in: Graham Searle, *Rush to Destruction*. A detailed critique of the government's first environmental impact report was published as: L. F. Molloy, comp., *A Critique of the Environmental Impact Report on the Proposed Utilisation of South Island Beech Forests to the Officials Committee for the Environment*. Also see: A. D. Thomson, ed., *Beech Research News*.

79. Recent scientific investigation indicates that the soil, plant, and animal communities in the forests in question are of considerable complexity and diversity. The deferment of the scheme on the environmental grounds announced by the New Zealand government in May 1975 gives hope that there will be sufficient time for a full ecological investigation and consequent reservation of the threatened biota.

80. UNESCO, *Biosphere Reserves.*

81. Franklin, Jenkins, and Romancier, "Research Natural Areas," p. 138.

82. Ibid.

83. Simon Kuznets, *Economic Change: Selected Essays in Business Cycles, National Income, and Economic Growth*; idem, *Economic Growth and Structure*; R. A. Easterlin, *Population, Labor Force, and Long Swings in Economic Growth: The American Experience*; James B. Shuman and David Rosenau, *The Kondratieff Wave: The Future of America until 1984 and Beyond.*

84. See the writings of Jane Jacobs and Robert MacArthur for more information on this principle.

85. The U.S. automobile monthly manufacturing rate in May 1975 was about 660,000 cars; only 518,000 were sold in April, and 343,000 in the first 20 days of May.

86. *Statistical Abstract of the United States 1974,* table 744.

87. Richard J. Barnet and Ronald E. Muller, *Global Reach: The Power of the Multinational Corporations.*

88. N. Mostert, "The Age of the Oilberg." Note particularly discussion on pp. 41–42.

89. Howard T. Odum and E. C. Odum, *Energy Basis for Man and Nature: Energy Growth to Steady State.*

90. Calculated from data in tables 1139 and 1141, *Statistical Abstract of the United States 1974* and corresponding tables in previous volumes.

91. Tomas Frejka, "Reflections on the Demographic Conditions Needed to Establish a U.S. Stationary Population Growth."

92. Kenneth E. F. Watt, *Principles of Environmental Science,* chap. 16; idem, *The Titanic Effect*; C. K. Varshney, "Food Potential of India."

93. Mihajlo Mesarovic and Edward Pestel, *Mankind at the Turning Point.*

4
Basic Human Needs: Problems of Poverty, Affluence, and Inequity

Although the concept "quality of life" has many dimensions, we have identified three as being of major significance: (1) the maintenance of ecosystem balance, (2) satisfaction of basic physical needs for human development, and (3) satisfaction of basic social needs. Of these three dimensions it is the satisfaction of basic physical needs that, perhaps more than any other, reveals the extent to which contemporary problems have intensified.

While it may be difficult to define basic physical needs precisely, food, health, and shelter seem to be primary categories. When worldwide data on these three needs are examined, the extreme conditions of need "undersatisfaction" and "oversatisfaction" that characterize present-day humanity become glaringly apparent.

However, we are not solely concerned with demonstrating the poverty that afflicts as much as 60 percent of the world's people, and the affluence that surrounds some 15 percent.[1] We are also concerned with investigating those factors that have created and perpetuated the extreme undersatisfaction and oversatisfaction of basic physical needs. The availability of resources, the way these resources are utilized, and the inequitable distribution of resources (a factor that takes on a staggering influence as more and more data are analyzed) are major determinants in the satisfaction of basic needs. These factors will be discussed as we explore the facts about food, health, and shelter in an attempt to understand the conditions of contemporary humanity.

Much of the material in the sections on food, health, education, and shelter, are the contributions of John Morgan (see the Preface).

THE FOOD DILEMMA

The quality and quantity of food is perhaps the most basic indicator of how adequately fundamental human needs are being satisfied. Although certainly not the only factor influencing the satisfaction of food needs, the availability of food vis-à-vis a society's population is of first importance. In analyzing availability, it is helpful to look first at the prevailing trend of food production per capita in various parts of the world.

In figure 4.1 it is clear that despite efforts to improve productivity through the Green Revolution, there has been little increase in per capita food production in the developing world, and that the disparity between the developed and developing regions of the world has increased during the last ten years. In the hard-hit areas, hundreds of millions of people are barely surviving under severe grain shortages. Domestic use and consumption quickly exhaust the inadequate grain supplies, so that in areas such as West Asia and parts of South America per capita consumption exceeds per capita production by as much as 60 kg (table 4.1); and yet the amount consumed is still far below minimum daily nutrition requirements. Although on a per capita basis some may claim that this is a small deficiency in food production with respect to consumption, its absolute magnitude is great due to the total number of people in the world and the fact that resources are inequitably shared.

However, in terms of the overall global food situation, it can be argued from data that the period 1951 to 1971 was a time of success; food production almost doubled, while population increased by only 50 percent. Thus per capita cereal supplies increased by 40 percent over the twenty-year period. But it is crucial to understand that the increase was not equally shared by the world's peoples. More than half of it was absorbed by the richest 30 percent of mankind while the rest was spread unevenly among the poor 70 percent: the 2.6 billion people of Asia, Africa, and Latin America. In these lands, food production grew at an average of 2.6 percent, barely keeping ahead of population growth which averaged 2.3 percent. The average net improvement in food supply per capita thus registered only 0.3 percent. Even this small gain was unevenly distributed among the poorer regions. Latin America fared best, with a 0.9 percent growth of food per capita. In the non-Communist countries of Asia, the gain was only 0.2 percent, and in Africa the volume of food consumption per capita actually declined by 1.1 percent over the eighteen-year period.[2] In short, in terms of food, the rich got richer and the poor got poorer from 1951 to 1971.

Part of the problem can be traced to rapid population growth; for even if efforts were to succeed both in increasing the food intake of the present

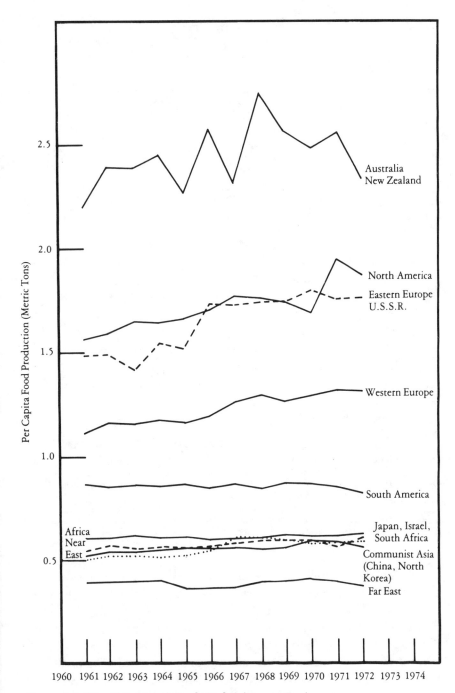

Figure 4.1. World Regional Food Production per Capita

TABLE 4.1   Per Capita Output of World Grain Production and
             Domestic Use in 1973/1974 (KG/Capita Total Grain)

Country/Region	Production	Domestic Use	Production Less Use
United States	1,120	833	+287
Canada	1,701	1,034	+667
E.E.C.-9	408	459	− 51
Other West Europe	345	337	+ 8
Japan	107	279	−172
Australia and New Zealand	1,075	419	+656
South Africa	389	298	+ 91
Total Developed Countries	618	550	+ 68
East Europe	695	744	− 49
U.S.S.R.	818	839	− 21
China	188	199	− 11
Total Central Plan Countries	363	378	− 15
Mexico, Central Am., & Caribbean	159	199	− 40
Brazil	213	234	− 21
Argentina	829	475	+354
Other South America	91	156	− 65
North Africa	162	206	− 44
Central Africa	105	111	− 6
West Asia	234	295	− 61
South Asia	158	170	− 12
Southeast Asia	209	182	+ 27
East Asia and Pacific	129	172	− 43
Total Less Developed Countries	164	181	− 17
World Total	312	313	− 1

Source: *World Agricultural Situation* (Dec. 1973), U.S. Department of Agriculture.
Note: 1. Domestic Use: production plus net imports, adjusted for stock change.
        2. Total grain was computed on the basis of total wheat, milled rice, and coarse grains (maize, barley, oats, rye, sorghum, and millets, mixed grains).
        3. Levels of domestic use should be dealt with carefully in compiling and reading this material. Some regional data are incomplete, lacking production or trade of some grains. Also stock data were not available for some countries, the largest being the U.S.S.R. and China.

population and in building up small stocks, before long the new mass of population would deplete stocks and respread the problem throughout the poverty areas of a society. When the disproportions of population growth in developed versus underdeveloped countries are considered (figure 4.2), the dilemma becomes even more severe.

It has often been suggested that one way of attacking the food problem is to increase the productivity per capita of farm land in those areas which presently have a very low per capita production rate. But in suggesting such a possibility, one has to keep in mind an essential interrelation, one which is environmentally significant. Food is obtained at an inevitable cost to the environment, a cost which is dependent on the number of people supported by a given area of farm land, the quality of food people consume, and patterns and techniques of agriculture used. A wealth of agricultural experience indicates that an increase in agricultural intensity will often be accompanied by increased environmental costs. So in evaluating any new technique aimed at increasing production, the economic capability of a society to meet the demand for matter and energy inputs, the prevailing social values, and the willingness to accept consequences of environmental deterioration must be considered.

Another interesting interrelationship is the one between productivity per capita and the percentage of people engaging in agriculture. Figure 4.3 in-

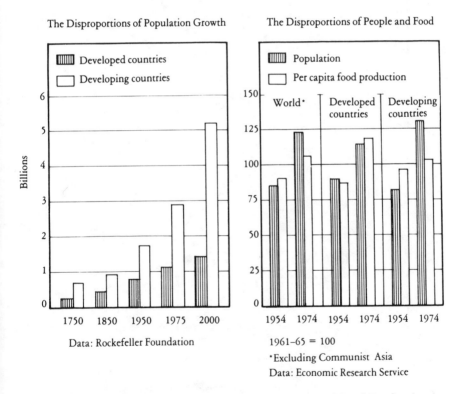

Figure 4.2. The Disproportions of Population Growth and Food Production in Developed and Developing Countries

Reprinted from the June 16, 1975 issue of *Business Week* by special permission. © 1975 by McGraw-Hill, Inc.

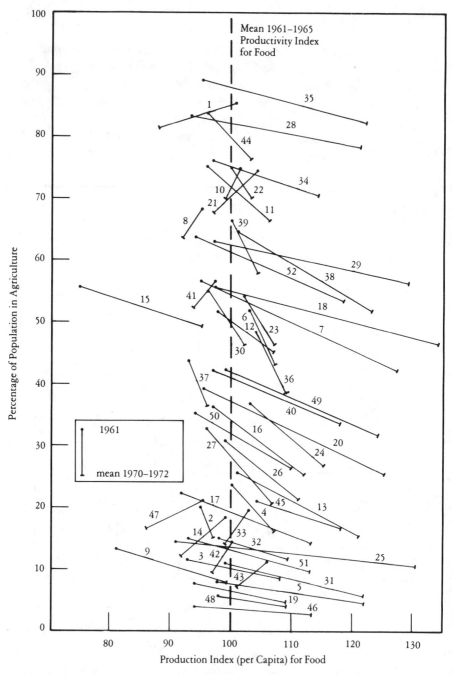

Figure 4.3. Production Index per Capita for Food in Relation to Percentage of Population in Agriculture

dicates the production index per capita of 52 countries during the period from 1960 to 1970/1973. Despite the fact that all countries show a consistent drop in the percentage of people engaging in agriculture, there is generally an increase in the production index per capita during the period. On the surface these statistics could lead one to conclude only that, generally, more is being produced with a smaller proportion of agricultural workers. But are agricultural workers being displaced by automated farming, and what effect does this have on unemployment and the accompanying disadvantagement of the unemployed? And although production shows an increase in many countries, what impacts are felt by the environment as a whole? A careful review of the data also reveals that increases in the production index are very marginal in many developing countries, such as Indonesia, South Korea, Iran, Brazil, Portugal, and others. For several countries, such as India, Burma, Afghanistan, Sri Lanka, Uruguay, Denmark, Norway, Sweden, and Switzerland, the production index shows a decrease from 1961 to 1970/1972.

The food dilemma in modern times is further revealed by figures 4.4 through 4.6 which indicate that people in poor countries have to spend as much as 60 percent of their income for food (contrasted with the U.S., for example, where on the average only 13 percent of disposable income goes for food). Even with such a high proportion of their incomes expended for food, they often fail to get the minimum amount of calories required for a healthy

Figure 4.3. Countries

1. Afghanistan	18. Greece	35. Papua/New Guinea
2. Argentina	19. Hong Kong	36. Poland
3. Australia	20. Hungary	37. Portugal
4. Austria	21. India	38. Romania
5. Belgium	22. Indonesia	39. South Korea
6. Brazil	23. Iran	40. Spain
7. Bulgaria	24. Ireland	41. Sri Lanka
8. Burma	25. Israel	42. Sweden
9. Canada	26. Italy	43. Switzerland
10. Chile	27. Japan	44. Thailand
11. China	28. Laos	45. Trinidad & Tobago
12. Colombia	29. Malaysia	46. U.K.
13. Czechoslovakia	30. Mexico	47. Uruguay
14. Denmark	31. Netherlands	48. U.S.A.
15. Fiji	32. New Zealand	49. U.S.S.R.
16. Finland	33. Norway	50. Venezuela
17. France	34. Pakistan	51. West Germany
		52. Yugoslavia

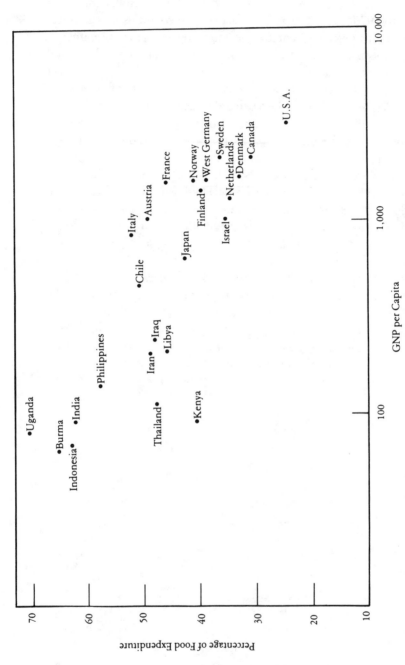

Figure 4.4. The Relation between Level of GNP per Capita in U.S. Dollars and the Percentage of Food Expenditure Relative to Total Family Expenditure of Twenty-four Countries

Data for GNP per capita from *World Bank Atlas of per Capita Product and Population*. Data on percentage of expenditure on food from the United Nations *Compendium of Social Statistics: 1967*, table 57. Graph plotted on semilogarithmic paper.

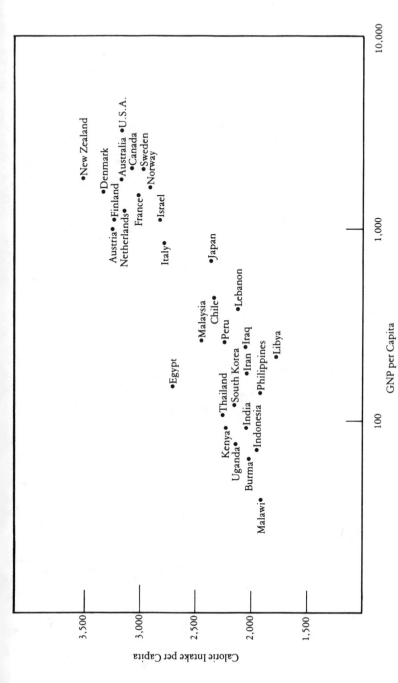

Figure 4.5. The Relation between the Level of GNP per Capita in U.S. Dollars and the Calorie Intake per Capita per Day

Data for GNP per capita from *World Bank Atlas of Per Capita Product and Population* (IBRD, 1966). Data on calorie intake per capita from *United Nations Statistical Yearbook 1972*, table 162. Graph plotted on semilogarithmic paper.

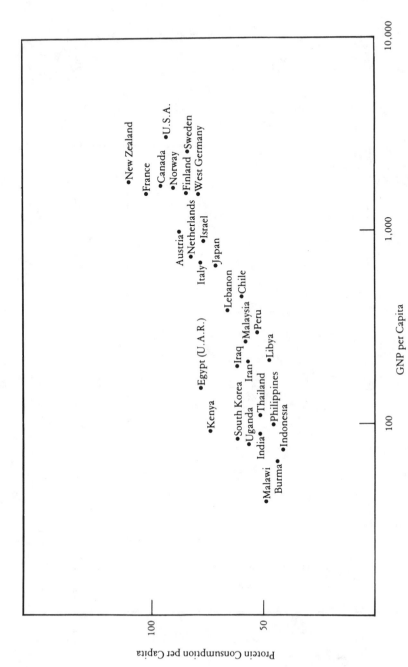

Figure 4.6. The Relation between the Level of GNP per Capita in U.S. Dollars and the Protein Intake/Consumption per Capita per Day in Grams

Data for GNP per capita from *World Bank Atlas on Per Capita Product and Population*. Data on protein consumption per capita from *United Nations Statistical Yearbook*, 1972, table 162. Graph plotted on semilogarithmic paper.

and decent life. On the other hand, people in the rich countries spend, on the average, only 25 percent of their income on food; yet the amounts of calories and protein they get are often far beyond the upper level of healthy consumption. As table 4.2 shows, this luxury consumption pattern intensifies efforts to convert grain into meat from cattle, hogs, chicken, and others, a highly inefficient process of conversion, since a large proportion of the food energy goes to the support functions (such as respiration) of the meat animal. It is estimated that if grain is grown to be fed to animals which are then fed to people (instead of feeding the grain directly to people), the total population which a given grain-growing area can support drops by a factor between five and eight.

Figure 4.7 indicates the demand elasticity for meat with respect to income. Although social and cultural factors may play an important part in determining the meat consumption pattern for some countries (for example, in India a substantial proportion of the population are vegetarians and few Indians eat beef; the Japanese traditionally eat more fish to satisfy their major protein intake than do people in other parts of the world; and Moslems will not consume pork, and so on), the graph shows a very strong correlation between the meat consumption level and the level of income, with relatively high elasticity. In other words, the data show that there is a correlation between higher income levels and increased demand for meat. To meet the in-

TABLE 4.2   Wasting Protein

	Commodity	Average Protein Content (%)	Proportion Fed to Livestock (%)
World Production	Grain	8–14	33–35
	Oil seeds (peanuts, palm kernels, etc.)	26–40	60–70
	Fish	15–25	25–40
	Milk products	3–33	25–40
U.S. Consumption	Corn, barley, oats	8–14	80–90
	Soybeans	35–40	90–95
	Wheat	11–14	24
	Milk, liquid	3–14	2*
	solids	30–33	
	Total crops		50

*Two percent of U.S. milk production is the equivalent of 1.7 billion pounds of milk, 1.4 billion pounds of nonfat milk solids, and 63 million pounds of milkfat.

Source: Frances Moore Lappé, "Fantasies of Famine," *Harper's* (February 1975), p. 90.
        (As corrected by the author in personal communication.)

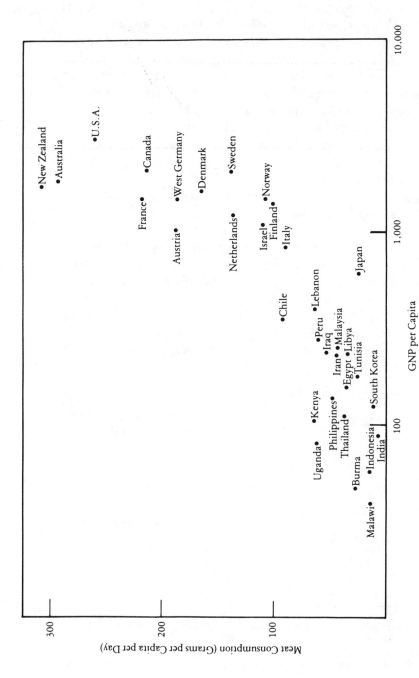

Figure 4.7. The Relation between the Level of GNP per Capita in U.S. Dollars and the Meat Consumption per Capita per Day in Grams

Data for GNP per capita from *World Bank Atlas of Per Capita Product and Population*. Data on meat consumption per capita per day from *United Nations Statistical Yearbook*, 1972.

creasing demand for meat, more grain must be converted into meat. Keeping in mind the facts of dwindling world food stocks and the power-politics basis of the international market mechanism, it is evident this trend to high meat consumption can contribute significantly to food supply failures in poorer countries.[3]

In defense of "carnivorousness," many nutritionists still insist that there is no substitute for meat in the diet. Data suggest they are mistaken. First, there are many other sources of animal protein that have a greater percent of utilizable protein than meat, such as eggs, milk, and cheese (see figure 4.8), and the production of those products is two to three times more efficient than the conversion to beefsteak. In addition, evidence has been found showing that past allegations claiming deficiencies in some meatless diets were based on ignorance of protein metabolism. The human body cannot synthesize eight of the amino acids required for growth. It requires these eight in fixed proportions. The "law of the minimum" operates here in that, if there is in the diet an ample supply of the first seven amino acids, but one is missing, the body will not be able to use any of the other seven. Protein deficiency symptoms will result from a prolonged diet of this kind. It turns out that, although there are no known single plant sources (except, significantly, for soybeans) which individually have close to the correct pattern of the eight amino acids, the required pattern of amino acids can be achieved by simple combinations of plant protein sources.[4]

We have already noted that people might eat too much, as well as too little. For example, figure 4.9, using data for countries in which more than twenty pounds of meat are eaten per person per year, suggests that a correlation between death due to cardiovascular disease and the excessive consumption of meat does exist.

Overconsumption of meat is, of course, not the only hazard of luxurious eating. Some nutritionists argue that high degrees of sugar consumption (especially of the sucrose type such as cane and beet) are harmful. There are also claims that many of the additives and preservatives in "convenience" foods may have bad health consequences, and that the lack of roughage in many prepared foods, plus excesses of fat, cholesterol, and refined grains, may be a prescription for obesity, tooth decay, heart disease, intestinal cancer, and diabetes.[5] Thus while some people around the world die from starvation, others may die prematurely from gluttony and harmful diets.

These insights also tend to support the previous argument about the maldistribution of world resources. Since the elimination of a pound of meat from the world diet makes theoretically possible the production (for human

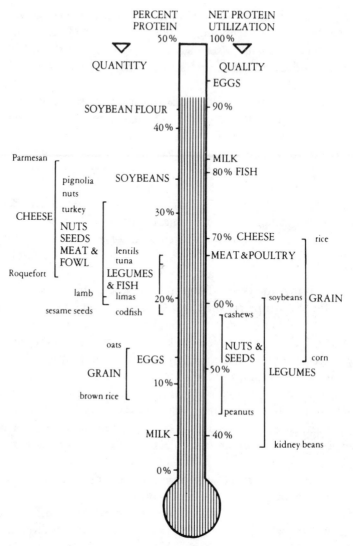

Figure 4.8. The Protein Continuum

From Frances Moore Lappé, "Fantasies of Famine," *Harper's*, February 1975, p. 87.

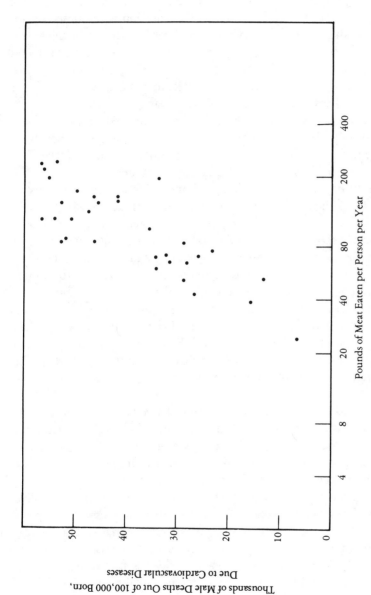

Figure 4.9. The Relationship between Meat Eating and Death due to Cardiovascular Disease

Statistics on meat consumption from *United Nations Statistical Yearbook*. Statistics on cardiovascular disease death rates from Samuel H. Preston, Nathan Keyfitz, and Robert Schoen, *Causes of Death: Life Tables for National Populations*.

consumption) of an additional several pounds of grain, it is clear that a solution of the overindulgence problem for some people might also help to solve
the starvation problem for others. But under the present patterns of world
trade, two-thirds of the world's agricultural production is consumed or utilized by less than one-third of the world's people.[6] The same wide discrepancy applies to the products of the seas, with only one-fourth of the ocean food
catches reaching consumers in the poor world. At the same time, many of
the poor nations have been traditionally devoting substantial portions of
their good soil, better irrigation systems, and managerial effort to the production of crops that are eventually sold to the developed world. In effect,
then, there is still a persisting process of net calorie and protein outflow from
the developing to the developed countries, an outflow often rationalized by
arguing that the need for currency justifies the loss of protein.

To show the dependence of nations on imported foods (but not necessarily the *source* of the foods), we can examine the "trade acreage balance"
among nations illustrated in table 4.3. Clearly Western Europe and Japan,
often praised as among the most developed parts of the world, are the major
users of the trade acreage. In other words, Europe and Japan are very much
dependent on calories and proteins produced by other parts of the world,
and actually import more in absolute terms than India and China combined. When Latin America and Africa are examined, we find that even
though these regions suffer serious nutrition deficiencies, they supply protein
and calories to developed areas of the world. Furthermore, when export data
for North America are examined, we find that the country with perhaps the
highest material standard of living in the world—the U.S.—is by far the major exporter.

The implication of this inequitable control over resources is reflected most
clearly in patterns of basic resources consumption. Table 4.4 illustrates just
how disproportionate consumption patterns have become between people
living in certain developed and underdeveloped countries. An American
consumes more than four times the primary calories, almost thirteen times
more animal protein, and close to fifty-six times more energy than his Indian
counterpart. These facts make it unfair to attribute pressure on world
resources entirely to the growth and size of the developing world's population. To the contrary, we contend that the excess of the per capita consumption of the rich minority over the poor majority has far greater effect on
resources use and depletion than the difference in their relative sizes of
population.

Thus it can be strongly argued that the overall maldistribution of wealth

TABLE 4.3   Trade Acreage Balance by Areas, 1965–1967

	(million hectares)		
	Import	Export	Net
Europe	63.6	5.9	47.7
Western, incl. Southern	53.2	11.1	42.1
Eastern	10.4	4.8	5.6
Asia	52.3	26.2	26.1
Japan	11.0	0.1	10.9
India	13.5	7.5	6.0
China	7.3	3.0	4.3
Hong Kong	2.6	0.1	2.5
U.S.S.R.	7.7	2.3	5.5
Latin America	21.0	32.1	−11.1
South America	11.6	26.6	−15.0
Argentina	0.05	18.4	−18.4
Central America	2.0	3.2	−1.2
Mexico	0.8	1.78	−0.98
Caribbean	7.4	2.3	5.1
Africa	10.9	24.3	−13.6
Nigeria	0.2	2.4	−2.2
Ghana	0.5	1.9	−1.4
Oceania	2.2	15.8	−13.6
Australia	0.4	12.7	−12.3
New Zealand	0.12	3.99	−3.4
North America	8.1	49.7	−41.6
U.S.A.	6.6	37.8	−31.2
Canada	1.5	11.8	−10.3

has led to abuse and misuse of world resources. While the majority of the world's population hardly gets sufficient amounts of grain to meet the minimum need of calories and proteins, the rich nations are converting available grain into meat by feeding the grain to livestock. The abundant supply of meat promotes overconsumption to such a level that it becomes injurious to health. The unchecked world food-market mechanism further reinforces the imbalanced distribution of food supplies by bringing large portions of the marketable surplus of grains and other food crops to the developed rather than to the underfed developing nations. A good example

TABLE 4.4   Balance Between the U.S. and India in Food,
            Energy, and Water, 1969

Substance	Per Capita/Day		
	U.S.	India	Ratio U.S./India
Food			
Calories	3,300	1,900	1.65
Primary Calories	11,900	2,910	4.10
Total protein (gram)	98.6	49.4	2.00
Animal protein (gram)	71.5	5.6	12.75
Energy (kg)	10,774	193	55.80
Water (for food, in agricultural production, in tons per cap/day)	14.4	1.8	7.97

From *The Food and People Dilemma* by Georg Borgstrom, p. 135. Copyright © 1973 by Wadsworth Publishing Co., Inc., Belmont, California 94002. Reprinted by permission of the publisher, Duxbury Press.

is the soybean crop, long touted as a major U.S. contribution to alleviating world hunger, which went mostly to Europe (two-thirds) and Japan (one-fifth) from 1967 to 1970. Less than 2 percent reached the hungry world.[7] (See tables 4.5 and 4.6) Rich countries such as Japan, the Netherlands, Norway, and the United Kingdom are among the top-ranking grain importers, much higher both in per capita and in absolute quantity than India or China. Given these facts, the statement made recently by the Organization for Economic Cooperation and Development that the developed countries have been increasingly supplementing the food supply of the developing countries[8] is grossly misleading.

HEALTH

Compiling data on global health is made extremely difficult by the fact that there exist good vital statistics for only about one-third of humanity.[9] For example, only an estimated 2 percent of infant death rates are recorded accurately. Data deficiencies are much more marked in developing countries, mirroring weaknesses in all health services there. In spite of these difficulties, some informed estimates of the world health situation can be uncovered.

Expectation of life at birth is generally accepted as the best single indicator of health, since (unlike crude death rates) it takes into account the effects of varying age distributions between countries. In the period 1965/1969 the average expectation of life at birth in developing countries was fifty years. (See table 4.7.) In developed regions during the same period, the expectation of life averaged seventy years. It should be noted that the variations in

TABLE 4.5   U.S. Soybean Export

Importers	1967–1968		1969–1970	
	Mill. Bu.	Percent	Mill. Bu.	Percent
West Europe	150.1	54.2	226.7	52.7
Japan	71.8	25.9	102.1	23.7
Canada*	29.3	10.6	53.9	12.7
Total	276.8	90.7	430.7	89.1
World Ranking				
1. Japan	71.8	25.9	102.1	23.7
2. Netherlands	39.8	14.4	57.4	13.3
3. Canada	29.3	10.6	53.9	12.7
4. West Germany	31.3	11.3	47.4	11.0
5. Spain	30.3	10.9	37.5	8.9
6. Italy	15.6	5.6	25.7	6.0
7. Taiwan	13.6	4.9	20.4	4.7
8. Denmark	13.7	4.9	19.9	4.6
9. Belgium	9.5	3.4	14.7	3.4
10. Israel	8.0	2.9	10.7	2.5
11. France	0.5	0.8	9.1	2.1

From *The Food and People Dilemma* by Georg Borgstrom, p. 131. Copyright © 1973 by Wadsworth Publishing Co., Inc., Belmont, California 94002. Reprinted by permission of the publisher, Duxbury Press.

*Including transshipments to Japan and Europe

TABLE 4.6   Soybean Importation, 1969

World Ranking in Kg/capita	Thousand Metric Tons	Population (millions)	Kg/capita	Protein Kg/capita
1. Denmark	416.1	4.9	85.0	28.2
2. Israel	207.9	2.8	74.0	25.8
3. Netherlands	915.1	12.9	71.0	24.8
4. Norway	177.3	3.8	46.7	16.7
5. Taiwan	472.2	13.5	35.0	12.2
6. Spain	1,026.5	32.7	31.4	10.9
7. Belgium	256.2	9.7	26.4	9.2
8. Japan	2,590.6	102.1	25.4	8.9
9. West Germany	1,397.8	58.1	24.0	8.4
10. Canada	384.3	21.1	18.3	6.4
11. Italy	606.7	53.1	11.4	3.9
12. United Kingdom	324.4	55.7	5.9	2.1

From *The Food and People Dilemma* by Georg Borgstrom, p. 131. Copyright © 1973 by Wadsworth Publishing Co., Inc., Belmont, California 94002. Reprinted by permission of the publisher, Duxbury Press.

TABLE 4.7   Expectation of Life at Birth
            Around 1970

Years	Percent of World Population
Less than 45	7
45–54	31
55–64	29
65 and more	33

Source: WHO, *World Health Statistics Report* 27:672.

standards of health are much greater among the developing countries than among the developed, reflecting greater differentials in successful health development among the developing nations. Thus for the twenty-five least-developed nations in 1970, the expectation of life at birth was only forty years, or about the same as was found in Western Europe around 1850.

Even this low level of life expectancy includes startling improvements when it is understood that expectation of life in the developing countries in the period 1935/1939 was at about the same level as it had been at the height of the Roman Empire—about thirty-two years. The global picture of life expectation, including continents, World Health Organization (WHO) regions, developed nations, developing nations, and the world (1970), is illustrated in figure 4.10.

Because certain features of science-based medical technology can be imported into developing countries and can succeed with little sophisticated medical infrastructure (for example, antibiotics and mass vaccination against infectious disease), a number of countries which had reached some minimum level of infrastructure have shown unprecedented rates of improvement in life expectancy. For example, in Brazil from 1940 to 1970, life expectancy increased an average of 0.6 year per year over the entire period, achieving in thirty years what took twice as long in developed countries.

The trends in life expectancy in the developed countries are a startling contrast. In general, the rate of improvement in expectation of life at birth has been declining since 1950. And there is accumulating evidence to suggest that among developing countries in the 1960s there emerged a trend toward actual increase in death rates for men in later years. The causes of death which are showing increasing rates are mostly heart diseases and cancers. Health authorities suggest that these increases in mortality may be attributed not to health care per se, but to overall environmental, cultural, and technical patterns, such as eating habits, exposure to exotic chemical

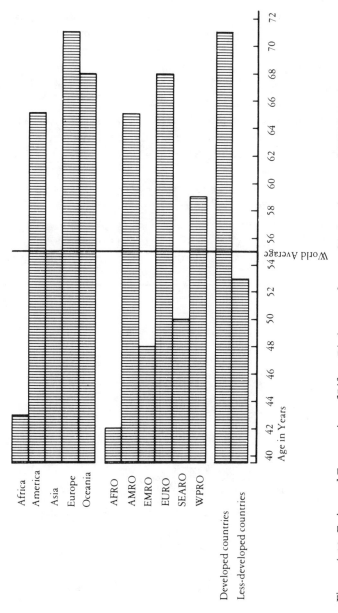

Figure 4.10. Estimated Expectation of Life at Birth around 1970, by Continent and WHO Region

From WHO, *World Health Statistics Report* 27:701.

substances in air, food, and water, and the pace of life in industrial civilization.

Fast advances in mortality control in some developing nations from use of exotic "portable" and proven medical technologies are contrasted by the relatively slow progress in finding a technical fix for what may turn out to be systemic environment-based ills in the developed countries. Together these trends have combined to produce an overall trend to decreased differentials in life expectancy in the world. The difference in life expectancy between developed and developing regions was 23.4 years in 1950. In 1970 it had been reduced to 20.8 years. Paralleling this trend is a less welcome one—the trend toward a widening of differences within the less developed regions, as some nations show progress in health care (and other sectors) while others stagnate.

Although the overall gap in life expectancy between developed and developing countries has narrowed slightly, the twenty-year gap that still remains represents great costs to developing societies. Figure 4.11 contrasts the survival from birth to age eighty of hypothetical populations of 100,000 males in typical low and high mortality conditions. From the figure the great

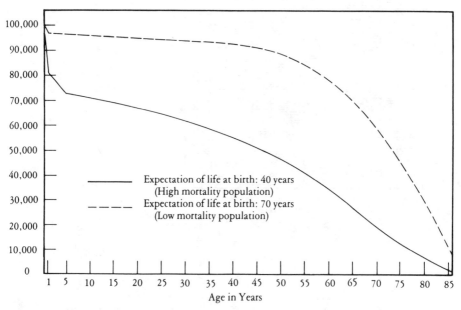

Figure 4.11. Male Survivorship Curves in a Low and High Mortality Population

From WHO, *World Health Statistics Report* 27:702.

differential in death rates in the first five years of life is clear. This differential represents a burden not only of human anguish, but also the loss of investments of time, energy, and materials. The differential in mortality rates among youths and adults under the two sets of death rates is not as great as that for the earliest years of life; but the differential persists. And here the cost to the society burdened with high mortality rates is great because those who die in these age groups are those in whom progressively more and more has been invested in terms of energy, materials, time, and education. To give some suggestion of the magnitude of this cost, it can be seen from figure 4.11 that in a low-mortality population some 97,000 of the initial 100,000 males would reach five years of age, when they might be expected to start school. Of these, 83,000 (approximately 85 percent) would reach fifty-five years of age—the period of peak contribution to society. In contrast, in a society with high mortality rates, of the initial group of 100,000, only some 72,000 males would survive until five years old, and of these, only some 42,000 (or 58 percent) would survive to age fifty-five. In effect, what these figures suggest is that to realize any number of trained and experienced senior people, a country experiencing high death rates has to support a population and make an investment of time, money, and education much greater than does a nation enjoying low death rates.

The Deaths of Infants

Mortality in the first year of life is sensitive both to the level of exposure to infections and to the resistance to them. Each is a function of environmental health conditions such as sanitation and nutrition. Since these determinants are themselves directly related to quality of life, infant mortality is inversely related to, and thus serves as an indicator of, social and economic development. The sensitivity of infant mortality to changes in social and economic development means that in developing countries where change is taking place, these rates may be expected to vary widely. Conversely, less variation in infant mortality rates may be expected among the developed nations. These expectations are verified by the data.

Where medical care is insufficient, deaths of infants in the first years are largely a function of infections and malnutrition. It is known that in many countries 100 to 200 of every thousand infants born alive die in their first year of life. For the group of developed countries the rate is 27 per thousand. In Sweden in 1969 the rate was down to 12. In contrast, for the group of developing countries in 1965 to 1969 the rate was 140—more than ten times as high.[10]

TABLE 4.8 Evolution of Public Health Patterns

State of Society	Environmental Health Problems	Predominant Patterns of Disease, Mortality, and Fertility	Goals, Type and Scope of Health Services	State of Nutrition
Traditional	Largely rural environment with contamination of water and food; proliferation of insects and rodents; periodic food scarcities.	Endemic infections, parasitisms, infestations, nutritional deficiencies. High death rate and high birth rate.	Indigenous systems of medicine based on traditional practices and beliefs.	Undernutrition as a result of food scarcities in a subsistence economy with practices and preferences of food production and consumption of a traditional, but youthful, society.
Early transitional	Largely rural environment with contamination of water and food; proliferation of insects and rodents; adulteration of foods and drugs; food scarcities.	Endemic infections, parasitisms, infestations, nutritional deficiencies. Intermediate death rate and high birth rate.	Medical relief and family planning in key centers; control of endemic diseases and environmental sanitation in selected areas; nationwide extension of categorical health services (malaria and small-pox eradication) requiring only minimal cooperation from the public and only minimal judgment from auxiliary staff with stereotype duties (residual spraying and vaccination).	Potential improvements in nutrition in areas of the monetary economy through possible modification of social, economic, and agricultural policies favoring the consumption of a variety of nutritious foods; facilitation of the extension of modern practices of agriculture, food technology and marketing, nutrition education, child-feeding and school lunch programs to the minority of the population within the scope of the nutrition programs of the health, education, and agricultural services.

Late transitional	Rural environment still resembles that of traditional society, whereas the urban environment resembles that of modern society.	Endemic diseases prevail at reduced levels in rural areas, whereas the disease patterns of urban areas resemble those of modern society. Low death rate and intermediate birth rate.	Comprehensive and integrated systems of preventive and curative health and medical services in key centers, with nationwide extension of medical relief, family planning, nutrition, basic sanitation, health education, and communicable disease control.	Continuing improvement of nutrition as a by-product of economic growth and as the result of progressive extension of nutrition programs nationwide, including the production of protein-rich foods and the fortification of staples.
Modern	Largely urban environment with pollution of air, water and food, plus hazards from use of cigarets, alcohol, food additives, new drugs, and narcotics.	Bronchopulmonary and cardiovascular diseases, malignant neoplasias, mental illness, accidents, obesity. Low death rate and low birth rate.	Nationwide extension of complex systems of comprehensive and integrated preventive and curative health and medical services, requiring a prosperous society and an enlightened public, as well as ample health manpower, qualified to exercise independent judgment.	Overnutrition as a result of an abundance of foods in an industrial economy of an affluent, sedentary, and aging society.

Source: Harald Frederiksen, "Feedbacks in Economic and Demographic Transition," *Science*, Vol. 166, 14 November 1969, table 1. Copyright © 1969 by the American Association for the Advancement of Science.

Since the mid-1930s there have been great advances in infection control, obstetrics, and nutrition. These advances have been applied to infant health care in both the developed and the developing countries. The result is that while the death rate of infants in their first year has declined almost everywhere, it has declined faster in developed regions. Thus the gap in this area has also been widening.

Reduction of death rates in infancy and early childhood (one to four years) was instrumental in reaching an expectation of life of seventy years in the developed countries. A recent study[11] showed that in developing countries nutrition was the most serious ultimate cause of death, most especially in ages one through four when children are weaned and have to make do directly on the available diet. The food dilemma is closely related to the health problems. The situation is made even more urgent by the recent findings that protein deficiencies in these early years can cause immediate impairment in mental development.

Patterns of Health Care

There can be distinguished two types of health problems: those which must depend on long-term developments for their solution, and those in which already established methods of control would, if satisfactorily applied, make an immediate and significant impact. The developing nations are plagued primarily by the latter problems. However, experience has shown that even for problems whose technical solutions, such as immunization programs, are well-known, such programs have often failed in developing nations because of lack of confidence in modern medicine among the poor masses and woefully weak national health services.

Thus the generalized pattern in health-services development worldwide seems to be that, initially, premodern societies lack trained manpower, bureaucratic and political organization, and even means of materials and information flow. Under these conditions even portable medical technologies are inoperable. Then, when a nation's infrastructure of health professionals, government efficiency, communications, roads, national integration, and the like, has surpassed some minimum, imported medical technology may bring about dramatic drops in mortality. Birth rates remain high, then later slow down as people become adjusted to a world in which infants do not die as often as they used to. Finally, the health levels reach those of developed nations and the rate of improvement slows markedly, seemingly because, as at the very beginning of the process, there are overriding environmental-systemic factors controlling mortality rates which cannot be dealt with from a narrowly defined health perspective. Table 4.8 distinguishes four plausible stages along this health care spectrum and posits characteristics for each. Table 4.9 presents actual data on twenty countries roughly grouped into the four theoretical stages.

TABLE 4.9   Vital Statistics, Health Services, and Socioeconomic Indices in Four Groups of Countries

Countries	Birth Rate*	Death Rate*	Infant Death Rate†	Deaths under 5 Years	Annual Population Growth Rate
	(1)	(1)	(2)	(%)(1)	(%)(3)
Group A					
Haiti	44	20	146	-	2.4
India	42	17	139	-	2.5
Indonesia	47	19	125	-	2.9
Nepal	45	23	150	50	2.2
Nigeria	50	25	200	56	2.6
Group B					
China**	30	13	-	-	1.7
Colombia	44	11	63	47	3.4
Iran	45	17	55	-	2.8
Mexico	43	10	68	44	3.3
Philippines	45	12	67	42	3.3
Group C					
Argentina	22	9	63	16	1.5
Puerto Rico	25	7	30	18	1.4
Singapore	23	5	21	12	2.2
Taiwan	28	5	19	17	2.3
Uruguay	21	9	50	13	1.2
Group D					
Japan	19	7	14	5	1.2
Australia	20	9	18	5	1.7
Sweden	14	10	12	2	0.4
U.S.S.R.	17	8	26	-	0.9
U.S.A.	17	9	19	5	1.0

Sources: (1)   *Demographic Yearbook 1970*, United Nations, 1971.
           (2)   *World Health Statistical Annual 1969*, WHO, 1972.
           (3)   The Population Council of New York.
           (4)   *FAO Production Yearbook 1971*, FAO, 1972.

(TABLE 4.9 Continued p. 128)

TABLE 4.9   (Continued)

Countries	Life Expec- tancy of Birth (Years)	Persons per Physician	Persons per Hospital Bed	Population in Cities of 100,000 or more	Food Calories per Capita per Day
	(1)	(2)	(2)	(%)(3)	(4)
Group A					
Haiti	32.6	13210	1350	8	1930
India	41.2	5240	1620	10	1990
Indonesia	47.5	27560	1470	12	1920
Nepal	40.6	49100	6750	4	2030
Nigeria	36.9	22090	1940	7	2290
Group B					
China**	50.0	333	440	14	2050
Colombia	45.0	2160	420	35	2140
Iran	50.0	3330	780	23	2030
Mexico	62.4	1850	510	21	2620
Philippines	51.1	10220	850	16	2040
Group C					
Argentina	66.0	620	180	61	3160
Puerto Rico	69.5	880	220	33	2530
Singapore	68.2	1520	260	80	2430
Taiwan	68.1	3170	2980	38	2620
Uruguay	68.5	950	160	53	2740
Group D					
Japan	71.7	900	80	55	2470
Australia	71.0	850	80	46	3380
Sweden	74.2	770	70	33	2850
U.S.S.R.	69.5	430	90	31	3180
U.S.A.	70.3	650	120	58	3300

*Rate per 1,000 population.
**Data for China from (1), (3), and various other sources.
†Rate per 1,000 live births.
Data compiled by R. W. Armstrong, Dept. of Geography, University of Hawaii.

The few statistics available indicate that in developing countries, health conditions are much worse in rural areas than in cities. These statistics reflect generally the development of dual economies and, specifically, the failure to provide modern medical care equitably to rural people.

In general there are great inequalities in the availability of health services in the countryside of developed nations as against the cities. Relatively few physicians, for example, are willing to forego the conveniences, comforts, and rewards of practicing in the capital cities for work in remote rural areas. The same combination of push and pull factors seems to be operating internationally. In 1973 one out of three newly certified physicians in the U.S. was a graduate of a foreign medical school. Of these, some 70 percent had emigrated to the U.S. from Asian countries where the shortage of medically trained personnel is most acute (refer to table 4.9). In effect, "the underdeveloped nations are educating thousands of physicians who ultimately end up practicing in what is perhaps the most developed nation of all."[12]

Future Prospects for a Healthy World

To see what might be done, it is important to understand exactly what are the major threats to health today. The proximate causes are quite different in the developing and in the developed regions of the world. For about 7 percent of humanity, conditions of socioeconomic development are such that modern medicine has barely touched them at all. Here the first need is to develop the minimal social and economic infrastructures. Where this work has developed, the most dramatic progress has taken place. The ranking of major causes of death in such societies is typically: infectious diseases (40 percent), circulatory diseases (20 percent), cancer (5 percent), accidents (5 percent), miscellaneous (30 percent). The prevalence of infectious diseases means there is room for great improvement in vaccination campaigns and the most rudimentary hygiene programs. In contrast, among developed nations, the major causes of death are ranked: heart disease (15 to 20 percent), accidents (3 to 6 percent), and lung cancer (5 percent for males, 1 percent for females).

When we look slightly afield for the *underlying causes* of world health problems, disparate factors begin to merge. Often the least developed nations are either exploited for raw materials or ignored for their lack of them by a world order largely guided by profit maximization priorities. Inside many developing countries this international pattern becomes *intra*national as the wealthy and powerful few enjoy excellent medical facilities while the neglected masses have little access even to basic health care. Inside developed nations, although disturbingly large numbers of poor and medically ignored peoples do indeed exist, illness and death often stem from the consequences of rapid industrial development.[13] In addition to numerous industrial and automobile accidents, energy flow rates and the by-products of industrial civilization can cause quite sudden and possibly pathological perturbations in the biosphere, perturbations whose effects we are just beginning to comprehend. A short list of sample by-products may suggest the dimensions of the situation: arsenic, cadmium, lead, mercury, asbestos, carbon monoxide, photochemical oxidants, smog, fluorides, nitrates, nitrites, nitroso compounds, DDT and related compounds, herbicides, plutonium, microwave radiation, laser radiation, ionizing radiation, crowding, and noise.[14]

A careful analysis of the data just presented clearly reveals that the basic human needs of health and health care are grossly undersatisfied among most of humanity. It is also becoming increasingly apparent that, in affluent societies, even though medical technology has attained unprecedented levels, good health is not an assured benefit, either because pockets of poverty persist, health care costs are prohibitively high, and/or affluent life-style diets and industrial growth by-products are proving harmful to health. And the data also reveal that the inequitable health-care treatment evident within societies exists in staggering proportions internationally as well. It seems glaringly obvious that the achievement of a high quality of life will perpetually be thwarted as long as one of the most basic of all human needs continues to go unmet.

SHELTER

The importance of shelter as one of the basic human needs was underscored once again by the 1974 UN Cocoyoc Declaration.[15] As with other patterns of resource use on earth today, the outstanding characteristic in the area of shelter is the great disparity between the conditions of the rich and the poor. While the fortunate minority live in what most of humanity would consider palaces, the UN estimated in 1972 that fully one thousand million people are living in substandard housing. Given world population growth rates, the UN estimates that the global housing need, A.D. 1970 to 2000, will be 1.4 billion dwelling units[16] if all mankind is to be even minimally sheltered. This means that dwelling unit construction must reach a rate of ten dwelling units per thousand persons per year. This rate may not seem awesome until one realizes that even most developed countries fail to achieve this construction rate. (See table 4.10.)

Achieving the necessary rate will thus call for a speedup of dwelling con-

TABLE 4.10   Rate of Construction of
Dwelling Units (DU)

Country and Census Year	No. of DU/1000 Persons/Year
U.S.S.R. (1965)	9.4
U.S.A. (1970)	7.1
Japan (1970)	4.9

Source: U.N. *Statistical Yearbook 1973*, table 198, "Summary of Housing Conditions," p. 724.

struction in most developed countries, and it will call for a revolutionary overhauling of the means for dwelling unit construction in the less developed countries, where the rates typically range from .5 to 3.0 dwelling units per thousand persons per year. The UN has adopted the standard that nations should aim to invest 4 to 5 percent of their total GNP in housing. Some nations are making heroic efforts in this direction. Sri Lanka's current plan calls for spending fully 25 percent of the government budget on housing. But, in fact, the least developed countries do well to spend even 1.5 percent of GNP on housing.

Aside from the pandemic shortage of funds in the developing world, there is a traditional body of economic theorizing which holds that housing is not a *productive* good, like capital equipment, but a *consumption* expenditure; thus housing should be delayed until investment in capital goods (like agricultural or industrial equipment) can raise the GNP. This position is forcefully opposed by the insight of Gunnar Myrdal, in his consideration of levels of living in Asia.

> . . . in the underdeveloped countries of South Asia, levels of living are so low as seriously to impair health, vigor, and attitudes toward work. Consequently, increases in most types of consumption represent *at the same time* "investment," as they have an immediate and direct effect on productivity (emphasis is Myrdal's).[17]

To this argument may be added, in defense of a high priority for housing expenditure, a consideration of its purely economic multiplier effects. The late Charles Abrams, a senior UN housing expert with wide experience in many countries, concluded that investment in housing in developing countries: (1) inspires material production industries, (2) absorbs urban unemployment, (3) spurs savings among new and would-be home owners, and (4) fattens tax revenues and speeds general industrial development.[18] This characterization of the economic impact of housing is emphatically borne out by the experiences of developed economies. In the U.S., for example, fully 25 percent of total investment is in housing, and the same percentage of average annual expenditures goes to housing. Housing has strong economic linkages to materials and construction industries, as well as to financial circles and public utilities planning. Indeed, activity in the housing sector is a major indicator of the economic well-being of developed country economies.

The existing deficits of housing are staggering. In Latin America 20 million housing units are needed now. In Asia, 22 million are needed in urban areas and 125 million in rural areas. Why these great deficits in housing? The three proximate driving forces are: (1) rapid population growth, (2) even more rapid urbanization, and (3) poverty (that is, the economy grows too slowly to compensate for the great dependency burden of youthful, fast-growing populations).

Urbanization

Of the three proximate driving forces mentioned above, one is increasingly becoming a major factor in the housing crisis: the rapid implosion of people to urban centers. As figure 4.12 shows, the rise in urban population has ever been greater than the well-known increase in total population. Thus we cannot understand the problems of shelter in the developing world until we consider this very rapid flow of people away from the countryside and into the cities. As an indicator, of the 148 countries for which population data are reported in the 1972 *FAO Production Yearbook*, every one recorded a drop in the percentage of the population economically active in agriculture. What is happening is that, as agricultural holdings become progressively subdivided by succeeding generations in which infants do not die off at the high pre-antibiotic rates, the size of holdings rapidly diminishes, unless many people leave the land and head for the cities. To this population factor are added the economic forces of farm mechanization and consolidation which, in many societies, are contributing to the urban implosion by leaving large numbers of rural people with no work to do. And then to these factors are coupled the ecological problems of exhausted soils, devegetated lands, eroded slopes, and dried-up springs and streams.

Before the forces of change were unleashed on the developing world, shelter, like other needs, was usually provided. A number of authors[19] have pointed out that the shelter techniques developed traditionally, and which contained the wisdom and empirical findings of countless generations of people living under nearly constant conditions, should not be abandoned carelessly. For, in many cases, traditional housing designs are not only aesthetic delights but models of economy, using only locally available building material, and little of that when the supply is limited. The structures tend to be culturally, climatologically, structurally, and ecologically appropriate, even though certain shortcomings such as poor lighting, inadequate ventilation, vulnerability to fire, and susceptibility to insect infestation certainly cannot be ignored.

In a traditional, stable agrarian society, most materials for a simple house are available locally, often free for the gathering from one's own land. Likewise, it is common to find that almost all adults command (at least in some degree) most of the skills involved in construction. The community spirit also plays a role, as neighbors usually cooperate in the most demanding aspects of construction. The result is that, where the resources base is still ade-

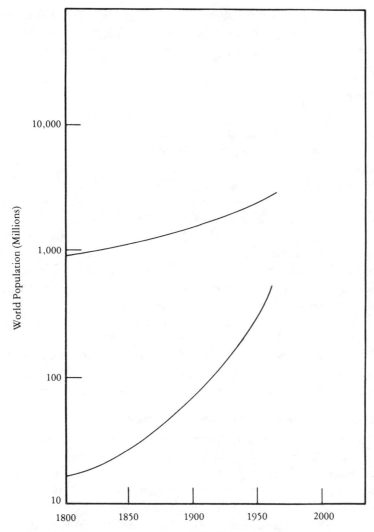

Figure 4.12. Urbanization of the World's Population

"Rapid urbanization of the world's population is evident in this comparison of total population (upper curve) with the population in cities of more than 100,000 inhabitants (lower curve) over more than a century and a half. The use of cities of 100,000 or larger to define an urban population shows a close correlation with other definitions of urbanism."

From Kingsley Davis, "The Urbanization of the Human Population," copyright © by Scientific American Inc., September, 1965.

quate and traditional patterns of rural life are little disturbed, housing can be constructed at little or no cost. And since there is little status differential among people concerning housing, most everyone is "adequately housed" by local standards.

Squatters

Today, however, with the pressures of dwindling resources, population growth, and technical change, people are flocking to the cities in search of a life that might be even marginally better than life in the countryside. They immediately find that the traditional housing techniques are impossible in the city. For instance, in Addis Ababa, Ethiopia, in 1974, it would have been far more expensive to build a traditional grass-thatched house than a tin-roofed one, because the urban dweller would first have to buy the grass from a farmer and then reimburse him for bringing it twenty kilometers on donkey-back. So, instead of using traditional building forms, the poor who flock to the cities use whatever materials they can get hold of, on whatever tiny plot they can find. Far too often the results are inadequate shelters. All these shortcomings are compounded by incredible crowding. The notorious Tondo squatter section in Manila reportedly houses 132,000 people in 137 hectares, suggesting a density for predominantly single-story structures of nearly one thousand people per hectare (four hundred people per acre). This is as high as the overall density of the New York City Metropolitan Statistical Area, a region of predominantly medium to high-rise residential structures.

Critical Urban Problems of the Population Implosion

Due to the centralization of government bureaucracies, limitations of funds, and the snowballing role of positive feedbacks as urban centers grow, the largest cities (most often one prime city) in developing countries experience the fastest rates of economic and industrial growth. At the same time they become the targets of significantly higher rates of in-migration from the countrysides than do the secondary cities. This concentration (seen in figure 4.13 in the case of India) further exacerbates the severe problems of the cities.

The case of Manila is a revealing example. The 1970 census was the first in the city's history to include data on housing. It was found that fully 42 percent of the city's dwelling units were classified as light construction and "temporary." Only 10 percent of the areas had access to electricity, and the last improvement to the sewage system was made in 1939. In the squatter areas at present drainage and flood control are particularly inadequate, meaning that periodically in floods, what goes down the few sewers is just as

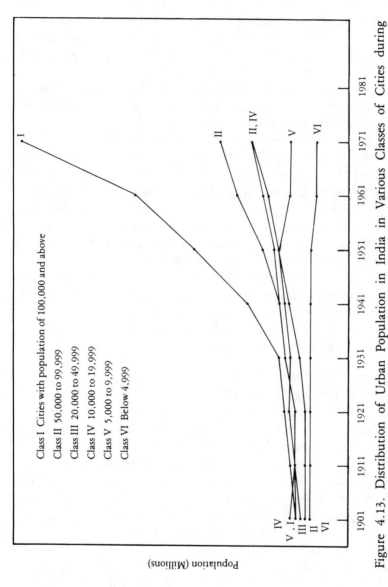

Class I Cities with population of 100,000 and above

Class II 50,000 to 99,999

Class III 20,000 to 49,999

Class IV 10,000 to 19,999

Class V 5,000 to 9,999

Class VI Below 4,999

Population (Millions)

1901 1911 1921 1931 1941 1951 1961 1971 1981

Figure 4.13. Distribution of Urban Population in India in Various Classes of Cities during 1901–1971

Source: *Indian National Report on Human Environment* submitted by the Government of India to the United Nations Conference on the Human Environment, May 1971.

likely to come up again. Water comes to the squatters primarily through shared standpipes, and these operate only in the evening. Current estimates suggest that the city should have 375 million gallons per day (MGD). There is available only 270 MGD, leaving a shortage of 100 MGD. The population of the city is growing at a startling 6 percent per annum, and the slum areas are growing at a frightening 12 percent. This means that the population will double in about six years, so that by 1980 the city's population will reach more than eight million, about twice the 1970 population. The water need then will be about 800 MGD. There is no way foreseen to meet this demand. The point is that when one deals with housing one must also deal with other basic services in addition to dwellings.

The squatter and slum housing problem in the developing world's burgeoning cities has two major dimensions: (1) overcrowding and (2) sanitation. Though the concept of crowding is to some degree culturally determined, by any standard it is clear that higher densities are a characteristic of the hungry world. (See table 4.11.) One basic indication of how bad things can become is that the first public housing units constructed in Hong Kong to relieve squatters consisted of one room of 110 sq. ft. with one door, no windows, and a bath shared with 50 other such units. Whole families with relatives (as many as ten people) lived in such cubicles. These units have since been recognized as unacceptably small, but the current standard for low-income housing in Hong Kong is only 35 sq. ft. per person.[20] Contrast this with the developed nations' standard of space by which a 1,000 sq. ft. house is considered small for four persons.

Housing and Sanitation

In addition to crowding, the lack of basic sanitation in the housing conditions of the poor, especially in the less developed countries, is severe. Especially dangerous is the public health hazard of contaminated water supplies or other sources of pathogen transmission resulting from inadequately treated sewage. Depending on soil and water-table conditions, human wastes in some cities may be handled by dug latrines (as in Addis Ababa) or by open ditches (as in much of Jakarta). Such conditions, amplified by crowding, increase the likelihood of many infectious diseases, of which typhoid fever and cholera are only the two best known.

In spite of advances in epidemiological techniques, the interaction of these problems of health and housing is so complex that the evidence from empirical studies is by no means conclusive.[21] But the data scatter in figure 4.14 does indicate a relation between the incidence of cholera and typhoid fever and the prevalence of piped water in a country. Indeed, there is con-

TABLE 4.11 Number of Persons per Room as Determined from National Censuses of the Total Population

Country and Census Year	No. Persons/ Room
Developing Countries	
Morocco (1971)	2.4
Algeria (1966)	2.8
Congo (1960–61)	2.7
Zambia (1969)	2.4
Mexico (1970)	2.5
Ecuador (1962)	2.5
Peru (1961)	2.3
Iran (1966)	2.3
India (1971)	2.8
Pakistan (1960)	3.1
Developed Countries	
Canada (1971)	0.6
U.S.A. (1970)	0.6
Israel (1971)	1.5
Japan (1970)	1.0
Australia (1971)	0.7
Denmark (1965)	0.8
France (1968)	0.9
Italy (1961)	1.1
Sweden (1970)	0.7
Switzerland (1960)	0.7

Source: *UN Statistical Yearbook 1973*, table 198, "Summary of Housing Conditions," p. 724.

siderable concentration at the level where deaths are low and homes with piped water are plentiful. Below this rarefied level, the data points for different countries are widely scattered. So even though the empirical confirmation may be hard to obtain, the causal pathway connecting housing conditions with health is well-known and convincing.

Poverty and filth are often closely associated with poor housing. Without a water supply, it is very difficult to maintain personal cleanliness, and wastes accumulate where there is no public service of refuse collection. Even when the occupants attempt, within the limits of their meagre resources, to improve the hygiene of their dwellings, the results are seldom lasting. This is mainly because the physical condition of the house, with leaking roof, cracked walls, and earth floors, facilitates the admission and accumulation of dirt, dust, and soot, and gives rise to dampness. Filth attracts lice, fleas, bugs, and mites that may transmit disease. Poor housing permits the harbouring of mice and rats, which can also be carriers and transmitters of disease, and the entrance of flies and mosquitos, with the resultant spread of such diseases as trachoma, malaria, yellow fever, filariasis, and dengue.[22]

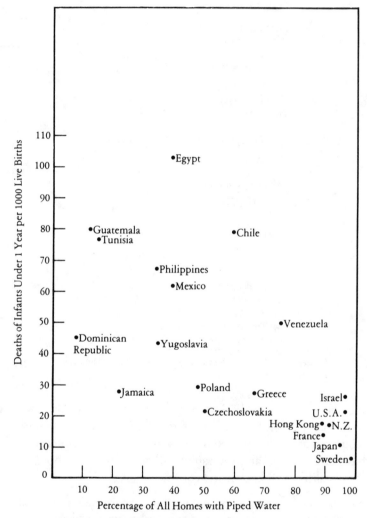

Figure 4.14. Deaths of Infants in Relation to Percentage of Homes with Piped Water

Data on infant deaths from *United Nations Demographic Yearbook*, 1973, table 13, pp. 256–261; on homes with piped water from *United Nations Statistical Yearbook*, 1973, table 198, pp. 724–758.

Poor Among the Rich

Though the degree of deprivation is less severe, inadequate housing conditions can also be found in the developed nations of the world. In the U.S. for example, government standards currently indicate that a family of four with an income of less than $10,000 per year will probably be unable to afford "decent" housing. In general, if a family's income is below this level, and if more than 25 percent of its income goes for housing, the family is considered deprived. An "overcrowded" house is one with more than one person per room. A "dilapidated" house is one in which plumbing is not working, the roof is leaking, or the like. Using these definitions, a Massachusetts Institute of Technology study of 1970[23] found that of the 63.4 million households in the U.S. in 1970, about 20 percent fell into one of these three categories of housing inadequacy, as shown in table 4.12.

Elements of the Problem of Shelter

1. *Land.* In many urban areas the availability of land for housing is a critical link in the total problem. Too often a few wealthy landowners are content to keep their land empty, speculating against the inevitable rise in the value of their real estate. Some societies have enacted legislation to try to combat these practices. A good example is Sweden, where there is an active program of long-term municipal land banking aimed at making land available for government housing projects projected ten years into the future. The availability of land far in advance of its scheduled development is claimed to be one of the elements in the success of the Singapore Housing and Development Agency which has built over 100,000 dwelling units from 1964 to 1974.

2. *Energy and Materials.* It is possible to calculate the energy cost of various building materials, and work of this kind has recently been done.[24] As we have argued previously, when societies exploit their environment to

TABLE 4.12   Dimensions of U.S. Housing Problem, 1970

Housing Condition	No. of Households (millions)
Dilapidated dwelling units	6.9
Overcrowded dwelling units (physically sound)	0.7
Other units where rent burden is high	5.5
Total	13.1

get materials, including of course, building materials, they run the risk of irreversibly disrupting environmental balance. The classic example of this pattern is the destruction of forests to obtain timber for building construction and logs for fuel, without provision for protected regrowth. This happened in Lebanon over two thousand years ago when King Solomon dispatched an army of cutters to fetch the bountiful cedars for construction of a temple. It also happened in northern Ethiopia in the early years of the twentieth century, and contributed to the recent drought and famine in that region. It is happening in Indonesia today, where the excessive felling of forests to be used in domestic and export consumption is not balanced by protected reforestation. The energy cost of natural materials like wood is relatively low for man, since trees are, with minimal protection, living, self-sustaining production systems. Industrialized building materials like cement and steel are, in contrast, energy intensive. With the recent sharp inflation in the price of energy in the world, the price of such energy-intensive industrial building materials has risen accordingly, causing havoc with the ambitious housing plans of many governments.

In contrast, for decades some have spoken in favor of less energy-intensive, more labor-intensive techniques of construction that are more closely related to the vernacular building styles. Some of these were innovations like the Cinvaram (a compressed brick of soil and cement) or the Stack Sack (a plastic or burlap bag filled with soil-cement). Others were calls to use traditional materials better, like impregnated bamboo, or unshored mud-block arches and domes. With the advent of the energy crisis, plus the realization that traditional capital-intensive strategies of development just were not trickling down fast enough to meet the insistent need for amelioration of living conditions, these ideas for "appropriate technology" are getting fresh emphasis for housing as well as other spheres of technology. E. F. Schumacher, a senior spokesman of this philosophy, has long pointed out that in conditions of severe underdevelopment, the prime need is not to maximize productivity, but the number of work places.[25] Schumacher argues that the worst curse is for men to be deprived of any chance to use their hands and minds to produce for their living. He suggests that as a first step to lift this curse, it is necessary to encourage those technologies that are intermediate (in scale, cost, and productivity) between the unchanged traditional technologies and the techniques used in highly industrialized societies. An example in the field of building construction is the research being done in India on the use of bamboo. A particularly interesting finding presents engineering data showing that bamboo can successfully replace steel as reinforcing in concrete slabs.[26]

In sum, there is always a ferment of action in the development of new building materials. For decades this activity has been in the direction of more synthetic, industrialized materials. Now it appears that there will be a harmonizing tendency in at least some spheres of research, seeking to combine efficient but energy-intensive materials with improved traditional materials and new natural sources.

3. *Technology.* Until rather recently, it was universally assumed that in building construction there was really only one best technology: the newest, biggest, most productive per man-hour. But as mentioned in the previous section, the turnabout in the costs of energy and materials vis-à-vis manpower, coupled with impatience with the slow equity effects of capital-intensive growth, is producing pressure for a reordered set of criteria in the still young field of technology assessment. Now, in addition to productivity, it is important to look at: (1) the employment-generating potential of a technology; (2) the degree to which technology promotes dependence upon or independence from foreign sources of materials, equipment, and/or expertise; (3) the ease with which the technology can be a base for development of ancillary technical developments (locally grown) and skill upgrading; and (4) the appropriateness of the product of the technology, including consideration of scale, infrastructural requirements, and suitability to local conditions and requirements. The Intermediate Technology Development Group (ITDG) out of London has done pioneer work in this area, generating portfolios assessing the technology alternatives in several areas, including building construction.

A further dimension is the equity question. It is becoming clear that in the absence of specific government policies, there is a tendency for higher-capitalization technologies to encourage the concentration of the value added into few hands—those of the big investors and entrepreneurs. In short, in the construction of human shelters, as in other areas of technology (notably, production industries and agriculture), there is an emerging awareness of an array of alternative technologies which must be measured, not by the single metric of productivity per unit of worker's time, but rather over a range of criteria. In the words of the UN's Cocoyoc Declaration, "Our first concern is to redefine the whole purpose of development. This should not be to develop things, but to develop man."[27] It seems clear that one of the causes of the tragic waste of human resources which stands behind all the grim statistics of world poverty, including those on shelter, is choosing technologies solely on the basis of profitability to the investor and entrepreneur.

4. *Labor.* Labor cost is necessarily an element in the total cost of shelter.

As explained earlier, in traditional, preindustrial rural societies most of the labor of shelter production was supplied by the owner and helpful neighbors. With urbanization and industrialization has come specialization and the accompanying emphasis on efficiency at the cost of individual self-sufficiency. The cost of labor relative to materials in a particular country and setting is a critical parameter in the decision as to which level of technology is most appropriate.

The implications of the reaffirmation of the development process as being for and about people requires a reexamination of the concept of labor. No longer can the comparatively recent notion that labor is a necessary evil, to be minimized and finished quickly with as much mechanized assistance as possible, be tolerated as the dominant view. Schumacher has put the point very well in his essay, "Buddhist Economics,"[28] harkening economists back to the classical view of work as an elevating experience for the individual. If the job does not elevate the person, then there is something vitally wrong with the job. This is an entirely novel criterion to most contemporary economic thinkers, one which could change the type and distribution of job tasks in construction, as well as in other technologies.

Still another aspect of labor has been the grotesquely unbalanced extremes in the value of workers' time in developing versus developed countries. In the less developed countries men may work all day and barely earn the equivalent of fifty U.S. cents, while in some parts of the U.S. it is reported that plumbers charge $25 per hour. Over an 8-hour day, the plumber earns 400 times what his brother laborer does in a developing country. Further, an extremely low cost of labor encourages wasteful use of manpower and constriction of buying power. The contrasting extreme of high labor cost in the industrialized nations encourages energy- and materials-intensive production of housing, which, with the explosion in the cost of energy and materials, has contributed to raising dwelling costs to such levels that new housing in developed countries is beyond reach.

5. *Taxation, Mortgaging, and Home Financing.* Under the conditions of the traditional, preindustrial society, home construction requires little cash outlay. Therefore, the need for mortgaging or other financing is absent. In postindustrial nations, especially in the case of capital-intensive construction (urban high-rises), a tremendous amount of capital must be invested in each dwelling unit. To raise this capital requires in turn the operation of a sophisticated money market. In this context there is a wealth of fiscal measures open to governments. For example, some nations have instituted government insurance for homes built to certain specifications. The U.S. Federal Home Loan Bank Board loans program is one example. In New

Zealand a government program of low-cost "State Housing" (with rental at approximately one-sixth of income) has been moderately successful in housing low-income families since 1937. The notably successful Singapore Housing Development Agency, riding the crest of a very high per annum growth rate of GNP and bolstered by total political support, has achieved an impressive record in public housing construction—over 60 percent of the island's population is housed in the Housing and Development Authority's (HDA's) buildings. However, in many cases the intentions of policies have not been achieved. Critics complain that the U.S. housing policy, especially the HDA scheme, has encouraged wasteful urban sprawl and the gobbling up of valuable open space; and that overall the system has failed to provide adequate housing for all people while playing into the hands of mortgage bankers.[29] In New Zealand, some point to those who artfully work to keep their income low enough to qualify for government estate housing, then push their income up as soon as they obtain the house and make no attempt to purchase their own home eventually.

More tellingly, it has been argued that in some developed countries the interacting facts of finance, labor professionalization, closing costs, taxes, mortgages, and building codes have gone too far. John F. C. Turner and Rober Fichter have called for freedom of the individual to get on with the task of building, unencumbered by the restrictions generated by these finance groups.[30]

Utilization of Resources for Shelter

As we mentioned earlier, the way in which resources are utilized has as much impact on the satisfaction of basic needs as does the availability of resources. Nowhere is this more true than in shelter needs. Numerous programs have been tried in various scenes throughout the world, from the countryside in the developing world, to cities where capital is severely lacking, to cities where capital is available. An investigation of resource utilization for shelter in these various scenes can perhaps offer hints for the solution of the extremely serious housing problems affecting most societies.

As has been explained above, in some senses the housing problem is not as acute in the developing world countryside as it is in the imploding capital cities of these nations. But traditional shelter, good as it may be, can often use improvement. There are problems in getting the useful technical innovations to the villagers. Many imply that villagers are irrationally conservative in matters of technology. That is clearly not true. When villagers are presented with a technical innovation that they believe has relevance to their way of life, that works, and that they feel is worth the price, they are quick to adopt it. Witness the use of corrugated metal sheet for roofing, carried by men and beasts to remote areas, because the metal perfoms a tough technical job well, is relatively easy to install, requires no exotic maintenance, and has proven to be worth its price. Furthermore, the farmer in most societies is the primary producer for the cities, so that he is linked through trade with the larger world. That is, there is in every developing, agricultural country, a highly evolved sector of traders catering to the needs of farmers, exchanging for foodstuffs the products of the urban world. This trading sector supplies some building materials to the village people now. If there are programs of research and development in housing in villages, these channels, reinforced by government demonstrations and mass media information, can be used to get improved housing technology widely disseminated and to do it quickly. Programs in this vein are well under way in many countries. The radio extension services in Mauritius serve as an example. Experimental programs have also been started in Chilalo governorate, Ethiopia.

In the area of research and development on building technologies appropriate to the villagers, there are several good examples of current efforts: the Central Building Research Institute in Roorkee, India; the Building Research Center at Kumasi University of Science and Technology in Ghana; the Intermediate Technology Development Group of London (both in research and development and in publishing construction and management guides);[31] and the work of Hassan Fathy in Egypt[32]—all attempt to focus directly on the shelter needs of rural areas.

Yet another approach is an attack on the problem of upgrading the level of building skills in the villages. One such approach that has shown some success is the brigade scheme of Botswana. In this program, school dropouts are organized into working teams called brigades. They are given an intense program of classroom and on-the-job training, and then the brigades actually function as building contractors in the community.

In sum, housing in villages, though often ingenious, needs improvement. Channels of communication do exist, and must be utilized to identify and develop appropriate technologies. Some promising pioneer work has been done, but much more is needed. It should go without saying that improvement in housing in the traditional villages of the world is impossible without improving the general standard of living of villagers, which in turn hinges on establishing a balanced, equitable, and productive relationship among the villagers, their ecosystem, and the national and international economic systems.

In cities where capital is severely lacking, "self-help" (having the owner build his own shelter) is a popular catchword among housing specialists. The squatter settlements ringing so many cities in the developing world are almost entirely the result of self-help building, and illustrate both the strength and the weakness of the approach. The strength is found in the great potential of energy inherent in most people; but this strength must be put to work. In most of the cities of the developing world, the energy of many people is wasted because there is no job for them to do. Self-help gets around this blockade, and can thus unleash a tremendous flood of manpower.

Experience suggests that self-help schemes work well when owners do some of the work, but leave the more demanding tasks for specialists. For example, owners can form pressed-earth blocks but hire masons to lay the walls. But self-help of this variety is not restricted to the developing countries. Self-help can also be made possible in the developed world, mainly by freeing the owner-builder from the encumbrances of the interlocking bureaucracies characteristic of industrial society construction.[33]

Mutual aid schemes represent another variety of self-help. A group of families is given basic training in house construction and then the families work together building each member's house. But the social-dynamic problems of such an undertaking are formidable, so that where alternatives exist, other self-help schemes seem more productive. One such alternative scheme is the "sites and services" idea, in which plots of land with minimal infrastructures (a water standpipe, a sewer line, an electric line) are provided. Through this scheme, scarce capital improvement funds are spread to more of the population, and new owners are given the responsibility of building their own houses. The "core house" concept goes one step beyond sites and services. It involves the provision of a utilities hookup, plus some sort of basic module of a dwelling (usually a bathroom, since maintaining sanitary standards in construction is technically demanding). Resettlement of squatters from choice downtown locations has also been tried. Squatter huts have been disassembled and reassembled on a new site, with all the same old neighbors (to preserve social networks), but with much more open space.

In many of these attempts at improvement, the human implications of housing-related programs are ignored, and/or housing agencies simply fail as bureaucracies. But sound efforts are being made in some areas. In Jakarta, for example, the city government is concentrating on the *service* level of the urban environment rather than on housing construction alone. The Kampong (neighborhood) Improvement Program includes work on vehicle and pedestrian roads and bridges, drainage canals, community wells and windmills for drawing water, community lavatories, garbage bins, and health clinics, in an effort to bring improved services to already developed sites.

In sum, there are many approaches being tried in the overtaxed cities of the developing world. Some succeed but many fail. There is, therefore, a great need to sift the accumulated experience and determine the factors that can bring success. Once done, the knowledge and necessary assistance must then be extended to the great majority of poor urban dwellers in the crowded cities whose shelter, water supply, and sanitation remain in a woeful state.

In the third scene—cities where capital is available—severe problems of housing can also be found. In 1975 New York City hovered on the brink of bankruptcy. Poor housing conditions and the failure of policy to alleviate these conditions were a part of the problem. New York had instituted rent control legislation to keep the rents on apartments down for low-income renters. However, in yet another example of counterintuitive, unanticipated behavior operating in a complex system, landlords who were unable to make a competitive profit from investment in their rent-controlled property simply stopped all maintenance services. The results were not only deplorable living conditions, but a steady exodus from the city of people who could afford to commute and were attracted by much better housing at similar prices outside the city. This situation, so characteristic of many large cities, in turn further restricted the tax base of the city, contributing to the 1975 money crunch.

Again using Singapore as an example, the Singapore Housing and Development Board (HDB) built 110,000 medium-rise dwelling units in its first ten years of existence. An insider's analysis of what was right with the HDB[34] shows that the success was based on several key factors:

1. *Political Will.* In Singapore, the HDB had strong support at the higher level. The president and his cabinet supported the program wholeheartedly.

2. *Competent Civil Service.* The Singapore civil service was quite competent and honest. Such people were essential to support the ambitious and complex program of the HDB.

3. *Comprehensive Administrative Structure.* The HDB is semi-autonomous, though attached to the Ministry of Public Works. The ministry controls all aspects of construction and financing; these include land assembly, materials production, physical design, contracting, allocation, and rent/mortgage control.

4. *Money.* During the HDB's first decade (1963–1973) Singapore's economic growth rate was fantastic, reaching 15 percent per annum, and the HDB enjoyed in effect a blank-check status with the city-state's treasury.

Another encouraging example is the Joint UNDP–Peruvian Government Experimental Low-Cost Housing Program.[35] The project called on a selection of Peruvian and international architectural/engineering firms to design a complete neighborhood of fifteen hundred low-rise, high-density dwelling units, complete with shops, community centers, schools, road and pedestrian networks. The emphasis was on innovative house design to cut costs. The resulting designs were so impressive that it was decided to build a prototype cluster of each of the designs submitted. The units were estimated in 1972 to cost between U.S.$2,000 and $5,000. This is an impressively low price compared with developed-country house prices, especially when the quality of the environments planned is considered. It remains to be seen to what proportion of the world's poor such a standard of housing can be supplied, given the present level of funding to such housing efforts. There is also the question of to what degree the plans and designs of architects, especially from overseas, can meet the needs of the poor who, in fact, have their own culture.

Few major cities of the world are without serious housing problems and without many programs and policy alternatives being tried to solve the problems. The core insight seems to be that the answer is not technical; it is one of economics and finance. Housing problems are related to the ecology, the economics, and in turn to the political, cultural, and social development of a society; and, overall, the societies of the world are falling behind in housing. Policymakers feel the desperation as human needs and desires increase rapidly. Today it is even more true than when Robert Louis Stevenson wrote, more than 80 years ago, that, "There is no cabinet science in which things are tested to a scruple: We theorize with a pistol to our head: we are confronted with a new set of conditions on which we not only have to pass judgement, but to take action, before the hour is at an end."

EDUCATION

It may strike some as odd that education would be classified as a basic human need. However, essential to all human development is the *knowledge* required to satisfy basic human needs. And although we strongly support the argument that formal education is not the only vehicle to basic knowledge, the role formal learning plays in providing tools for meeting basic needs should not be underestimated. For in most societies of the world, education serves as a vehicle to the acquisition of society's benefits and is the prime means of improving the human capital on which development should be largely based. Finally, the challenges of shifting to some form of organic growth cannot be met by merely extending basic education to all. A conscious reeducation of all people so that they know more of how the planetary system works, and can work, is essential to qualitative growth. Thus in our description of the conditions of present-day humanity, it is important that we investigate the degree to which the basic need of education is being met. Tables 4.13 and 4.14 provide us with some indication of the relative importance education is given by various national governments.

Table 4.13 shows that in most regions of the world today, more money is allocated for military expenditures than for public education. It can also be seen that in those regions where economic and ecological problems are especially damaging to basic needs (Latin America, South Asia, and Africa), the smallest proportion of available GNP is spent on education. This finding comes as no surprise, for in many ways, education is an investment in human capital for the future and, as such, often takes a lower priority than seemingly immediate programs defined by leaders as "urgent." It is also true, of course, that as GNP per capita rises above basic subsistence levels, expenditures for education seem to be given a higher priority than before.

The *magnitude* of the discrepancy in spending on education may not be so commonly understood. From table 4.13 it can be quickly calculated that, overall, developed countries are devoting to education a somewhat larger slice of a much larger pie; in fact, they spend about twenty times as much per capita on public education as do developing countries. Of course this figure is somewhat misleading since it equates expenditures by using international money-exchange rates which characteristically undervalue the actual domestic buying power of "soft" currencies. But the figures do suggest the great economic barrier developing nations face if they wish to develop an education system that depends on the technology and infrastructures of the developed-country models.

But beyond the great disparity in buildings, audiovisual equipment, high salaries, and highly trained teachers, there remains the fact that a dedicated, gifted teacher even sitting out under a tree can still impart much to students who want to learn. Figures on percent of GNP invested in education cannot accurately show the degree to which even this kind of basic educational opportunity is available in a country.

Table 4.14 moves in this direction by presenting data from selected countries on the ratio of students to teachers. It can be seen that, although not as appalling as the 20:1 disparity in dollars spent, there is still a great disparity in the chances that a student will be able even to hear or be heard by any teacher. As an indicator, the average ratio of the total of school-age children to the total of primary and secondary school teachers in the selected developed countries is about 23:1. The average ratio among the selected developing countries is four times as great. In short, there is a serious shortage of teachers relative to the school-age population in developing countries.

What this shortage of teachers means is that developing nations must

TABLE 4.13 GNP and Selected Public Expenditures, by Region, 1970

Region	GNP		Public Expenditures			
	Total (U.S.$ billions)	Per Capita ($)	Military		Public Education	
			Total (U.S.$ billions)	% of GNP	Total (U.S.$ billions)	% of GNP
World	3,219.3	881	208.5	6.5	167.7	5.3
Developed countries	2,663.9	2,701	180.4	6.7	147.8	5.5
Developing countries	555.4	208	28.1	5.0	19.9	3.6
North America	1,058.8	4,670	79.7	7.5	61.2	5.8
Europe	1,439.5	1,948	100.8	7.0	79.7	5.5
Latin America	142.1	510	2.9	2.1	4.1	2.5
Far East	372.0	290	15.5	4.2	15.6	4.2
South Asia	74.9	103	2.5	3.2	1.6	2.1
Near East	35.7	366	4.3	12.1	1.5	4.2
Africa	57.9	202	1.3	2.2	2.2	3.8
Oceania	38.3	2,504	1.4	3.7	1.6	4.2

Source: U.S. Arms Control and Disarmament Agency, *World Military Expenditure*, 1971.

TABLE 4.14   School-Age Population and Supply of Primary
and Secondary School Teachers, Selected Countries,
ca. 1970

Country and Census Year	(1) School-Age Population (5–19 yrs.)	(2) 1st & 2nd Level Teachers	(1)/(2) No. of School-Age Children per Teacher
Developing Countries			
Algeria (1970)	4,455,000	55,000	81
Morocco (1970)	5,983,000	49,000	122
Nigeria (1970)	19,628,000	120,000	164
Ecuador (1969)	2,569,000	40,000	64
Mexico (1969)	19,173,000	291,000	66
Peru (1970)	5,136,000	101,000	51
India (1965)	198,125,000	1,781,000	111
Indonesia (1970)	35,025,000	464,000	76
Iran (1970)	11,680,000	123,000	95
Pakistan (1969)	39,132,000	327,000	120
Total	340,906,000	3,351,000	
Mean			101
Developed Countries			
Japan (1970)	25,081,000	853,000	29
U.S.A. (1970)	59,815,000	2,340,000	26
France (1970)	12,537,000	435,000	29
Italy (1970)	12,482,000	557,000	22
U.K. (1969)	11,111,000	479,000	23
Total	121,025,000	4,664,000	
Mean			26

Source: Calculated from *UN Demographic Yearbook* 1972, table 6, p. 158.

choose a policy position between two extremes. They must either concentrate
their scarce educational resources on a small percentage of their children,
leaving the majority uneducated, or they must spread their resources so
thinly—overcrowding classrooms, underpaying and overworking teachers,
lowering teaching standards—that finally every child can be reached with
some sort of diluted educational experience. Both alternatives seem unac-
ceptable.

The education dilemma defines yet another of the vicious circles (or in-
herently unstable systems) feeding into current world conditions: the prob-

lem that education is the sine qua non for breaking out of the cycles of underdevelopment. Yet it is the disadvantaged societies that cannot seem to find adequate resources, capital, and personnel to support the Herculean programs of education that the situation demands. But another look at resource-allocation data reminds us that the problem cannot be blamed solely on a *lack* of funds in many societies of the world. If the perceptions, skills, and behavior so crucial to organic growth, ecosystem-economic system stability, and an improved quality of life are to be learned, education will have to become a top priority.

INEQUITY

The numerous statistics we have thus far presented reveal that human society is saturated with poverty, affluence, and extreme inequity. In the industrialized nations and among the elite in many developing nations, standards of conspicuous consumption in housing, furnishings, and clothing have soared in postwar years. For example, aerial photographs of favored suburban locations in southern California are richly jeweled with sparkling blue swimming pools. Italian and Danish designers continue to lead the world in design with extraordinarily imaginative and expensive chairs, couches, beds, and objets d'art. Others make coffee tables out of matching pairs of Rolls-Royce radiators. Magazines devoted to "Better Homes and Gardens" display in rich, full color the endless flow of desirable environments and accoutrements. The fortunate masses in the rich nations come to believe that they really *need* three bathrooms, chrome and leather lounge chairs, each season's newest fashions, microwave ovens, and, of course, a bigger house in which to stow and display all of these new conveniences. Meanwhile, thousands sleep and die on the streets of Calcutta; the cardboard, tin, and scrap squatter settlements of Latin America grow prodigiously; nearly seven million households are still inadequately housed in the United States;[36] and a leprous beggar in Ethiopia relates rather incredulously how the urban poor are less free with their alms now that the outlandish habit of having more than one suit of clothes is spreading, draining off more and more of the people's meager funds.

These problems of inequity are closely linked with basic need satisfaction and with the broader context of environmental problems. On a planet of finite resources where the power to obtain, develop, and distribute these resources is monopolized by a small minority of people and institutions, gross inequity can spell starvation, depletion, dependence and, in general, an intolerably low quality of life for the overwhelming majority of mankind.

Thus equity becomes a priority component of the quality of life. A conceptualization of equity suggested by Dudley Weeks sheds light on the global dimensions of this complex phenomenon.

> In contemporary human society equity can be defined as a condition in which the dominant patterns of interaction not only promote justice and fairness, but also (1) facilitate for all people a condition of life beyond that of bare survival (a "survival-plus" condition), (2) limit the unequal distribution of power, resources and benefits to a differential too low to facilitate monopolization and exploitation, (3) promote a sufficient degree of autonomy so that each society's sustenance and development is not merely a dependent consequence of another society's activity, but rather the result of its own decisions. The key component of equity, then, is equal *access* to the benefits of existence, and to the tools essential to self-development.[37]

Using this definition, it is now important to note the difference between equity and equality. The utopian ideal of all humans having an *equal* quantity and quality of resources, although perhaps desirable to many, is not our main concern in the examination of need-satisfaction disparities. Rather, we are directing our attention to the need for a drastically more equal *access* to power, resources, benefits, and information. In this sense, inequality becomes a major indicator and result of inequity, one that can be measured statistically.

The age-old argument over man's alleged innate inequality will no doubt continue ad infinitum. Without becoming lost in that debate, it is still possible to deal with inequality if we focus on the extreme degrees to which disparities have been allowed to develop. As the numerous data previously discussed demonstrate, inequality has intensified to such an intolerable degree that the very quality of human life and survival for the disadvantaged masses are now threatened.

But the effects of inequity and inequality extend beyond basic physical needs into the broader areas of growth, development, and environmental problems. In our analysis of the relationship between inequality and growth we begin with two versions of the dominant growthmania model we originally discussed in chapter 1. Figure 4.15 shows the process of economic growth that the proponents of quantitative growth claim as being accurate, while figure 4.16 shows what we contend is the actual process that occurs within the growthmania model.

As figure 4.15 shows, man has consumption demands that must be satisfied. In order to satisfy these demands, enough utilities, or objects of consumption, must be available. This, of course, requires adequate production. The best incentive to get people to produce is the chance to reap and maximize economic profit. As the population increases and as man's desires for consumption naturally continue to increase, more and more production is required. To continue maximizing profit, it also becomes necessary to make sure that the products will be consumed; thus efforts to create and increase more and more consumption desires become important. The freedom to be able to accumulate as much as a person can becomes not only a right but an additional incentive to the consumption-production-consumption process. More production requires more labor which thus provides jobs and benefits for the citizenry. As production, consumption, and labor increase, so does the growth rate of the gross national product. Since a higher GNP means more aggregate benefits, it is only a matter of time before all members of society receive a share of benefits proportionate to their contribution to the national economy. Whatever minimal inequality may exist, then, is due to the differences in ingenuity and hard work expended by various members of the populace.

Such a simplistic view of growth omits several crucial ingredients. The finiteness of resources is completely ignored; thus, the increased exploitation of resources and their resultant depletion and the increase in prices are also ignored. The fact that profit maximization and freedom of unlimited accumulation lead to a demand for cheap energy, automation excesses, unemployment, increased needs and expenses for service and "repair," decreased consumption power, and ultimately less growth and benefits, is simply left out of growthmania's vision. Also ignored is the fact that unlimited accumulation and profit maximization give the already powerful more ability to monopolize benefits, thereby increasing inequality, the underutilization of human resources, and the rush toward debilitating growth.

Thus at least two important feedback loops must be added to the growthmania model if it is to depict reality. In one loop, demand for goods and services stimulates the rate of exploitation of natural resources. The higher these rates are relative to the supply of nonrenewable, or stock resources (such as petroleum or coal), the higher the price will rise when depletion of the entire resource is approached. In the case of renewable resources (fish, forests, cattle, rice), prices rise when the exploitation rates surpass or approximate the maximum rate at which the resource can be harvested without destruction. This price rise, caused by depletion of stock resources or overharvesting of renewable resources, dampens demand and puts the brakes on economic growth. In a second important loop, increasing resource prices finally rise at a higher rate than wages, even in an inflationary situation, and a sharply increasing proportion of the labor force must curtail its expenditures, except for the bare essentials of life. This means sharply reduced demand for manufactured products, decreased demand for a labor

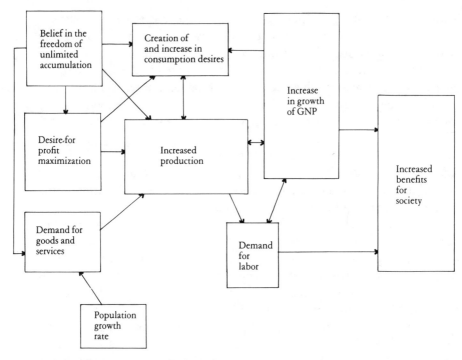

Figure 4.15. The Growthmania Model: The Claim

force to work in manufacturing, and high unemployment. This leads in turn to sharply lowered equity of income distribution.

We now turn to an analysis of pertinent data that further reveal the consequences of the growthmania model. Our central question focuses on what happens to comparative levels of income distribution as demand for resources overwhelms supply.

First, we consider the hypothesis, popular in the conventional wisdom, that population growth stimulates economic growth. As shown in figure 4.17, the data indicate that just the opposite is true: higher rates of population growth *inhibit* rather than stimulate growth in per capita GNP.

We now consider, in some detail, the course of events as depicted in the bottom of figure 4.18. Data from the United States are used as an example, partly because data are readily available, and partly because the U.S. can, perhaps as well as any other country, serve as an example of how national systems behave wherever these causal pathways are operating and this particular time sequence of events is analogous.

First, if we seek evidence that some commodities are becoming scarce, we would expect such evidence to be revealed in either of two forms. If a coun-

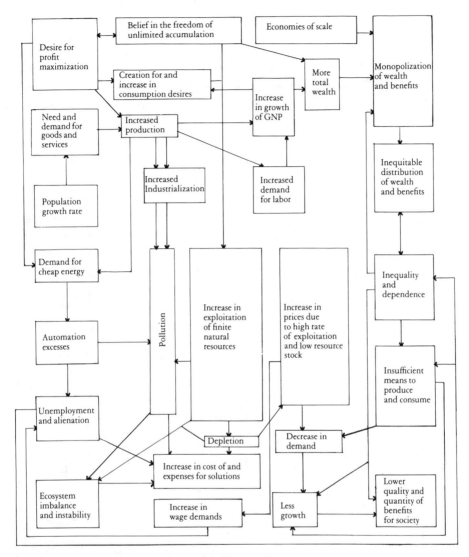

Figure 4.16. The Growthmania Model: The Reality

Source: Dudley Weeks, *Learning Alternative Futures* (doctoral dissertation, University of Hawaii, 1976), graphic 2.32.

try is running out of an essential commodity, the scarcity would show up in the form of sharply increased imports from other countries to compensate for domestic supplies nearing depletion. Alternatively, a sharp increase in exports of a commodity could exacerbate domestic shortages. Figure 4.18 illustrates both patterns: increasing imports of fuel and metal, and increasing

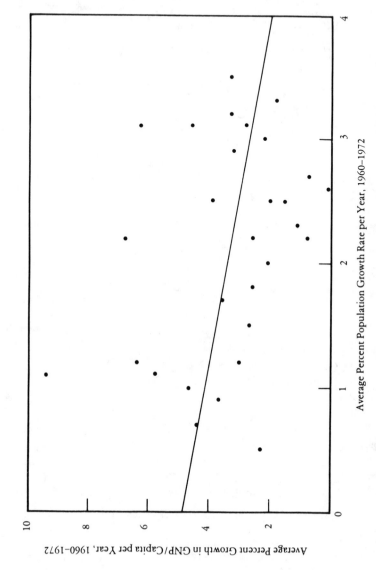

Figure 4.17. The Relation between the Rate of Population Increase and Rate of Increase in GNP per Capita

The data depicted are for the 30 largest countries in 1972, as compiled in the *World Bank Atlas: Population, Per Capita Product and Growth Rates*, 1974. The straight line was fitted by regression analysis.

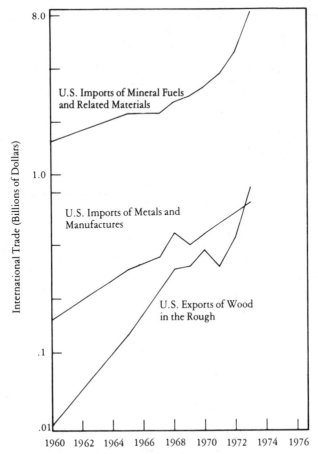

Figure 4.18. Volume of U.S. International Trade in Three Basic Commodity Groups

Data from *Statistical Abstract of the United States,* 1974, tables 1328 and 1321.

exports of wood. In the case of fuel and wood, the rates of international trade are increasing sharply. As these commodity groups show shortages, we would expect to see prices of goods which utilize these commodities increase. To verify this expectation, and to see if wages fail to keep up with prices, we use as our measure "average spendable earnings"/the wholesale commodity price index for the respective commodity group (figure 4.19). Earnings are defined very precisely in the statistical series we use, so there can be no doubt that we are tracking the impact of prices on the typical worker's ability to pay. (The full definition of "average spendable earnings" is the average

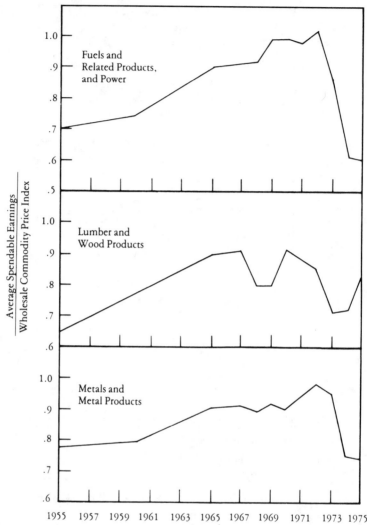

Figure 4.19. Impact of Resource Shortages on the Ratio of Average
Spendable Earnings to Wholesale Commodity Prices

Data on earnings from table 574, and on prices from table 662, *Statistical Abstract of the United States*, 1974.

spendable weekly earnings of a worker with three dependents, in current dollars, in private nonagricultural industries after subtracting social security and income tax payments.) The data indicate the impact of resource shortages on prices. In all three cases, "average spendable earnings" slowly increased relative to wholesale price, finally reaching a peak between 1970 and

1972. Then after 1972, when resource shortages became more acute, in all three cases wages suddenly collapsed relative to prices and the gains of the two previous decades were lost.

As one might expect, these dramatic changes in *wholesale* prices relative to wages are quickly reflected in *retail* prices relative to wages. Figures 4.20 and 4.21 show the time trends in the ratio of wages to prices for private transportation (cars and operating costs) and houses, respectively. After 1973 for cars, and after 1972 for houses, these commodities rapidly became less accessible to the poorest segment of society. What comes as a surprise is how large the "poorest segment" is, and how rapidly the change is occurring. In 1973, 21.5 percent of U.S. families could afford a median-priced new house, but by 1974 only 15 percent of families could afford one. Thus, there is a clear connection between resource shortage and the unavailability of commodities to the less-advantaged.

Returning to our flow chart (figure 4.16), we hypothesize that when prices outstrip wages inequality in income distribution is one of the results. To check this hypothesis against data, we used as a measure of inequality (or "equity index") the percentage of aggregate incomes going to the lowest fifth of all families (by income rank) relative to the percentage going to the highest fifth. As figure 4.22 reveals, lower wages relative to prices (and prices have already been shown to be affected by resource shortages) do result in less equitable income distribution. We can only conclude that the "environmental problem" of resource availability per capita, and the equity problem are the same underlying problem in two different guises. Either can be solved in part by increasing resource availability *per capita*, or decreasing the number of people relative to the availability of resources.

The preceding results lead us to ask, more generally, how equity changes through time as a society evolves, and how income inequality presently varies from country to country. These data are often difficult to obtain (for obvious political reasons), but at least some results are arrayed in figure 4.23 and table 4.15. The data obviously suggest that there is very little evidence to support the claim that economic growth leads to greater equity in income distribution.

Another aspect of inequity, one with highly interesting ramifications, has recently been noted by Illich.[38] As society uses energy at higher and higher rates in transportation, or elsewhere in the economy, a powerful force is created which promotes inequities in the distribution of both capital and political power and influence. As Illich points out, we have a very inadequate view of the real costs of any activity if we measure cost only in money. In the case of transportation, we must also examine the cost of movement in

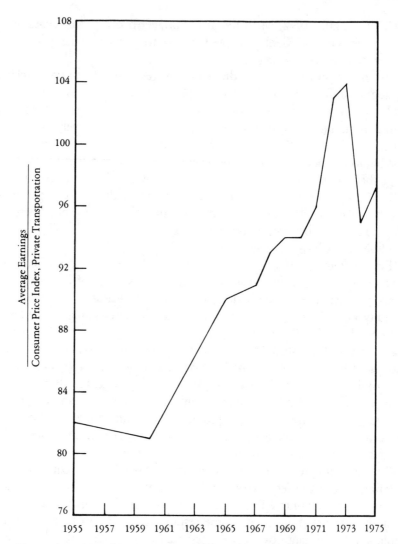

Figure 4.20. Trend in the Ratio of Average Earnings to the Consumer Price Index for Private Transportation

Data from *Statistical Abstract of the United States*, 1974, tables 574 and 665–666. The price index for private transportation is based on the consumer prices of new and used automobiles, gasoline, and automobile insurance.

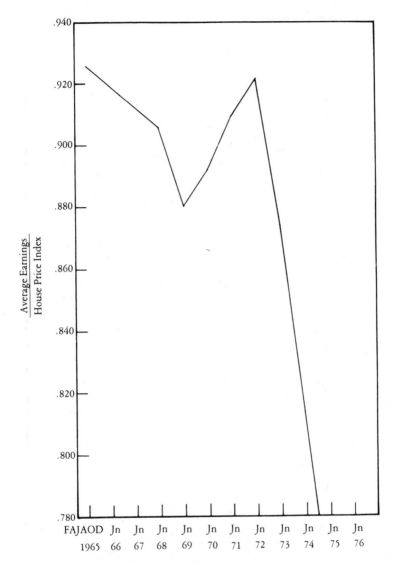

Figure 4.21. Trend in the Ratio of Average Earnings to Home
Ownership Cost Index

Data from *Statistical Abstract of the United States*, 1974, tables 574 and 665–666.

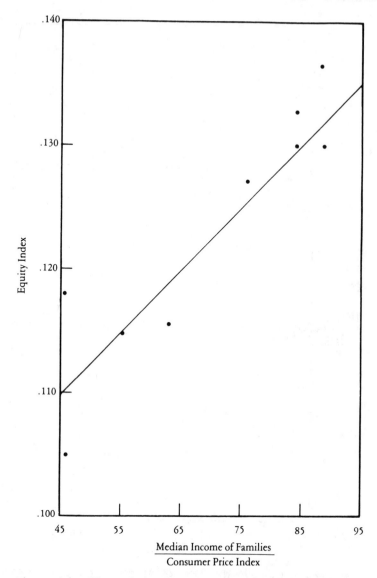

Figure 4.22. The Relation between Equity, and the Ratio of
Median Family Income to the Consumer
Price Index

Data from *Statistical Abstract of the United States*, 1974, tables 619, 614, and
665. The "equity index" used is percentage of aggregate income going to the
poorest fifth of all families, relative to the percentage going to the richest fifth.
The line was fitted by regression analysis; the relationship accounts for 83 percent
of the variance in the equity index. The dots represent different years.

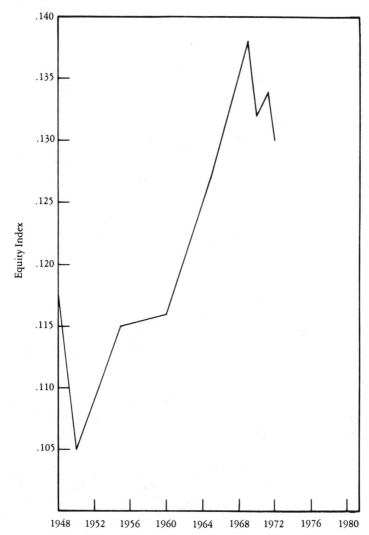

Figure 4.23. Trend in Income of Poorest Fifth of All U.S.
Families Relative to Income of Richest Fifth

Data from *Statistical Abstract of the United States*, 1974, table 619.

TABLE 4.15   Share of All Income
Received by the 40 Percent of
Households with Lowest Incomes

Country	Percent
Malaysia (1970)	11.6
Philippines (1971)	11.6
Thailand (1970)	17.0
Indonesia (1973)	15.0
Mexico (1970)	10.5
Brazil (1970)	10.0
Venezuela (1971)	8.0
U.S.A. (1972)	17.3

Sources: Data for Indonesia from Sumitro Djojohadikusumo, *Indonesia Towards the Year 2000*;
data for U.S. from *Statistical Abstract of the United
States 1974*, table 619; remainder from *Redistribution with Growth*, joint study by the World Bank's
Development Center and the Institute of Development Studies at the University of Sussex (Oxford
University Press, 1974).

time units (hours). The trick in this calculation is that the time-cost of motion is not only the portal-to-portal time-cost of the movement, but also the
time that must be worked to pay for the ticket and the vehicle. Further com-
plications arise because with poor workers a much higher proportion of all
the time they work goes into providing the basic necessities of life. Since only
a small proportion of their work time is available to pay for luxuries, a very
long time must be worked to pay for a luxury item such as a jet ticket. All
the figures necessary to make up curves for an analysis of the relations between energy and equity are available from standard government statistical
compilations, and from other sources as well. The results are displayed in
figure 4.24. This is a plot of the total cost of travel, per mile, in hours, at different speeds (in miles per hour). For the wage-earner with an income in the
top 7 percent, his cost per mile at 580 miles per hour (the cruising speed of
most jet planes) has still not been optimized. On the other hand, for the
worker with an income in the top 30 percent, and for the average worker as
well, the optimum-cost travel velocity is at 55 miles per hour. A further com-
plication occurs because when the high wage-earner travels, typically all or
part of his costs will be absorbed by taxpayers or shareholders. By being able
to exploit the potential advantage of great speed (a high rate of energy consumption), the person who is already wealthier than his fellows gains the
chance to increase the inequity. For example, while all taxpayers share in the
ticket cost for a government consultant, he derives an above-average amount

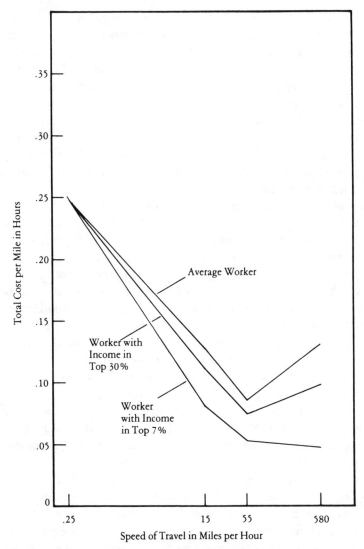

Figure 4.24. The Relation between Cost per Mile of Travel (in
           Hours) and the Speed of Travel, for Workers in
           Different Income Groups

of benefit from the flight (gain in prestige which increases the opportunity
for future consultation, higher wages, and the like). Thus, when we hear
people encouraging a high rate of energy use per capita in society, we have
legitimate grounds to question their real motives. Higher rates of energy
consumption for whom?

The severe inequalities we have attempted to reveal are in large measure the consequences of certain major beliefs and structures. Beliefs that place great emphasis on man as a consumer, on material profit as incentive and goal, on unlimited accumulation as a cherished right, and on man as the master over unlimited resources, all become institutionalized through numerous socioeconomic and political structures; these, in turn, then create and perpetuate extreme inequality and dependence. These structures permeate both international and domestic interactions, creating a center-periphery dichotomy in which the center nations, corporations, and individuals consistently gain advantage over the peripheral nations and peoples *because* of the way the structures operate.

Three of the structures that most clearly demonstrate the center-periphery inequality are trade, aid, and investment. The poor countries on the periphery have become greatly dependent on international trade, aid, and investment, a dependency that gives the highly industrialized center nations enormous power over the periphery's development. In the case of trade, the periphery's dependence is compounded by the fact that exports from the underdeveloped world constitute only a small portion of total world commerce. Using data from the 1950s and 1960s, the period during which many of the present patterns were formed and institutionalized, we find that the underdeveloped nations of the world accounted for only 21.6 percent of total world exports in 1965, even when the oil-exporting countries are included. Exclude the oil-exporting nations and the figure drops to 15.2 percent. Indicative of the fact that the export inequality has worsened is the annual rate of export growth from 1950 to 1965. The export growth rate in the developed countries was 8.5 percent while in the underdeveloped countries (excluding the major petroleum producers) it was 3.6 percent.[39]

These highly unequal export growth rates have resulted in a great loss of purchasing power for the underdeveloped world. United Nations economists have shown that the losses due to decline in terms of trade reached $2,752 million in 1966 for the underdeveloped countries. The magnitude of these losses becomes even more staggering when we realize that they canceled out 42.8 percent of the total aid received by these nations.[40]

One of the reasons why the trade picture looks so bleak for the underdeveloped world can be traced to the drop in the price of food and raw materials relative to the price of manufactured goods (a dilemma further compounded by the production of synthetic raw materials in the industrialized nations). An increase in the export of finished products from peripheral nations, then, is an obvious way of improving the situation. But this logical step is thwarted by the enormous power of foreign investors, primarily the transnational corporations based in the U.S., Western Europe, and Japan. Foreign interests have successfully captured the most potentially productive areas of manufacturing activity in underdeveloped societies, thereby blocking indigenous export-sector development while adding to the foreign investor's share of total development production. Gaining control over production, manufacturing, and prices as a tool for maximizing profits thus becomes a major strategy of foreign investors. The real per capita value of an underdeveloped country's exports is greatly diminished, as most of the raw materials are sent by the foreign firms to their mother countries, and as the bulk of production and trade is kept within the family of corporate subsidiaries. Add to this problem the numerous tariff restrictions the industrialized nations place on manufactured imports from the underdeveloped world,[41] and it is easy to understand how the dominant trade structures exploit peripheral societies.

As exports continue to stagnate in the underdeveloped world, less and less foreign exchange is available to purchase those imports necessary for development. This balance of payments deficit creates a dependency on aid from the same countries primarily responsible for the unequal balance in the first place. The aid structures that dominate the world economy further exacerbate global inequality. Aid generates more economic profit for the donor than for the recipient, and provides the wealthy nations with a formidable leverage in influencing the political policies and development goals of the underdeveloped world. The following quote from William S. Gaud, former head of the U.S. Agency for International Development, illustrates how present aid structures increase the advantage of the donor, thereby perpetuating inequality.

> The biggest single misconception about the foreign aid program is that we send money abroad. We don't. Foreign aid consists of American equipment, raw materials, expert services, and food—all provided for specific development projects which we ourselves review and approve. . . . Ninety-three percent of AID funds are spent directly in the United States to pay for these things. Just last year (1967) some 4,000 American firms in 50 states received $1.3 billion in AID funds for products supplied as part of the foreign aid program.[42]

A closer look at the composition of foreign aid flowing from one donor nation (the U.S.) also raises questions about aid as a vehicle of basic need satisfaction. In 1972, 52 percent of all U.S. foreign aid went for "security assistance" and only 6 percent for welfare and emergency relief.[43]

But even if it could be argued that aid does provide a significant contribution to the periphery, not much of it actually travels to the underdeveloped world. Again using the U.S. as an example, we find that from 1957 to 1967 only 50 percent of U.S. aid went to those underdeveloped areas not classified as "clients" (areas with special military importance to the U.S.), even though these areas contained 70 percent of the world's population.[44]

In a recent book commissioned by the Overseas Development Institute (a book, by the way, whose publication was discouraged by the World Bank, according to the author and the publisher), Teresa Hayter emphasizes that the three major aid institutions in the world, the World Bank, the International Monetary Fund (IMF), and the U.S. AID, often reach agreement together on which aid projects will be funded before negotiations with a recipient underdeveloped country ever take place. According to Hayter, the guidelines followed by the three major aid agencies strengthen the present patterns of trade, investment, and servicing and repayment of debts.

> There is a strong emphasis in the agencies' policies and demands on the principles of free enterprise, on reliance on market mechanisms, and on the respect of private property, domestic and especially foreign. The need for change is, to some extent, acknowledged; but the first priority is stability. Right-wing and military dictatorships with little or no concern for development, in the sense of raising the standards of living of all sections of the community, are acceptable, and indeed typical, recipients of aid so long as they offer the prospect of economic and financial stability.[45]

This information should not be surprising since the Western industrial giants as of 1974 controlled 72 percent of the voting power of the IMF.

For a closer look at how aid often contributes to increased inequality, we turn once again to the Green Revolution, the original research for which was started by the Rockefeller Foundation in Mexico in 1943. Consisting primarily of improved varieties of rice and wheat, heavy introduction of fertilizers, and tightly administered irrigation flow, this well-known project has had as its stated goal the rapid increase in grain output in underdeveloped countries. In 1965 an international team of economists and agricultural technicians, also trained primarily by the Rockefeller Foundation, AID, and the Agricultural Development Council (ADC), began carrying the message of the Green Revolution to various peripheral nations. In most areas grain yields rapidly increased. But as is true with so much of aid (and indeed with most other areas of present-day planning), the concomitant effects have frequently increased inequality and harmed the quality of life. The cost of fertilizers and mechanized agriculture has been such that most of the poorest farmers have been unable to become a part of the Green Revolution. The wealthier farmers thus have been able to buy the original supplies, increase their wealth, and then replace the extremely poor tenant-farmer with machines. But the effects go even deeper. The ADC handbook preaches the value of teaching peasants to become heavier consumers and to cast off the traditions of collectivist farming for the more businesslike drive for personal gains.[46] The farmer who is wealthy enough to participate in the Green Revolution thus becomes more dependent on the market, as he finds it necessary to buy the manufactured inputs and to sell his crop for the cash necessary to purchase the inputs for the next year. The system on which he is becoming more dependent is, of course, a system that brings great profit to the fertilizer manufacturers, agrobusinesses, and their local agents. The net result is often a substantial increase in inequality between the industrialized nations and the underdeveloped nations, and between the center in the underdeveloped country and its own massive periphery.

The point here is not to suggest that the Green Revolution has been a total failure. Rather, the important message is that once again we find more than meets the eye when a close examination is undertaken of the effect of aid programs on the increasing dilemma of global inequality.

The Green Revolution is often hailed as a technological breakthrough. As such it serves us well in introducing yet another global structure of inequality: the transfer of technology. Nowhere is the world's inequality more evident than in technology. The UN estimates that 98 percent of all expenditures on research and development (R & D) within nonsocialist nations occurs in wealthy nations, with as much as 70 percent taking place in the U.S. alone.[47] But it is not only the location of technological R & D that disadvantages the underdeveloped world; it is also the substance of the research. Much of the research undertaken by the highly developed countries and the transnational corporations is, at best, of little use to peripheral societies and, at worst, is actually detrimental. As much as 46 percent of the central nations' research goes into military and space pursuits, while another 7 percent goes to atomic energy.[48] And, as has already been pointed out, much of the new R & D is aimed at making synthetic raw materials (plastic to replace jute sacks, synthetic rubber products, and others), which, of course, have a serious negative effect on the already struggling export economy of many underdeveloped countries. Thus, rather than transferring much needed technology to peripheral societies, the highly developed world either monopolizes research, development, and patents, or provides a kind of technology that is often heavily capital-intensive and culture-bound, with great emphasis on entrepreneurship training and mechanized agriculture.

The inequality in technological R & D spills over into growth rates. Whereas growth in the highly developed countries seems to depend primarily on an increase in *primary* factors of production, growth in the underdeveloped world appears to be more dependent on an increase in the *productivity* of the factors of production.[49] In other words, technological change is significantly more important as a source of growth in wealthy nations than in poor ones. The transfer of technology, or in other words the transfer of the power to generate new growth sources, remains locked within the exchange channels that link together the highly developed countries of the world.

The transfer of technology and its impact on increasing inequality cannot be fully understood without a more in-depth look at transnational corporations (TNCs). Indeed, a rather sound understanding of how the entire international economic order operates can be gained by an examination of these immensely powerful corporate giants.

Led by oil companies, banking concerns, key transportation and utilities companies, and huge industrials specializing in consumer goods, the TNCs have as their major objective one overriding purpose: the allocation of resources on a worldwide basis so as to increase corporate growth and maximize profit. Essential to this objective is the generation of the highest possible returns on investment (within a corporation's planning horizon) and the maximization of power over management. The growth imperative, global expansion through investment and increased centralization of corporate power, interests in maintaining export markets and supplies of raw materials, vested interests in government contracts for defense and R & D related to defense—all are priority drives that form the guiding policies of TNCs. Their power and structure give them the ability to influence social, political, and cultural directions throughout the world, and the ability to shape an environment that greatly determines which problems and conflicts occur and which groups receive what kind of consequences.

Arguments claiming that TNCs represent a generally positive step in socioeconomic evolution usually point to at least five major contributions TNCs make to world development.[50] The first contribution usually cited focuses on the TNC as an integrative force that ties the nations of the world together in an interdependent system of mutually beneficial interaction. That the TNCs draw numerous nations into an economic network of interdependency cannot be disputed. But in a world of staggering and sanctioned inequality, interdependence invariably means that the benefits of interdependency will be defined and distributed by the dominant powers. Without adequate checks on accumulation, such a system of interdependency translates into greater dependency and fewer home-grown alternatives for peripheral societies.

The second contribution pro-TNC writers discuss is the integration of the world's economies into a worldwide economic system which ultimately reduces the numerous distortions found all over the world. But these "distortions" the TNCs define as obstacles to their profit maximization goals are often those particular domestic economic systems of peripheral societies that may be much more appropriate for their own individual cultures and states than is the global model pushed by the TNCs.

A look at an alleged third contribution returns us to the area of technology transfer. Advocates of TNCs claim that corporations provide the technical knowledge, expertise, and equipment so essential to development. This argument assumes, of course, that industrialization and highly mechanized agriculture are synonymous with positive development. That industrialization and mechanization often lead to serious negative consequences has already been discussed; but the question of technology transfer goes even deeper. In the first place, not all *that* much technology is transferred to peripheral societies. The large majority of the technology exported from the parent TNC (estimates are as high as 90 percent)[51] remains within corporate channels, much of it staying within the same corporation's network of subsidiaries. Even when a substantial quantity of technology is given to a peripheral society, all is not as mutually beneficial as one might think. Key bits of knowledge and equipment are often withheld, so that it becomes impossible for the recipient society to reach technological independence. Few if any institutions capable of handling the transfer or the technology are encouraged in the developing countries. Furthermore, the center elements in the peripheral societies often benefit from the technology with dubious benefit filtering to the masses. And as has already been mentioned, the composition of the technology that is transferred often favors capital over labor, security and military desires over basic needs, and, in general, continued monopoly by the TNCs over indigenous self-development capabilities.

A fourth popular justification for TNCs is that they provide needed capital for development. Again, at least two disturbing assumptions are made: that underdevelopment is due to a *lack* of capital rather than under- and/or poor utilization of capital, and that development emanates from a leading sector, a takeoff process. But, more to the point, several factors are ignored. Statistics reveal that TNCs take out more wealth from peripheral societies than they put in.

> In the underdeveloped regions almost three times as much money was taken out as was put in . . . [and] investors were able to increase the value of the assets owned in these regions manifold: in Latin America, direct investments owned by United States business during this period [1950–1965] increased from $4.5 to $10.3 billion; in Asia and Africa, from $1.3 to $4.7 billion.[52]

Other authors, notably Ronald Müller, make the same point. Müller emphasizes that the average rate of return in Colombia in 1968 reached 136.3

percent for 15 TNCs, while the average rate of return to Colombia tax authorities was only 6.7 percent.[53] These new profits are then often used to gain control over (or to buy out) the most significant sectors of the economy, including capital-producing sources. The results are that local investment is retarded and the local economy is absorbed into the TNC-dominated system. It is also important to note that much of the heralded capital transfer, like technology, takes place within the closed TNC-subsidiary channels.

A fifth alleged contribution is the introduction of new products to new consumers. Once again the basic assumptions of the claim need to be examined. As we and others have attempted to show, placing high priority on consumerism may well be one of the more serious causes of present environmental problems. This is especially true when one realizes that the goods produced are often nonessential items that are both too expensive and virtually useless to the majority of people in nonaffluent societies. So even if a case could be made that TNCs flood the world with new products, the negative consequences of such a contribution may well outweigh the positive. And when one studies the facts, it becomes apparent that even the ''more-products-for-underdeveloped-societies'' claim may be a myth, since a large portion of TNC-made products utilize the raw materials and cheap labor in peripheral societies and then ultimately end up on the shelves of the Western industrialized nations.

The conditions and structures of inequity that permeate the modern world are inseparable from the problems of detrimental growth and environmental instability. If growth is to occur in a manner that improves the quality of life, great attention must be paid to *equitable* growth. In her excellent work on development, Irma Adelman describes the priorities required in equity-oriented development strategies.

> To achieve equitable growth, two extreme strategies are in principle possible: (1) grow now, redistribute and educate later; (2) redistribute and educate now, grow later. I am convinced that, for equitable growth to become prevalent, there must be a deliberate application of the second strategy on a wide scale.[54]

We have consistently argued that the qualitative growth and development of society necessitate the satisfaction of basic human needs. As the numerous and varied data in this chapter show, the basic needs of the vast majority of contemporary humanity are undersatisfied, while the needs of others are grossly oversatisfied. These conditions of poverty, affluence, and inequity, when coupled with the increasing disruption of ecosystem balance and the destabilization of economic systems, constitute the core of the world's environmental problems. Only by attempting to understand the causal pathways and interrelationships that link these problems to certain belief systems and patterns of growth will societies be able to design and implement healthy development strategies. Thus it is to an analysis of these interrelationships that we devote the following chapter.

Notes to Chapter 4

1. S. H. Ominde, "Environmental Problems of the Developing Countries."

2. Roger Revelle, "Food and Population."

3. Norman Borlaug and Ramon Ewell, "The Shrinking Margin."

4. Frances Moore Lappé, *Diet for a Small Planet.*

5. See D. P. Burkitt, A. R. P. Walker, and N. S. Painter, "Dietary Fiber and Disease." See also "Stamp Out Food Faddism."

6. Georg Borgstrom, *The Food and People Dilemma*, p. 130.

7. Ibid., p. 131.

8. Ibid.

9. WHO, "Health Trends and Prospects, 1950–2000." Note: Unless otherwise specified, other data on health in this section are from this source.

10. *UN Demographic Yearbook 1973*, table 13, pp. 256–261.

11. R. R. Puffer and C. V. Serrano, "Patterns of Mortality in Childhood."

12. Stephen S. Mick, "The Foreign Medical Graduate," p. 14.

13. Warren Winkelstein, Jr. and Fern E. French, "The Role of Ecology in the Design of a Health Care System."

14. Reproduced by permission of the World Health Organization, *Health Hazards of the Human Environment*, p. 111.

15. The Cocoyoc Declaration, adopted by the participants in the UNEP/UNCTAD Symposium on "Patterns of Resource Use, Environment, and Development Strategies," held at Cocoyoc, Mexico, 8–12 October 1974.

16. Stephen Yeh, head of the Research Department, Singapore Housing and Development Board, personal communication, 1975.

17. Gunnar Myrdal, *Asian Drama: An Inquiry into the Poverty of Nations*, 1:530.

18. Charles Abrams, *Man's Struggle for Shelter in an Urbanizing World.*

19. Among them: Heinrich Engle, *The Japanese House: Tradition for Contemporary Architecture;* Hasan Fathy, *Architecture for the Poor;* Lloyd Kahn, ed., *Shelter;* Aprodicio A. Laquian, *Slums Are for People;* Paul Oliver, ed., *Shelter in Africa;* Bernard Rudofsky, *Architecture Without Architects;* John F. C. Turner, "The People Build with Their Hands."

20. Luke S. K. Wong, "An Overview of Housing Provision and Housing Needs in Hong Kong."

21. WHO, *Health Hazards*, p. 112.

22. Ibid., p. 111.

23. David Birch et al., *America's Housing Needs, 1970 to 1980*.

24. Graham Brown and Pete Stellon, "The Energy Cost of a House."

25. E. F. Schumacher, *Small Is Beautiful*.

26. UN, Department of Economic and Social Affairs, *The Use of Bamboo and Reeds in Building Construction*.

27. The Cocoyoc Declaration.

28. E. F. Schumacher, "Buddhist Economics."

29. Michael E. Stone, "Federal Housing Policy: A Political Economic Analysis."

30. John F. C. Turner and Robert Fichter, *Freedom to Build*.

31. Intermediate Technology Development Group, *Kit 5, Planning and the Contractor*.

32. Fathy, *Architecture for the Poor*.

33. Turner and Fichter, *Freedom to Build*.

34. Stephen Yeh, head of the Research Department, Singapore Housing and Development Board, personal communication, 1975.

35. "Experimental Low Cost Housing Project—Peru," *Architectural Design*.

36. Birch et al., *America's Housing Needs*.

37. Dudley Weeks, "Learning and Teaching Alternative Futures."

38. Ivan Illich, *Energy and Equity*.

39. Compiled from data found in Hal B. Lary, *Imports of Manufactures from Less Developed Countries* (1968), p. 2, as cited in Harry Magdoff, *The Age of Imperialism: The Economics of U.S. Foreign Policy*, p. 156.

40. UN Conference on Trade and Development, *Review of International Trade and Development*, pp. 35–36.

41. See Magdoff, *Age of Imperialism*, pp. 164–165, for an excellent summary of some of the more damaging tariff restrictions.

42. This quote is from *Rules of the Game*, a pamphlet prepared by Thomas Fenton and published by The Christophers (12 E. 48 St., New York, N.Y.), p. 14.

43. Ibid., p. 13.

44. Magdoff, *Age of Imperialism*, p. 124.

45. Teresa Hayter, *Aid as Imperialism*, p. 152.

46. Harry M. Cleaver, Jr., "The Contradictions of the Green Revolution," p. 179.

47. UN, *Science and Technology for Development: Proposals for the Second U.N. Development Decade*, p. 23.

48. Keith Griffin, "The International Transmission of Inequality," p. 4.

49. Ibid., p. 5.

50. The counter points discussed in this study's treatment of TNCs are from Dudley Weeks, "Learning Alternative Futures." There are numerous good sources on multinational corporations, a few of which are: *Annals of the American Academy of Political and Social Science*, especially the articles by Lawrence B. Krause, Richard D. Robinson, and Chadwick F. Alger; Arthur Barber, "Toward World Corporate Structures"; Richard J. Barnet and Ronald E. Muller, *Global Reach*; Nasrollah Fatemi and Gail Williams, *Multinational Corporations*; Andre G. Frank, *Capitalism and Underdevelopment in Latin America*; Pierre Jalee, *The Third World in World Economy*; Harry G. Johnson, "Thrust and Response"; Charles P.

Kindleberger, *American Business Abroad*; Harry Magdoff, *The Age of Imperialism*; Robert Stauffer, *Nation Building in a Global Economy*; Raymond Vernon, *Sovereignty at Bay*.

51. From an address by Prof. Karl Wolmuth, University of Bremen, at the Inter-University Centre of Post-Graduate Studies, Dubrovnik, January 1975.

52. Magdoff, *Age of Imperialism*, p. 198.

53. Ronald Muller, "The Multinational Corporation and the Underdevelopment of the Third World," p. 145.

54. Irma Adelman, "Growth, Income Distribution and Equity-Oriented Development Strategies," p. 75.

5
The Interrelationships:
Technology, Culture,
and the Environment

An analysis of the interrelationships linking together the numerous themes introduced thus far leads us into interesting conceptual and statistical territory.* First, to establish firmly the point that environmental problems follow from defective belief systems, three statistical generalizations are introduced which describe the dependence of national economies on environmental determinants. These generalizations are used to help explain certain fallacious statements emanating from the conventional economic wisdom, and then are supported by analysis of all available national data. Next we present a systems analysis of the mechanisms that produce this economic behavior, and subsequently introduce data to document existence of these mechanisms. This leads to discussion of, and presentation of data on, "degree of deviance from the expected level of realism" as a cross-cultural trait, followed by presentation of data on this phenomenon. We conclude by outlining the way in which ecological theory bears on the systems behavior of nation-states and their economies, and finally show how deviance from realistic behavior and environmental factors constitute one big system.

---

*The central arguments in this chapter are controversial, and some readers will want to see the details of the data and methodology used in deriving them. However, to avoid distracting the reader from the main flow of the argument, this material is relegated to an Appendix, which follows this chapter. We have also not inserted references at each point; the reader will find this technical support in the Appendix. But we wish to point out that the methods and results in this chapter are intended to be suggestive rather than definitive.

This is especially true of our "expected level of realism" concept. Our purpose in using this idea is to accentuate the relationship between beliefs and perception systems and the patterns of behavior and policy that lead to environmental problems. As we have repeatedly stated, each society defines its own quality of life components *within certain crucial parameters*. These parameters, stated in general terms, are ecosystem balance, basic human need satisfaction, and organic growth development. Thus we are attempting to stimulate introspection and expand ways of analyzing patterns of behavior by suggesting that societies are often "unrealistic" in the sense that many of their policies and habits run counter to quality-of-life requirements for their own society and for the global community as a whole.

THREE FUNDAMENTAL FACTORS CORRELATED WITH THE
ECONOMIC HEALTH OF NATIONS

We postulate that among environmental factors, three are most strongly correlated with the growth of national economies: (1) the use of energy per
capita, (2) the population growth rate, and (3) carrying capacity (the
availability of arable land per capita). The first two of these are already major
determinants of economic vitality in all countries—between the two of
them, they account for 25 percent of the variation between countries in
average rate of growth in GNP per capita. The third will be of increasing importance in the future, and is already a major factor for Japan, the
Netherlands, and Switzerland.

The first factor, use of energy, is illustrated by figure 5.1. This graph is
based on analysis of data from 67 countries. The countries chosen were those
for which we could obtain energy consumption per capita data for 1968, the
midpoint of the period 1965–1972, less two countries (Cuba and Vietnam)
for which the data were aberrant due to well-known causes. The smooth
curve was obtained from the following equation, developed by Kenneth
E. F. Watt:

$$R = 4.62 \left[1.0 - \exp^{-(\exp^{-6.3-.000188E})E} \right]$$

where   R represents the average annual rate of growth in GNP per capita,
              1965 to 1972
and   E represents the 1968 consumption per capita of all sources of energy
              in pounds of coal equivalents.

We call this relationship *Energy Stimulation and Suffocation* (equation 5.1).

Figure 5.1 indicates that as energy consumption per capita increases, rate
of growth in economic product per capita also increases, up to a maximum at
about fifty-four hundred pounds of coal equivalents, in all forms of energy.
Beyond that amount, further increases in energy consumption per capita cor-
relate with a decrease in rate of growth in economic product per capita. This
is, of course, quite different from the view held and widely trumpeted by the
conventional wisdom. Distinguished leaders in government, science, and industry often make pronouncements to the effect that constantly increasing
rates of energy consumption per capita are necessary to promote economic
growth. If this graph is an accurate representation of the relation between
energy consumption and economic growth in the real world, then, if the
conventional wisdom had its way and energy consumption increased steadi-

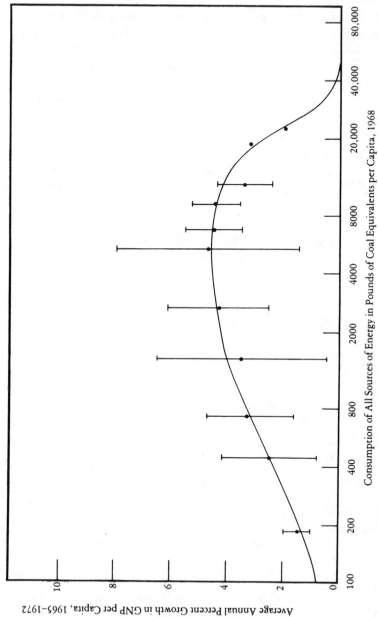

Figure 5.1. Energy Stimulation and Suffocation

Data on energy consumption per capita in 1968 in pounds of coal equivalents from *Statistical Abstract of the United States*, 1970, table 1267. Data on average annual growth rate in GNP per capita, 1965–1972, from *World Bank Atlas: Population, Per Capita Product and Growth Rates*, 1974. Where a dot is based on more than one country, the total length of the bar above and below the dot is two standard deviations (which would enclose about 68 percent of the range in a normal distribution).

ly, economic growth would soon grind to a halt. Indeed, figure 5.1 suggests the highly counterintuitive conclusion that the way for many countries (such as the United States, Canada, Russia, West and East Germany) to stimulate economic growth would be to reduce energy consumption per capita. This conclusion is so contrary to the conventional view that we will devote considerable space later in this chapter to explaining it, and outlining and documenting the causal mechanisms involved.

To expose most clearly the effect of the second fundamental factor, population growth rate, on rate of economic growth, we first adjusted the growth rate in GNP per capita of all the countries in the analysis for the effect of energy consumption, using equation 5.1. Then the residual economic growth was computed, and the data for countries was collected into groups on the basis of population growth rates. The group means are plotted in figure 5.2, which shows an inverse linear relationship between rate of population increase and rate of growth in GNP per capita. The fitted linear equation implies that the higher the rate of population increase, the lower the rate of increase in GNP per capita, all other things being equal. On average, when all countries are considered together, this graph reveals an important fundamental generalization, which we call *Population Growth Rate Anemia*. This means that when population growth rate is excessive, a much higher proportion of the population is under age twenty-one. This, in turn, means that relative to the rate of GNP and tax production per person of wage-earning age, there is a greater demand for consumption of youth-oriented items such as education, recreation, health care, food, and clothing. Capital and tax revenue must then be utilized for these purposes instead of being used for urban renewal, mass transit, improved sewage disposal, cultural amenities, and so on. Indeed, if population growth rates become extremely high, the economic resources of the society may be so strained in attempting to provide adequate services for the great number of young people, that these services, as well as many others, cannot be adequately provided. Thus excessive population growth rate works against the interests of the young, as well as the interests of their parents.

Some readers will be disturbed by the great length of the standard deviation lines relative to the variation accounted for by the fitted equation. However, a study of the tables on which these two graphs are based (see the Appendix) will reveal that much of this variation is due to factors which are not relevant to the discussion here—low per capita military costs (Japan), unusual levels of external assistance (Israel, Taiwan, Korea), or economic disruption due to war (Egypt) and internal instability (Uruguay).

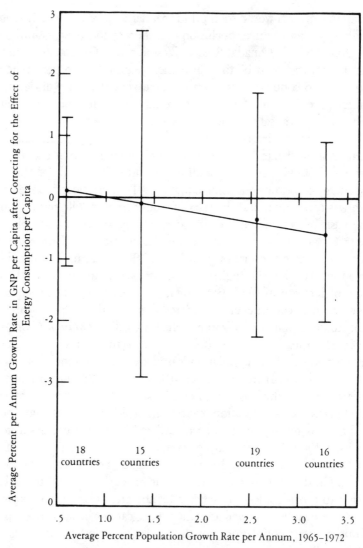

Figure 5.2. Population Growth Rate Anemia

The relationship between average annual percent population increase and average
annual percent growth in GNP per capita, after correcting for the effect of energy
consumption on growth in GNP per capita. This graph is based on data from 68
countries, all with populations of one million or more. Data from *World Bank Atlas: Population, Per Capita Product and Growth Rates*, 1974. The bars are two
standard deviations long.

Where R = average annual rate of growth in GNP per capita, in percent from

1965 to 1972,

E = 1968 consumption per capita of all forms of energy in pounds of coal equivalents, and

P = the rate of population growth, in percent from 1965 to 1972 (annual average),

then the data are described by Watt's equation

$$R = 4.62 \left[1.0 - \exp^{-(\exp^{-6.3-.000188E})E+.26-.237P} \right]$$

We conducted a statistical test to discover how much of the variance from country to country in R could be accounted for by just the part of the equation expressing the effect of E, and by the entire equation. The analysis showed 22 percent of the variance is accounted for by E alone, and 25 percent is accounted for by E and P. This is not large; however, the other factors previously mentioned obscure the role of energy consumption and population growth rates on growth in GNP per capita.

The third fundamental factor which operates on economic growth rates is the availability of arable land per capita (carrying capacity). This effect is illustrated in figure 5.3. The more the population of a country exceeds the carrying capacity of the soil to provide food for the population, the more food the country must import. This in turn constitutes an increasing outflow of cash, a tendency toward an adverse merchandise trade balance, and a brake on economic development. The greater the excess of the population over the carrying capacity, the more important the brake becomes. We call this the *Restriction of Economic Growth by Inadequate Carrying Capacity*.

The countries for which points are plotted in figure 5.3 are those for which the annual average total amount of cereal imports during 1967–1969 exceeded one million metric tons. For these countries, the number of hectares of arable land per capita in 1969 accounts for 24.3 percent of the country-to-country variance in cereal grain imports.

Two features of figure 5.3 are particularly noteworthy. First, we note that, despite all the discussion in the news media about imminent starvation in the countries of the underdeveloped world, these are not the countries which import large amounts of cereals per capita. Rather, the major cereal importers, on a per capita basis, are highly industrialized countries whose populations are now far in excess of the carrying capacity of their soil. Several examples are the Netherlands, Switzerland, Japan, and the United Kingdom. A second most interesting feature of this graph is the relatively

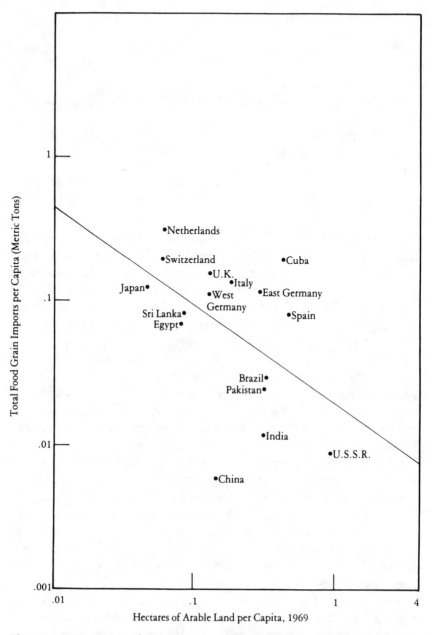

Figure 5.3. Restriction of Economic Growth by Inadequate Carrying Capacity

The effect of low availability of arable land per capita in forcing higher food grain imports, and consequently draining off capital that might otherwise go into economic development.

Data on arable land from *FAO Production Yearbook*, 1973; data were for either 1970 or 1971, whichever was most recently reported. Data on cereal imports from Georg Borgstrom, *Harvesting the Earth*, p. 217. The straight line is for the equation which best fits the data, $Y = aX^b$, where $a = .0196$, $b = .685$, and $r^2 = .243$.

low level of cereal importation by China and India, given their rather small amount of arable land per capita. The reason for this low level of cereal importation is that in those two countries cereal is fed directly to people. If it were used to feed animals whose meat would then be eaten by humans, they would have to import more than seven times the amount of cereal they now import. Of course, the low level of cereal grain importation by many countries is also the reason why they have a high level of starvation.

THE MECHANISMS OF ENERGY SUFFOCATION: THE SYSTEM

We now turn to the mechanisms that operate to slow down economic growth at high rates of energy consumption per capita. The relationships of the various components in the causal system are displayed in figure 5.4. Starting from the left side, we notice that the breakdown in traditional values has three principal effects on the economy. There is an increased preoccupation with purely monetary measures of social efficiency, increased pressure for constantly higher wage rates, and population-wide political pressure to keep resource prices down. These three forces operating together create overwhelming pressure for managers of all enterprises to replace expensive labor with cheap energy (that is, to automate). This, in turn, has two principal effects: it causes constant increases in resource use, at an exponential rate, and it elevates the unemployment rate.

The elevation of the unemployment rate is exacerbated by operation of another causal pathway (bottom of the flow chart). The economic-demographic system which regulates the birth rate operates with a long delay, which means that twenty years into the future, the number of births will exceed job availablity. The high unemployment rate can be a powerful stimulus to certain crimes and violence, especially as the disparity widens between the image of middle-class life propagandized by mass media and advertising, and what is actual *reality* for most people. The constantly increasing consumption of matter and energy implies worsening pollution and resource depletion. These problems, coupled with the increasing crime rate, lead to large social costs for such things as pollution control, sickness resulting from pollution, police protection, and welfare and unemployment benefits. A remarkable panoply of problems is included in these social costs: drug addiction, alcoholism, divorce, suicide, legal problems, and so on. This array of social costs associated with excessive energy use absorbs so much capital that there is significantly less available for investment in productive enterprises. Ultimately, the resultant decrease in economic growth leads to dissatisfaction with the existing economic system, paving the way for adjustments which lower the rate of energy consumption, and lead to a stable state with a high rate of economic activity.

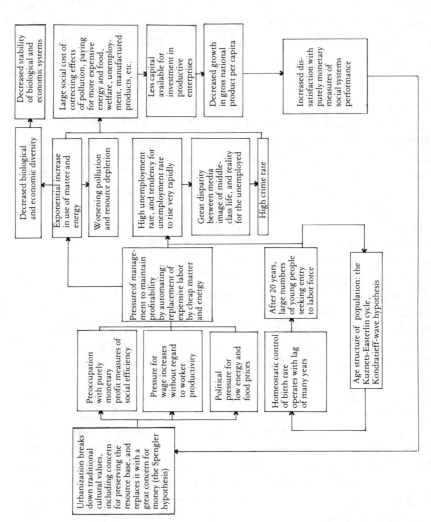

Figure 5.4. Systems Model of Environmental Problems

An important causal pathway is indicated at the top right corner of the flow chart. As was discussed in chapter 3, the high rate of flux of matter and energy through the socioeconomic system decreases biological and economic systems diversity, which, in turn, leads to decreased stability of biological and economic systems.

To this point, all we have presented is an elaborate hypothesis as to how the system works. We now present the supporting data.

THE MECHANISMS OF ENERGY SUFFOCATION: THE DATA

Two related sets of phenomena are basic to understanding the driving mechanisms of the system just outlined. One is the relation between the ratio of wages to energy prices and output per man-hour of work. The other is the relationship between energy prices relative to gross national product per capita, and the unemployment rate.

In developed nations, we find many social beliefs and cultural barriers that interfere with the solution of environmental problems. Indeed, these factors often lie close to the heart of the system that causes the problems. One of the most important of these factors is deficiency in perception by individuals. Despite the fact that modern society is a complex system, few people think in terms of the relationship between diverse parts of the entire system. Such failure to understand the system, of course, effectively blocks any attempt to solve the environmental problem; for problems cannot be solved if they are not understood. Deficiency in perception allows vested interest groups to push hard and often for new policies which, if effected, can actually bring catastrophe for everyone. Two of the most interesting examples of this phenomenon are the failure by labor union members to see what they are buying for themselves when they strike for higher wages, and the failure of society at large to perceive the ultimate consequences of insisting on low energy prices.

As shown in figure 5.5, the ratio of wage cost to energy cost accounts for almost all the year-to-year change in the man-hours of work input to attain a unit of output in manufacturing industries.* This means that as wage rates increase relative to the cost of energy, managers compensate by increasing the productivity of labor. The implication of this action is that part of the compensation is not just in terms of automation (exploiting cheap energy) but also in the form of unemployment (gradually eliminating expensive labor). The result can best be shown in an international comparison (figure 5.6). It is in the countries with the most expensive labor and the cheapest

---

*Unfortunately, we have had to use the cost of a barrel of crude oil as a surrogate variable for the cost of energy input to production. However, we are assuming that this is a useful index of country-to-country differences in the cost of all energy sources.

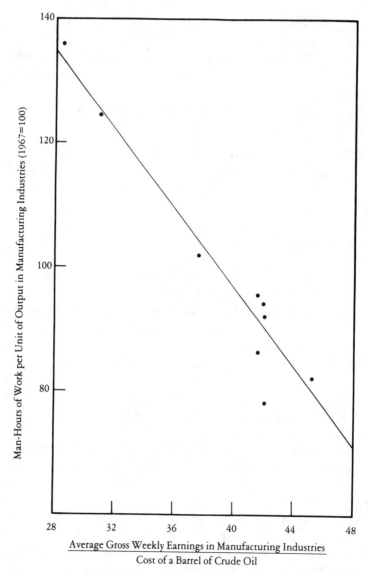

Figure 5.5. The Relationship between Man-Hours of Work
         Input to Obtain a Unit of Output, and the Ratio of
         Wage to Energy Cost

All data from *Statistical Abstract of the United States*, 1974: crude oil prices
from table 1129, gross weekly wages from table 574, labor productivity the
reciprocal of data in table 573. Each point represents one year.

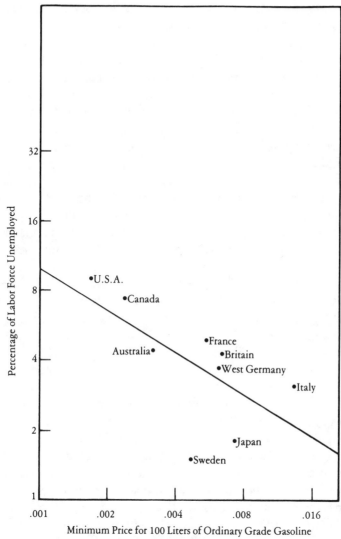

Figure 5.6. The Relationship between the Unemployment Rate
and the Ratio of Energy Cost to GNP per Capita
(a Surrogate for Wage Rates)

Gasoline prices from *World Road Statistics*, 1973, The International Road
Federation (1023 Washington Bldg., Washington, D.C.). GNP per capita
from *Statistical Abstracts of the United States*. Unemployment rates from the
U.S. Department of Labor, as quoted in *U.S. News & World Report*, 2 June
1975, p. 69. The figures were for the latest month available in each country.

energy that unemployment tends to be highest in a severe economic slow-down. This is not surprising since managers are expected to operate as profit-ably as possible, *especially* in times of economic insecurity.

The conventional wisdom of the technoculture has somehow failed to grasp the reality of the relationship between energy, labor prices, and unemployment. Consistently, this reasoning has claimed that although managers will indeed automate (for profitability reasons) when wage rates go up relative to raw materials costs, this really does not matter, because, as society becomes more automated, the increasing labor productivity in primary industries that leads to unemployment will be compensated for by increased need for workers in secondary industries. Then as secondary in-dustries also achieve higher worker productivities, the unemployment in those industries will be compensated for by development of exponentially increasing need for workers in tertiary industries. However, no one seems to have reasoned that there might come a limit to the rate at which tertiary and quaternary industries could expand fast enough to absorb the workers displaced by increasing worker productivity in primary and secondary in-dustries. By 1975, the consequences of (1) high wage rates, (2) low energy costs, and (3) great concern by managers with economic profit had become starkly revealed, as indicated in figure 5.6.

Clearly, economies equilibrate gradually to a state in which high wage rates relative to low energy costs will be translated into high unemployment. Those countries with more expensive energy, or less expensive labor, or both, will have lower unemployment rates than those countries in which energy is cheap, or wages are high, or both.

Pursuing this line of argument further, we would expect to find that since unemployment tends to contribute to higher crime rates, crime rates tend to be higher in countries with cheap energy and expensive labor. This indeed proves to be the case, showing once again that forces such as cheap energy, expensive labor, and automation, which lead to pollution and rapid resource depletion, can contribute to a variety of additional undesirable effects on socioeconomic systems.

Figure 5.7 reveals how homicide rates vary with GNP per capita (which is highly correlated with energy consumption per capita). As the level of af-fluence increases from the lowest levels, homicide rates drop spectacularly. At about fifteen hundred dollars per capita they reach a nadir, from which they increase again slowly, with increasing GNP per capita. But then homicide rates rise again, very rapidly, when GNP per capita levels of Canada, Kuwait, and the United States are reached. This phenomenon of a nadir in homicide rates at intermediate levels of GNP per capita is also

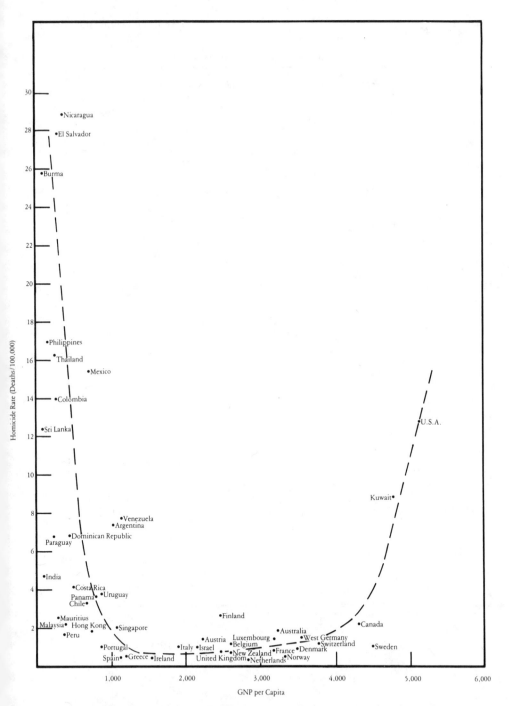

Figure 5.7. Relation of Homicide Rates (by Country) to GNP per Capita   (1971 Data)

Note: The line on this figure is the author's, and is not statistically fitted.

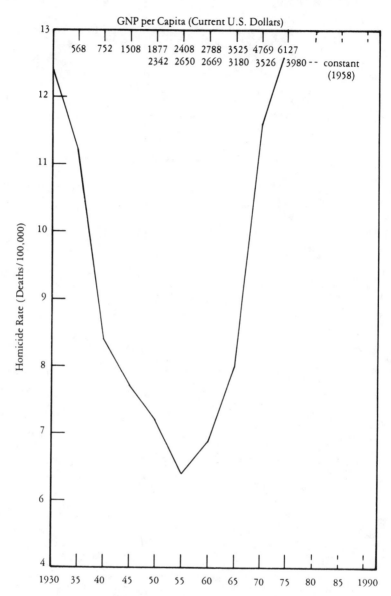

Figure 5.8. Homicide Rates and GNP per Capita, 1930–1975, U.S. Data

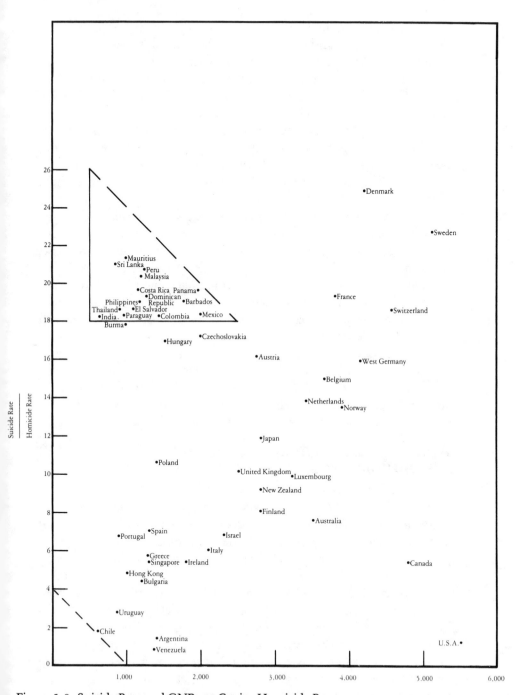

Figure 5.9. Suicide Rate and GNP per Capita Homicide Rate

revealed in the time trend for the U.S. (figure 5.8). The rate dropped steadily to 1955 but has been rising ever since. At the time this book went to press, the homicide rate was still rising rapidly in the United States

Suicide rates, on the other hand, do not exhibit a nadir at intermediate levels of GNP per capita but, in contradistinction, rise steadily in rectilinear fashion from the lowest levels of GNP per capita. There is an excellent linear relationship between the suicide/homicide ratio and GNP per capita (figure 5.9). Suicide stands out as a dominant social manifestation of dissatisfaction, alienation, and the like in many affluent societies, except those such as the U.S.A. and Canada, which have a history of homicide as well as of high suicide rates.

In attempting to gain further insight into the effects of increased GNP per capita on crime, the major difficulty lies in how to deal with numerous cultural variants, and with variables such as the comparative strictness of laws and crime-detection, law-enforcement policies of various societies. Thus, although figure 5.10 admittedly biases crime rates toward those countries with good detection and enforcement procedures, there is enough evidence to support the hypothesis that the overall rate of all types of crime rises with increasing GNP per capita.

Thus, there can be no doubt that "affluence," as presently understood, is a very mixed blessing. The problems accompanying affluence are numerous, and are linked together in a network in which crimes, unemployment, inequity, psychological problems raised by constantly rising personal expectations, and rapid economic growth all seem to feed each other.

DEVIANCE FROM EXPECTED LEVEL OF REALISM: A CROSS-CULTURAL TRAIT

Thus far we have demonstrated that nations can be unrealistic. Economies are managed so as to become ever more violently oscillatory. Living resources are so intensively harvested that valuable species approach extinction; habitat destruction produces the same result, often unwittingly. Indeed, species of great interest and value may be destroyed in great numbers simply by a long series of thoughtless accidents, as in the capture of porpoises in fishnets. Stock resources such as petroleum and natural gas, both of which have been accumulating on the planet over millions of years, will have been removed in just two centuries, largely through profligate waste. Government policy shows inadequate concern with the quality of life, and with equity. The misallocation of resources is truly mind-boggling. Vast resources go into freeways, atomic energy, missiles and space shots, while the resources for mass transit, urban renewal, solar energy, education, culture, medical ser-

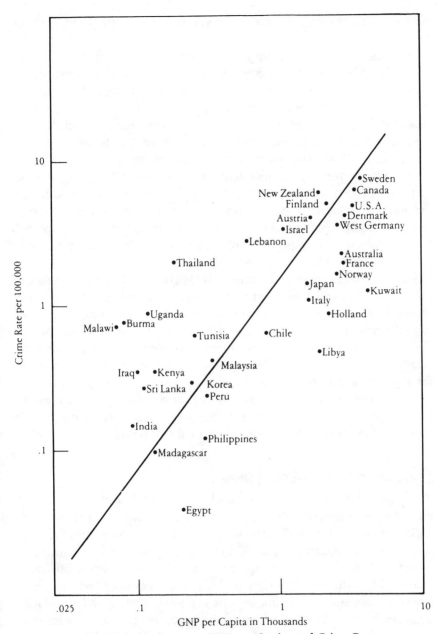

Figure 5.10. The Relation between GNP per Capita and Crime Rate
          per 100,000

GNP data from *United Nations Statistical Yearbook*, 1973, pp.596–598. Crime rate data from
International Crime Statistics, The International Criminal Police Organization.

vices, and environmental beautification and preservation are pitifully inadequate.

But these phenomena cannot be explained simply by saying they are the expression of callous governments pursuing policies contrary to the will of the electorate.[1] Rather, the electorate often votes in support of the present patterns of allocation. Further, the personal behavior of many people suggests that the governments now in power are accurate reflections of the people's attitudes. Personal resources are often squandered on frivolous, useless, and even self-destructive expenditures, while money never seems to be available for desperately essential items. Thus we cannot help but conclude that when nations and government are grossly unrealistic, it is very likely that the unrealism is an accurate reflection of the attitudes and beliefs of the majority of the population. In short, the degree of deviance from the expected level of realism is an important characteristic of cultures and civilizations, and one which is an important topic for analysis.

Such an analysis raises many questions. Might it be possible to quantify the degree of deviance from expected realism of a nation, using available statistical data? Suppose we could develop such measures, would they reveal large differences between nations with respect to the degree of unrealism? Could we isolate unrealism into different components? Would there be parallels between the degrees of unrealism indicated by different measures for a particular country? What would differences between countries with respect to unrealism tell us about the *origins* of unrealism? Is unrealism purely a product of affluence, or are there other causes? What might such analysis tell us about how we might decrease the degree of unrealism within nations?

DEVELOPMENT OF INDICES OF UNREALISM

We reason that if a culture is unrealistic, this attitude will reveal itself in quite diverse types of statistics. For example, if a society were unrealistic with respect to energy use (profligate), we would expect it to be unrealistic also with respect to international trade and monetary relationships with other countries. That is, we would expect the country consistently to buy more than it sold, leading to a situation in which its currency would accumulate in other countries and soon decline in value as normal supply and demand relationships operated. One way of testing this hypothesis is to examine the gold and foreign exchange holdings of various countries. We would expect to find that countries making unrealistic use of energy resources would have a shortage of gold and foreign exchange holdings on hand, relative to GNP. This would signify an adverse trade balance, leading to the shortage. The data reveal just such a pattern (figure 5.11).

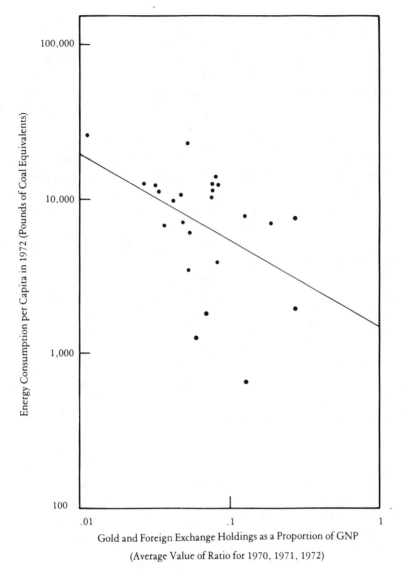

Figure 5.11. The Relation between Energy Consumption per Capita, and Gold and Foreign Exchange Holdings as a Proportion of GNP

All data are from tables in the *Statistical Abstracts of the United States:* data on gold and foreign exchange holdings from tables 1382 (1974 volume) and 1348 (1973 volume), GNP data from tables 1363 (1974 volume) and 1329 (1972 volume), and energy consumption per capita from table 1372 (1974 volume).

Such findings give us confidence that there is such an attribute as national degree of deviance from expected realism, that it can be quantified, and that different indices of national unrealism from the same country would be related to each other (be highly correlated). Accordingly, we have constructed such statistical indices for many nations, using a variety of published data (the "expected level of realism" being the average level of realism as defined by statistical analysis of the data for all countries). We are fully aware that the statistical methodology we have used is crude and in much need of development and refinement. However, new quantitative techniques in the social sciences, coupled with the high speed and massive storage capacity of modern computers, would facilitate such refinement and development. We are also sure that if another team had adequate time to assemble many more sets of data for the calculations than those we were able to assemble in a short time, the measure we developed would be altered and the conclusions might be different, or at least modified.

However, even bearing in mind these caveats, the analyses which we have done (described in detail in the Appendix) lead to some fascinating conclusions. There are large differences between countries with respect to the degree of deviance from the expected level of realism. Further, countries fall into meaningful groups with respect to such indices. Among both developing and developed nations, we find startlingly different sets of countries, with respect to deviance from expected realism. Further, two entirely different types of analysis have led to the same grouping of countries. The two groups can be epitomized by the following scheme.

	Developed Nations	Developing Nations
Examples of Nations with Less Realism than Expected from Average for All Nations	United States Canada Australia Netherlands	Venezuela Colombia Mexico Brazil
Examples of Nations with More Realism than Expected from Average for All Nations	New Zealand Norway Japan Sweden Finland Austria	Portugal Argentina Costa Rica India Burma Syria

We encourage readers to peruse the statistical findings in the Appendix. The startling contrasts between such pairs of countries as the United States and Norway, or Costa Rica and Colombia, in Appendix tables 3, 4, and 5, illustrate vividly the profound differences in social organization, national beliefs, and national economic strategies.

Our analyses show that affluence (GNP per capita) was the major factor in accounting for differences between countries in deviance from expected realism. However, a second factor has also shown up as being of significant importance: the proportion of a country's use of energy that comes from electricity. Additional analyses showed that the critical variable is probably the proportion of the energy used that comes from hydroelectricity. Our explanation is that if hydroelectricity is a principal source of power, it becomes a national characteristic to assess the ultimate capability of the nation more realistically, because it is much easier to agree on an assessment of the ultimate capability of hydroelectric systems than is the case with other forms of energy. Anyone can go and look at rivers and waterfalls and see how many there are and how large they are. Geophysicists and geologists can argue indefinitely, along with petroleum economists, about the ultimate size of petroleum or gas or oil reserves. In other words, self-delusion is much more possible in the case of fossil or nuclear energy than is the case with hydroelectric power. And perhaps, subtly, self-delusion about energy, or, in contradistinction, long experience in being realistic about energy, begins to have an effect on national beliefs which gradually pervades other areas of perception, and finally becomes a pervasive part of national character.

If a broader base of support for these hypotheses can be developed by further research that uses more components in the national index of deviance from expected realism and a larger number of countries, then an interesting conclusion is suggested. It should be made a crucial part of the educational program in countries that are heavily dependent on fossil fuels to point out the nature of this dependence and its extent, and to explain the sensitivity of scenarios about the future of the country to variations in estimates of fossil-fuel reserves. Then the estimates made by different people should be compared, and the basis for making the estimates should be widely explained and discussed. It is entirely possible to do this, as M. King Hubbert has so admirably demonstrated in a variety of important writings.[2] In short, if the whole future of nations is critically dependent on estimate of fossil fuel reserves, then everyone in the nations involved ought to know a great deal about these estimates—where they come from, and how they are derived. Such knowledge should facilitate a great improvement in national realism.

SOME ECOLOGICAL THEORY

Ecology has developed a body of theory that has relevance for figure 5.4 (the flow chart). It has been argued that productivity (the rate of energy flow through natural systems) divided by biomass (the standing crop in a system, such as a forest or cornfield) is a measure of systems efficiency, and that this, in turn, is negatively correlated to diversity, or variety in the system. Further, diversity, in turn, is supposed to be related to stability. (Here, we speak of the first type of cause for instability mentioned in chapter 3.) Thus, decreasing the diversity of a system decreases its stability, but also increases its efficiency. In biological systems, or in animal communities to be more specific, this implies that a particular predatory species is less likely to become extinct (be subjected to extreme instability) the more species of food it has. In the economic domain, the city is less likely to face economic extinction the more types of industries it has from which to derive economic benefit. Thus, the concepts of stability, diversity, and efficiency are all related, and further connect to biomass (amount of material) and productivity (energy flow rate). When we examine the present world economic system in the light of these generalizations, we see a most alarming trend. Increasingly, economic power both nationally and internationally, because of efficiency through economies of scale, is tending to be concentrated in a relatively small number of giant corporations. The consequence is just what we would expect from ecological theory: increasing tendency towards wide-amplitude fluctuations.

The basic issue here is that mankind must make a decision concerning the same trade-off faced by natural plant and animal communities: What is to be most desired, efficiency or stability? By not facing the trade-off in these terms, stability is losing out to efficiency by default. What we have now is an oligopolistic system which, by concentration of economic power, prevents the spreading of risk, and hence ensures increasing systems instability. In other words, we are calling attention to the same set of problems now being pointed out by many economists, including Galbraith, Daly, Heilbronner, Theobald, Boulding, Georgescu-Roegen, and many others.

THE BIG PICTURE

We now try to put together all the relationships noted up to this point. The picture which emerges is the flow chart in figure 5.12. Population size and age distribution (the expression of population growth rate), soil and water (the food production capability of a nation), energy availability and technology development, and cultural outlook toward human values and their paths to fulfillment, all combine to influence greatly the pressure of population on the environment. If the pressure on resources at home seems slight, or if new resources are constantly being developed through technological expansion, a nation can come to think of itself as having an unbroken series of successes. That perception and sequence, if long and relatively unbroken, makes a nation very unrealistic about itself and its long-term capa-

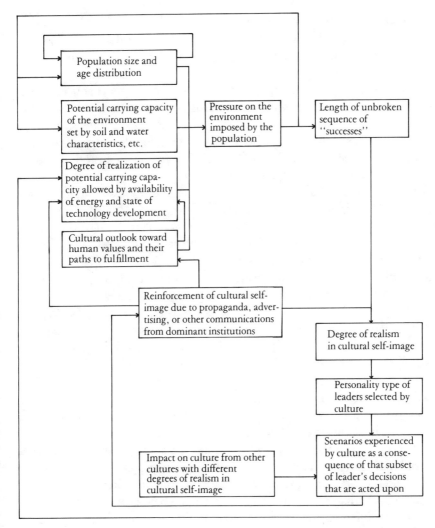

Figure 5.12. Abbreviated Sketch of the Causal Pathways Operating to Produce
Cultural-Environmental-Economic Problems

bilities. This, in turn, influences which leaders a nation either chooses or follows. A leader's personality type then influences to some degree the experiences a nation undergoes, although a leader's range of choices is limited and
is affected by numerous other influences, such as the impact of other cultures
possessing either similar or quite different self-images, and the characteristics of the national style in which the leader must operate. Thus, a small,
realistic nation may have its destiny temporarily affected by a large, powerful, exterior country which is temporarily highly unrealistic. However, in the

fullness of time, the exterior power will wane, and the small, realistic country can return to a policy of realistic management of its own affairs.

We now need to look more closely at several controversial points included in the rough theory of history just discussed. First, the basic argument of the theory is based on the Tolstoy hypothesis that history is not chaotic, but that civilizations and cultures operate according to definite laws which can be understood and even quantified.[3] Also, and more specifically, we follow Tolstoy in believing that the choice of leaders by a populace is not as random a process as appears to be the case, particularly in chaotic historical epochs. Even then, the leader being followed at any time is an expression of the will of the masses, or their representatives at that time. Despots ultimately sow the seeds of their own self-destruction or removal.

We agree with Toynbee and many other historians that civilizations are born, grow, flourish, then decline and disintegrate. However, we do not accept fully the explanations of Toynbee and most other historians as to why this happens. Rather, we agree with such writers as Hyams, Dale, Jacks, Carter, Whyte, and Loudermilk, who explain the rise and fall of civilizations in terms of the care with which the resource base is managed. Widespread dissemination of the belief in high school and university history texts that this is not the key to rise and fall of civilizations is critical. It is the widespread dissemination of a belief, rather than the truth or falsity of a belief, that determines what a civilization does. In short, the media, advertising, and powerful institutions which filter, distort, and perhaps withhold information, play critical roles in the causal system operating on a culture or civilization, and in determining the scenarios experienced by countries.

The pressure imposed by a population on the environment increases as population increases and resource consumption per capita increases. The consequence of more and more pressure is that resources are used up, depleted, overharvested, or destroyed outright. Before this occurs, a culture thinks of itself as having a long period of unbroken successes. This makes for a highly unrealistic cultural self-image. This self-image, in turn, leads a culture to select active-negative leaders. These are leaders often characterized by an unwillingness or inability to admit failure, and a strong, unswerving commitment to dogmatic positions and ideologies rather than to pragmatic, experimental approaches to policy-making with a realistic acceptance of failure.[4]

An additional problem, especially important in contemporary times, arises when a leader attempts to respond to the rising expectations of the citizenry in a rapidly changing global environment. Great pressure for the institutionalization of new values, either internally generated or imported via alien social institutions, can serve as a powerful impetus to the growth of authoritarian governments which either attempt to resist imported ideas or force particular changes on the populace.

THE UNDERLYING PATTERN BEHIND ALL ENVIRONMENTAL PROBLEMS

We can now perceive a pattern common to all environmental problems.

(1) If society were to manage environmental systems so as to ensure long-term stability, we could discover the rate or level of each activity that optimized the long-term stability of the managed system. For all types of management problems, strategies that are optimal in terms of such stability could be found.

(2) Instead of using stability criteria as the basis for selecting optimal management policies, the criterion of money output/money input, or profitability, is used to make policy selections in all kinds of situations. Invariably, this leads to use of strategies which are suboptimal in terms of long-term stability. If anything, with the passage of time, there is more and more emphasis on profitability, to the exclusion of stability.

(3) It should come as no surprise, therefore, that society shows more and more signs of instability, with the amplitude of various fluctuations increasing: sales rates, stock- and bond-market quotations, numbers of births, inflation rates, rates of resource depletion, and so on. Each of the problems discussed in this chapter is an example of this underlying pattern.

(4) As time passes, the increasing stresses that man is applying to the planet imply that local stresses, shortages, or difficulties must be dealt with by importing a solution or a resource from elsewhere. Thus, the world and its problems become a pattern of more and more intensely coupled interdependency. Environmental problems cannot be solved by perceiving and treating a part of the whole lifted out of context; the total system must be dealt with as an interconnected whole.

After a culture overwhelms its resource base, it may have the sense to start selecting active-positive leaders, who are less regulated by rigid ideological commitment and more regulated by an experimental, pragmatic approach and outlook. In any case, only a subset of the leader's goals and program will be acted upon by the masses (the Tolstoy hypothesis), so that what happens, in any case, will more than likely be what the *masses* want, not what the leader wants. As the flow chart indicates, the technological level of a culture can be affected either through reinforcement of the cultural image due to propaganda, or by the passage of events. To illustrate the former, a culture can be told that because it is the ''greatest,'' it is right, proper, and meaningful to demonstrate this by spending enormous sums to land men on the moon. Alternatively, modern nations may ''understand'' that they are so obviously superior in all ways to ancient nations that have survived for millennia, that it makes sense for Russia to build a high dam at Aswan for the Egyptians, or for Canada and the United States to help India and Middle Eastern powers enter the nuclear club. In the latter type of situation, a scenario may be so catastrophic as to wipe out the technological foundation of a civilization, as was aptly illustrated by the gradual decline of the irrigation system of Iraq, due to war and neglect.

Contact between nations may not have favorable consequences, even when the self-conscious intent of the donor culture is purely benevolent. Thus, as noted elsewhere, the Green Revolution and mechanized agriculture may have harmful effects on balance in the developing countries, even though the intent was to be helpful.

Thus the interrelationships among basic human needs, cultural beliefs, growth patterns, and environmental problems are often as close as they are revealing. But unless the masses who are affected by environmental problems—and that mass includes every human and every society—develop realistic perceptions of the causal pathways leading to these problems, the chances for solution will be minimized. Since information dissemination plays such a crucial role in the development of perception, chapter 6 will investigate the control of information about the environment.

Notes to Chapter 5

1. In comments on an earlier draft of this chapter Dr. Theodore Herman of Colgate University raised the crucial question, "Is it possible that a *decline* in economic growth could lead instead to a rigidly stratified society favoring the elite minority, such as happened in 17th century to 20th century Spain?" Of course such a condition could occur, but not simply because economic growth declined. But in any society where the elite minority controls the distribution of the benefits of growth (and, of course, that is the case in most every contemporary society), *increased* economic growth will favor the elite minority while also increasing the likelihood of environmentally destructive results. Thus, as the concluding pages of chapter 4 suggest, we cannot support the contention that increased economic growth will assure greater benefits for all of society or for the total physical and social environment.

2. For example: M. King Hubbert, "Energy Resources," pp. 43–150; idem, "Energy Resources," pp.157–242.

3. Leo Tolstoy, *War and Peace*, Epilogue, pp. 1351–1455. The conclusion of this vast novel about the apparently chaotic history of Europe in the Napoleonic era is an essay asking the question, "Is history as chaotic as it appears to be?" The penetrating, well-developed response is that it isn't, and that apparently random shifts in leaders represent shifts in the will and perceptions of their followers.

4. James D. Barber developed this theory of leadership character and illustrated it with biographies of American presidents.

Appendix to Chapter 5

THE DERIVATION OF FIGURES 5.1 AND 5.2

For each country for which the three variables were available, we made up a deck of hand-sort cards with (1) the name of the country, (2) the average annual population growth rate, 1965–1972, (3) the energy consumption per capita in 1968, and (4) the growth rate in GNP per capita, 1965–1972. These cards were then sorted in order with respect to the second item (energy), and the entire deck was subdivided into homogeneous subdecks to produce Appendix table 1. The U.S.A. and Canada were so different from all other countries, and from each other, that they were treated as separate data units. It will be clear from the table how countries were grouped with respect to energy consumption per capita (all those with 10,000–13,000 pounds of coal equivalents, 8,000–9,999, 6,000–7,999, and so on). Finally, means and standard deviations were obtained and plotted for all the subgroups. Equation 5.1 was arrived at as a minor variant of the well-known differential equation

$$\frac{dR}{dE} = a\ (R_{max} - R)$$

where R represents growth rate in GNP per capita, and E represents energy consumption per capita. This equation is based on the notion that the rate of increase in the dependent variable decreases regularly with increasing values of the independent variable, because of some saturation phenomenon. It integrates to yield

$$R = R_{max}\ (1 - e^{-aE})$$

R_{max} is the growth rate at which the saturation effect becomes complete, so

APPENDIX TABLE 1   The Relationship between Growth Rate in
                    GNP per Capita and Energy Consumption per Capita*

Consumption of All Sources of Energy per Capita in 1968 (in pounds of coal equivalents)	Country	Growth Rate in GNP per Capita 1965–1972
22776	United States	2.0
18702	Canada	3.2
12734	Czechoslovakia	4.5
11876	German Dem. Rep.	3.5
11817	Sweden	2.5
11543	Belgium	4.6
11296	Australia	3.1
11032	United Kingdom	2.0
10340	Denmark	3.7
Mean = 11520		Mean = 3.41
		Standard Deviation = .97
9885	Germany, Fed. Rep. of	4.1
9389	Norway	3.8
8948	U.S.S.R.	5.9
8845	Netherlands	4.3
8435	Poland	4.0
Mean = 9100		Mean = 4.42
		Standard Deviation = .85
7361	Finland	4.9
7324	Bulgaria	5.9
7235	France	4.8
6640	Switzerland	2.9
6354	Ireland	3.7
6292	Austria	5.0
6208	Hungary	4.2
Mean = 6773		Mean = 4.49
		Standard Deviation = .98
5999	South Africa	2.1
5904	New Zealand	1.8
5606	Venezuela	1.1
5545	Japan	9.7
5260	Romania	6.7
4883	Italy	4.3
4440	Israel	7.1
Mean = 5377		Mean = 4.69
		Standard Deviation = 3.24

APPENDIX TABLE 1 (Continued)

Consumption of All Sources of Energy per Capita in 1968 (in pounds of coal equivalents)	Country	Growth Rate in GNP per Capita 1965–1972
3111	Argentina	2.8
2896	Spain	5.0
2873	Panama	4.5
2749	Yugoslavia	5.5
2537	Chile	2.2
2346	Mexico	2.8
2242	Greece	7.3
Mean = 2679		Mean = 4.30
		Standard Deviation = 1.82
1799	China, Rep. of (Taiwan)	6.9
1737	Uruguay	0.4
1515	Lebanon	1.4
1420	Iraq	1.8
1396	Peru	1.1
1270	Colombia	2.4
1224	Korea, Rep. of	8.5
1193	Portugal	5.3
Mean = 1444		Mean = 3.48
		Standard Deviation = 3.02
992	Brazil	5.6
992	Turkey	4.3
957	Syria	3.8
769	Nicaragua	1.5
763	Costa Rica	4.1
657	Egypt	0.6
626	Liberia	4.0
575	Ecuador	3.8
547	Philippines	2.4
529	Guatemala	2.2
519	Tunisia	3.7
Mean = 721		Mean = 3.27
		Standard Deviation = 1.44
478	Honduras	1.7
456	Bolivia	1.4
452	Dominican Republic	5.0
441	El Salvador	1.2
437	Thailand	4.2
406	India	1.4
Mean = 445		Mean= 2.48
		Standard Deviation = 1.67

APPENDIX TABLE 1   (Continued)

Consumption of All Sources of Energy per Capita in 1968 (in pounds of coal equivalents)	Country	Growth Rate in GNP per Capita 1965–1972
311	Paraguay	2.1
282	Ghana	1.0
251	Sri Lanka	2.0
212	Pakistan	1.7
126	Burma	1.0
71	Haiti	1.3
49	Ethiopia	1.2
Mean = 186		Mean = 1.47
		Standard Deviation = .46

*Data on energy consumption from table 1267, 1970 *Statistical Abstract of the United States*; Data on growth rate in GNP per capita from the 1974 *World Bank Atlas*.

that no further growth is possible. The equation is modified in 5.1 on the assumption that a is not a constant, but that processes inimical to growth operate with increasing severity as energy consumption per capita is increased. Thus, in equation 5.1, the constant a is replaced by the term

$$e^{-b-cE}$$

$$\text{The equation} \quad R = R_{max}\left[1 - e^{-(e^{-b-cE})E}\right]$$

was fitted, first using algebraic transformation to obtain trial values of the parameters, then using an ad hoc gradient method on a Hewlett-Packard 65 electronic calculator.

Then the growth rates in GNP, after correcting for the effect of energy consumption per capita (observed values less values calculated from equation 5.1), were entered on the hand-sort cards. The deck was then sorted with respect to average percent population growth rate. Four subdecks were made up, and all countries used for the computation of means are tabulated in Appendix table 2. It will be noticed in this table that the very large standard deviations relative to means make sense in terms of well-known perturbations (foreign aid to Greece, the Republic of Korea, the Dominican Republic, the Republic of China, Thailand; low military spending in Japan; war in Vietnam; trade embargo against Cuba). Over a long period of time such perturbations would average out, and the effect of environmental variables would be more starkly revealed. Thus in figures 5.1 and 5.2 we want to show how certain underlying factors determine rate of economic growth, after correcting for a variety of short-term perturbations (wars, embargos, special political situations) which are not our concern in this book.

APPENDIX TABLE 2   The Relationship between Population Growth
Rate and per Capita Growth in GNP*

Average Percent Population Growth Rate per Annum, 1965–1972	Country	Growth Rate in GNP per Capita, 1965–72 (after correcting for effect of energy, as expressed in Equation 5.1)
.2	Finland	.44
.3	Czechoslovakia	.43
.3	Belgium	.39
.3	Hungary	−.29
.4	United Kingdom	−2.26
.4	Austria	.51
.6	Italy	−.19
.6	Ireland	−.79
.6	Germany, Fed. Rep. of	−.25
.6	Greece	2.99
.6	Bulgaria	1.44
.7	Sweden	−1.68
.7	Denmark	−.62
.8	Norway	−.58
.8	Poland	−.43
.8	France	.33
.9	Portugal	1.48
.9	Yugoslavia	1.11
Mean = .60		Mean = .11 Standard Deviation = 1.21
1.0	United States	−.03
1.0	U.S.S.R.	1.50
1.0	Switzerland	−1.58
1.1	Japan	5.21
1.1	Spain	.59
1.2	Netherlands	−.11
1.2	Uruguay	−3.76
1.3	Romania	2.21
1.3	New Zealand	−2.69
1.5	Canada	.24
1.6	Argentina	−1.63
1.6	Haiti	.74
1.8	Cuba	−5.31
1.9	Korea, Rep. of	4.65
1.9	Australia	−1.13
Mean = 1.37		Mean = −.07 Standard Deviation = 2.84

APPENDIX TABLE 2   (Continued)

Average Percent Population Growth Rate per Annum, 1965–1972	Country	Growth Rate in GNP per Capita, 1965–72 (after correcting for effect of energy, as expressed in Equation 5.1)
2.1	Chile	−2.16
2.2	Burma	.07
2.3	Sri Lanka	.36
2.3	India	−.90
2.4	Ethiopia	.81
2.4	Turkey	.70
2.5	Paraguay	.18
2.5	Egypt	−2.43
2.6	Bolivia	−1.08
2.6	Dominican Republic	2.54
2.6	Vietnam, Rep. of	−3.86
2.6	Ghana	−.79
2.7	Lebanon	−2.65
2.7	Israel	2.61
2.8	Peru	−2.88
2.9	Honduras	−.85
2.9	Brazil	2.00
2.9	Costa Rica	.85
2.9	China, Rep. of (Taiwan)	2.72
Mean = 2.57		Mean = −.25
		Standard Deviation = 1.97
3.0	Nicaragua	−1.76
3.0	Tunisia	1.03
3.0	Philippines	−.35
3.1	Liberia	1.04
3.1	Thailand	1.79
3.1	Panama	.09
3.2	Colombia	−1.48
3.3	Syria	.24
3.3	El Salvador	−1.23
3.3	South Africa	−2.39
3.3	Iraq	−2.19
3.4	Ecuador	.97
3.4	Guatemala	−.50
3.5	Mexico	−1.53
3.6	Venezuela	−3.39
4.1	Pakistan	.26
Mean = 3.29		Mean = −.59
		Standard Deviation = 1.47

*Data on population growth and growth in GNP per capita from 1974 *World Bank Atlas*.

The methods and results are intended to be suggestive rather than definitive.

Means were computed for groups pooled on the basis of integer value for population growth rate, except for Pakistan, which was pooled with countries having a 3 percent growth rate.

COMPUTATION OF INDICES OF NATIONAL DEVIANCE FROM EXPECTED DEGREE OF REALISM

There were two steps in the construction of these national indices: computing separate components of the ultimate composite index, then combining these into a composite index for the degree of national deviance from the expected level of realism. We now describe the two steps.

Each component of the composite index is obtained by selecting two variables for which data are available on a large number of countries, one of which appears to be a measure of realism. A sample pair is: national cigaret production in billions (unrealism measure), and number of book titles published (realism measure). These two measures, for a particular base year, are then plotted on graph paper, one country per point, to discover the type of mathematical equation required to describe the data by a straight line. For this example, a straight line is obtained on log-log graph paper (Appendix figure 1), so we know that the data can be described by an equation of the form

$$\log_e Y = a + b \log_e X,$$

where Y represents the volume of cigaret production, and X represents the volume of book production. Then the constants a and b are calculated statistically (regression analysis) so that the line best describing the data from all countries can be plotted, as in Appendix figure 1. Now, while we have made a subjective, culture-affected judgment about the selection of the variables, and which is X and which is Y, the fitting of the line is by an objective mathematical procedure. The index of unrealism is then computed by dividing the observed value of each data point by its value expected on the basis of the line fitted to the data for all countries. Thus, the behavior of each country is not being compared to an abstract yardstick, but rather to the average behavior of a large number of countries. To illustrate how this works out, consider a country which published three thousand book titles a year. From the line fitted to the data points from all countries, the expected cigaret production would be sixteen billion. If the country produced exactly that many cigarets, then the index of deviance from expected realism would be the observed cigaret production divided by the production expected from

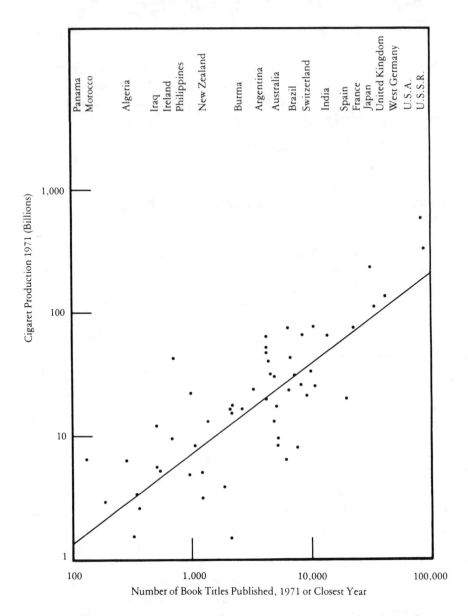

Appendix Figure 1. Illustration of the Technique for Computing Indices of National Unrealism

In this example, cigaret production is expressed as a function of number of book titles published. The straight line is fitted statistically to the data for all countries. Each point represents one country. Because of the great range of values encountered, not all the 61 countries used in computing the line are included on the graph. Data on number of book titles published are from *Statistical Abstract of the United States*, 1973, table 1361, and on cigaret production from the same volume, table 1342. The equation which describes the data best is $Y = .0494 X^{.7222}$, where Y represents the 1971 national cigaret production, in billions, and X represents the 1971 national number of book titles published. This equation accounts for 67.1 percent of the variance between countries with respect to cigaret production. The parameter-fitting was based on analysis of data from 61 countries.

the line calculated from all countries, or $16/16 = 1.00$. Thus, with respect to this particular pair of variables, we would say that the deviance from expected realism was exactly the average expected on the basis of the data for all countries. If, on the other hand, cigaret production was forty-eight billion, the index of deviance from expected realism would be 3.00, indicating that the country was quite unrealistic, by comparison with average behavior of all countries. On the other hand, if cigaret production for this country was only four billion, then the index would be $4/16$, or .25. In this case the index is much lower than what we expect from the average behavior of all countries. As will be noted in Appendix figure 1, it is rare for a country to have an index of deviance from expected realism lower than .25 or higher than 3.0.

Many readers will object that a variety of cultural biases can interfere with the meaning attached to measures of this sort. For example, we would expect to find unusually low levels of cigaret and alcoholic beverage production in Moslem countries, and we find just that. However, *we argue that when enough such measures are combined, such effects tend to cancel each other.* Thus, if we combine many such measures into a composite national index of deviance from expected realism, the resultant compound will tend to be culture-invariant, and the larger the number of component parts, the greater will be the extent to which that is true.

We now consider the technique for combining several such measures for any given country into one composite index of national unrealism. A simple, unsophisticated technique for combining five numbers into a composite index is to add them up and divide by the number of items to obtain the arithmetic mean. The difficulty with this procedure is that one really unusual component will have an inordinate effect on the resultant composite index. To compensate for this, we have used instead the geometric mean of all components. Thus, to take the mean of n numbers we multiply them all together and take the nth root of the product (in practice, add all their logarithms, divide by n and take the antilogarithm). To illustrate how this dampens the effect of the extreme outlier, suppose the five component indices used to make a national index of deviance from expected realism for Italy are as follows.

Index of Deviance from Expected Degree of Realism

Beer production relative to public expenditure for education	115.56
Cigaret production relative to number of book titles published	2.01
Television sets relative to hospital beds	1.05
Airplane use relative to train use	2.48
Automobile use relative to train and bus use	2.51

Composite index (arithmetic mean)   24.72
Composite index (geometric mean of first three multiplied by
   geometric mean of last two, then geometric mean of product taken): 3.95

Obviously, taking the arithmetic mean allows one very unusual value to have an inordinate effect on the composite index. Taking the geometric mean more faithfully exploits the strength associated with the combining process.

We thought of many pairs of measures that could be used to express national degree of deviance from expected realism.

   drug use relative to expenditures on food, clothing, and housing average
   expenditures relative to the savings rate
   automobile fatalities relative to the number of cars
   the birth rate, relative to the average availability of arable land per person
   total consumption of all alcoholic beverages relative to public expen-
      ditures for education
   cigaret production relative to book production
   use of airplanes relative to use of trains
   use of cars relative to use of trains and buses
   national GNP relative to holdings of gold and foreign exchange

Because we were limited with respect to time and computer budget, it seemed preferable to research the application of a few such indices in some depth, rather than attempt to number-crunch on a large number of them rather blindly. Accordingly, our efforts have been concentrated on the following five measures, for just thirty-three countries for which all the required data were available.

   1. Beer production relative to public expenditures for education.
   2. Cigaret production relative to book production.
   3. Number of television sets relative to number of hospital beds.
   4. Use of airplanes relative to use of trains.
   5. Use of cars relative to use of trains and buses.

The first three indices have been combined to get an index of national realism in the educational and cultural area, and the last two were combined to yield a measure of realism in the transportation-energy area. Finally, all five have been combined to obtain a composite measure of national deviance from expected level of realism (Appendix table 3).

We can now answer the questions posed earlier, in the light of a program of statistical analysis of the available data.

First, the indices do seem to be measuring something real, and there is a considerable degree of consistency from component to component. To illustrate, consider the difference between Colombia and Costa Rica in Appendix table 3. Colombia scores markedly higher than Costa Rica on four of the five scales. Similarly, Norway scores below the United States in four out of five, and markedly so in three. We feel reasonably safe in asserting, therefore, that since several measures based on such utterly different types of data yield the same pattern, the pattern is telling us something meaningful. In each continent, there were countries which scored very low on four measures, or very high relative to the rest of the continent on four. The composite indices of deviance from expected realism (Appendix table 4) ranged from .16 for the lowest country to 4.97 for the highest. Also, most people seeing the composite indices will be surprised at the extent to which they were correlated with other well-known attributes of the countries.

For the rest of this discussion, we employ a technical concept to describe the relation between various measures: "the proportion of the variance accounted for." If we have two variables, say Y and X, and we wish to express the extent to which X appears to be implicated in determining the variation in Y, then we compute the preceding statistic. (It is the square of the correlation coefficient, which measures the extent to which variation in two measures is co-related, or varies together.) To illustrate, if the variation from country to country with respect to the composite index of deviance from expected realism is purely a function of GNP per capita, so that all the variation is accounted for by this variable and no other variable has any effect on the index at all, we would say that the proportion of the variance in the index accounted for by GNP per capita is 1.00. This is the highest value that could be computed for that statistic and, in practice, is never encountered in actual data. Indeed, owing to the vagaries of data collection and the complexity of the phenomena involved, to account for more than 60 percent of the variance in any variable in the social or biological sciences is a considerable achievement. (This corresponds to a correlation coefficient of .77.)

If there were relationships between the different components of the index of unrealism, we would expect to find that, taking the geometric mean of the first three and the geometric mean of the second two, the proportion of the variance in one mean accounted for by the other was significantly greater than 0.00. In fact, it was .24 for the 47 countries in Appendix table 4. Given the cultural biases not yet canceled out with this small a number of components (Communist countries, Moslem countries, Catholic or Latin countries), this seemed to indicate that this type of index has some validity. We would expect to find higher levels for this statistic, for example, if the

Comparison of Various Indices of Degree of Deviance from Expected Level of Realism

Country	Beer Production Relative to Expenditures for Education	Cigaret Production Relative to Book Titles	Television Sets Relative to Hospital Beds	Airplane Use Relative to Train Use	Auto Use Relative to Train and Bus Use
Argentina	1.40	1.41	1.68	1.19	.66
Australia	3.11	1.32	1.41	3.52	1.24
Austria	2.50	.57	1.41	.31	1.04
Belgium	2.70	.98	2.24	1.26	2.53
Bolivia	1.26	.46	NA	.34	.24
Brazil	12.46	2.74	1.50	2.59	1.26
Burma	.10	.12	NA	.25	.29
Canada	.72	2.55	2.09	8.52	1.27
Chile	.97	1.08	1.06	.95	.42
Colombia	9.21	3.56	1.26	4.33	1.13
Costa Rica	.25	.48	1.86	.92	.66
Cuba	.80	3.12	NA	.42	.74
Czechoslovakia	2.80	.60	1.55	.39	1.44
Denmark	1.57	.39	2.69	1.15	1.65
Finland	.84	.25	1.33	.90	1.98
France	6.67	1.09	2.02	3.19	1.35
Germany, Fed. Rep. of	1.85	1.31	1.41	2.31	4.16
Greece	.70	1.36	.15	1.43	.72
Hungary	1.11	.84	1.61	.20	.56
India	.054	1.38	.0028	.65	.31
Iran	.17	1.46	.81	.53	1.46
Iraq	.063	1.26	1.59	.37	.59
Ireland	4.08	1.14	1.12	1.44	3.10
Israel	.21	.35	.17	2.45	.87
Italy	115.56	2.01	1.05	2.48	2.51

Japan	1.31	2.68	.93	1.85	.35
Korea, Rep. of	.40	2.30	1.77	.41	.28
Mexico	3.78	1.93	2.49	2.14	.80
Morocco	.39	4.11	.70	.58	.95
Netherlands	1.16	.64	3.82	2.55	2.55
New Zealand	2.29	.61	2.58	2.11	.54
Norway	.44	.041	2.24	1.98	1.65
Pakistan	.019	1.41	.18	.75	.68
Peru	1.89	.69	1.34	.96	.75
Philippines	.76	7.46	.68	2.47	.56
Poland	.37	1.96	1.08	.27	.52
Portugal	2.07	.36	.57	1.62	1.21
Spain	3.57	.32	2.78	2.51	1.17
Sweden	.39	.26	2.22	1.80	4.81
Switzerland	1.28	1.03	1.41	1.99	2.87
Syria	.063	.76	NA	.54	.62
Turkey	.18	1.55	.034	.47	.28
United Kingdom	3.44	1.22	2.13	5.84	2.19
United States	1.14	3.40	2.44	84.39	1.62
Venezuela	2.32	NA	2.25	4.97	1.31
Vietnam, Rep. of	3.18	2.76	NA	1.15	.33
Yugoslavia	1.95	.90	1.11	.48	2.04

NA = Not available.

APPENDIX TABLE 4   Composite Indices of Degree of Deviance from
Expected Level of Realism

Country	Social-Educational-Cultural Component of Composite Index	Transportation-Energy Component of Composite Index	Composite Index
Argentina	1.49	.89	1.15
Australia	1.80	2.09	1.94
Austria	1.26	.57	.85
Belgium	1.81	1.79	1.80
Bolivia	.76	.29	.47
Brazil	3.71	1.81	2.59
Burma	.11	.27	.17
Canada	1.57	3.29	2.27
Chile	1.04	.63	.81
Colombia	3.46	2.21	2.77
Costa Rica	.61	.78	.69
Cuba	1.50	.56	.91
Czechoslovakia	1.38	.75	1.02
Denmark	1.18	1.38	1.27
Finland	.65	1.33	.93
France	2.45	2.08	2.25
Germany, Fed. Rep. of	1.51	3.10	2.16
Greece	.52	1.01	.73
Hungary	1.15	.33	.62
India	.059	.45	.16
Iran	.59	.88	.72
Iraq	.50	.47	.48
Ireland	1.73	2.11	1.91
Israel	.23	1.46	.58
Italy	6.25	2.49	3.95
Japan	1.48	.80	1.09
Korea, Rep. of	1.18	.34	.63
Mexico	2.63	1.31	1.86
Morocco	1.04	.74	.88
Netherlands	1.42	2.55	1.90
New Zealand	1.53	1.07	1.28
Norway	.34	1.81	.78
Pakistan	.56	.71	.63
Peru	1.20	.85	1.01
Philippines	1.57	1.18	1.36
Poland	.92	.37	.59
Portugal	.75	1.40	1.02
Spain	1.47	1.71	1.59
Sweden	.61	2.94	1.34
Switzerland	1.23	2.39	1.71
Syria	.22	.58	.36
Turkey	.21	.36	.28
United Kingdom	2.08	3.58	2.73
United States	2.11	11.69	4.97
Venezuela	2.28	2.55	2.41
Vietnam, Rep. of	2.96	.62	1.35
Yugoslavia	1.25	.99	1.11

geometric mean of four components were statistically compared with the geometric mean of another four.

We discovered immediately that affluence (as measured by GNP per capita) is the most important influence on unrealism. The more affluent the country, the more unrealistic. However, by making graphs, we discovered that certain countries had values for the composite index of deviance from expected realism that were not accounted for by affluence. By examining the groups of countries which deviated from the basic pattern (the importance of affluence), we were able to determine which other factors were important. It quickly became apparent that the other factor had something to do with the source of a nation's energy. If a nation derived a very high proportion of its energy from electricity, it was much more realistic than what we would expect from the level of affluence alone. (Norway, New Zealand, Costa Rica, Switzerland, Sweden, Japan, Austria, and Finland illustrate this pattern.) If, on the other hand, a very high proportion of the country's energy came from fossil fuels, particularly crude oil, then the index of national deviance from expected realism was far higher than one would have expected from affluence alone. Accordingly, we experimented with various mathematical equations which would express the combined effect of affluence and the proportion of a nation's energy coming from electricity, or hydroelectricity alone, on the composite indices of unrealism. (See data on hydroelectricity and affluence in Appendix table 5.) It turned out that the highest proportion of the variance, country to country, in the unrealism indices was accounted for by assuming an interactive effect between affluence and the proportion of energy coming from electricity. This interaction was best expressed by combining affluence and the electricity term as a single variable, with the former as the numerator and the latter as the denominator.

The results are gathered together in Appendix tables 6 and 7. The transportation-energy component of the national unrealism index is most easy to account for statistically, the cultural and educational component is most difficult, and the combined index is intermediate. In table 6, for both the cultural and educational components of the composite index, there is a significant increase in the proportion of the variance country to country accounted for if we include the effect of the proportion of the energy used by a nation that comes from electricity. In table 7 (hydroelectricity instead of electricity), only the first subcomponent is raised by including the effect of hydroelectricity.

ANOTHER APPROACH TO CHARACTERIZING NATIONAL STRATEGIES: ENERGY AND GNP ALONE

L. F. Molloy, interested in obtaining a cross-check on the conclusions obtained from the preceding analysis, explored with K. E. F. Watt the relationship

APPENDIX TABLE 5   Variables Used to Account for Differences
                    between Countries in Indices of Degree of Deviance
                    from Expected Level of Realism*

Country	X_1 1969 GNP per Capita (U.S. $)	X_2 1964 Hydroelectric Production (billions of kWh)	X_3 1969 Consumption of All Sources of Energy (millions of short tons in coal equivalents)	$\dfrac{X_1}{X_2/X_3}$
Argentina	828	1.236	40.818	27344
Australia	2476	6.898	70.481	25299
Austria	1687	13.179	24.339	3115
Belgium	2372	.115	59.756	NA
Bolivia	190	.421	1.157	504
Brazil	337	22.097	48.215	735
Burma	78	.280	1.709	476
Canada	2997	113.344	204.422	5405
Chile	610	3.723	12.765	2092
Colombia	360	3.721	13.338	1290
Costa Rica	489	.495	.617	610
Denmark	2860	.025	27.723	NA
Finland	1944	8.501	18.541	4240
France	2783	35.218	195.294	15433
Germany, Fed. Rep. of	2512	12.101	325.245	67516
Greece	858	.749	11.199	12829
India	84	14.807	114.375	649
Iran	295	.270	NA	NA
Iraq	279	NA	6.426	NA
Ireland	1169	.784	9.513	14185
Israel	1663	NA	6.702	NA
Italy	1548	39.328	142.461	5607
Japan	1626	68.957	319.006	7522
Korea, Rep. of	227	.750	22.002	6659
Mexico	566	6.866	56.305	4642
Morocco	212	1.171	NA	NA
Netherlands	2196	NA	66.138	NA
New Zealand	1918	7.753	8.024	1985
Norway	2528	43.864	18.805	1084
Pakistan	140	NA	13.007	NA
Peru	291	2.448	9.039	1074
Philippines	340	1.554	10.670	2334
Portugal	529	4.220	6.360	797
Spain	872	20.646	49.438	2088
Sweden	3315	43.022	50.728	3909
Switzerland	2965	22.663	21.837	2857
Syria	188	NA	NA	NA
Turkey	380	1.652	17.471	4019

APPENDIX TABLE 5 (Continued)

Country	X_1 1969 GNP per Capita (U.S. \$)	X_2 1964 Hydroelectric Production (billions of kWh)	X_3 1969 Consumption of All Sources of Energy (millions of short tons in coal equivalents)	$\dfrac{X_1}{X_2/X_3}$
United Kingdom	1976	4.022	7.915	3889
United States	4664	180.302	2413.431	62430
Venezuela	944	1.223	23.810	18378
Vietnam, Rep. of	178	.056	6.944	22072

*X_1 and X_3 from *1971 Statistical Abstract of the United States*, tables 1279 and 1283. X_2 from N. B. Guyol, *The World Electric Power Industry* (Berkeley: University of California Press, 1969).
NA = Not available.

APPENDIX TABLE 6   Proportions of Variance between Countries with Respect to Indices of Degree of Deviance from Expected Realism Accounted for by Independent Variables

	Dependent Variable (alleged effect) Y		
Independent Variable (postulated cause) X	Cultural and Educational Component of Index of Deviance from Expected National Realism (first two components only)	Transportation-Energy use Component of Index of Deviance from Expected National Realism	Composite Index of Deviance from Expected National Realism
X = GNP per capita Form: $Y = a X^b$	.07	.59	.32
X_1 = GNP per Capita X_2 = Electrical Energy Production Relative to Total Energy Consumption Form: $Y = a \left(\dfrac{X_1}{X_2}\right)^b$	.14	.51	.38

APPENDIX TABLE 7   Proportions of the Variance between Countries with Respect to Indices of Degree of Deviance from Expected Realism Accounted for by Different Independent Variables (Regressions of Form $Y = aX^b$)

Independent Variable	Dependent Variable Y		
	Cultural and Educational Component of Index of Deviance from Expected National Realism (3 components)	Transportation-Energy Use Component of Index of Deviance from Expected National Realism	Composite Index of Deviance from Expected National Realism
X_1 (table 5)	n = 33 a = .109 b = .349 r^2 = .155	n = 33 a = .027 b = .575 r^2 = .567	n = 33 a = .053 b = .464 r^2 = .409
$\dfrac{X_1}{X_2/X_3}$ (table 5)	n = 33 a = .088 b = .309 r^2 = .191	n = 33 a = .199 b = .285 r^2 = .221	n = 33 a = .101 b = .298 r^2 = .267

between energy use per capita and GNP per capita. A simple linear regression was calculated for climate-adjusted energy per capita values (E_T/p); ($n = 54$, $r^2 = 0.68$).

$$GNP/p = 491.21 + 0.53\ E_T/p$$

In so doing, the energy use per capita figure was thus corrected for the requirement to keep warm, using the mean temperature for the center of population in the country. A graph of the energy index against the GNP index was subsequently plotted (Appendix figure 2), revealing that different groups of countries are pursuing very different national economic development strategies. Most of the points on the figure were then grouped into four crude categories:

(A) Underdeveloped or developing
(B) Inefficient energy use; generally developed
(C) Efficient energy use; developed
(D) Very high energy use; probably wasteful use in nonproductive, consumer luxuries.

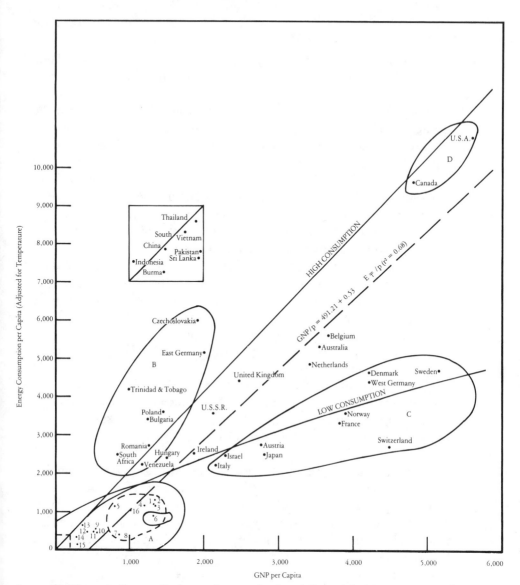

Appendix Figure 2. Energy Consumption per Capita, Adjusted for Temperature (EṪ/p) and GNP per Capita

GNP/p=491.21 + 0.53 EṪ/p
S_{yx} = 858.6
S_o = 169.13
S_1 = 0.05
r^2 = 0.68

Data from the Environmental Fund sheet on 1972 energy consumption and *United Nations Statistical Yearbook*, 1973 (for GNP data). Where GNP data were unavailable, data were computed using growth rate projections or rates given in Fremont Felix, *World Markets of Tomorrow*. Values for Eastern Europe and Communist bloc countries are Net Material Product.

Overall it appears that the four groupings (A, B, C, and D) may indicate different "development paths" which involve, among other things, cultural variables.

Group A countries are at a low level of economic development, but the nature of their future energy consumption (assuming they can get it) will determine toward which categories (B, C, or D) they will eventually move.

Group B countries include those with abundant oil and high energy use in refining (Trinidad & Tobago, Venezuela) or those with energy-intensive heavy industry (Eastern Europe). It should be noted, however, that the GNP values for Eastern Europe and Communist bloc countries are actually *Net Material Product*, not GNP, and therefore are not strictly comparable.

Group C consists of Western European countries with a particular mix of precision/industrial and agriculture (Scandinavia, West Germany, France, Italy, Switzerland). This group also includes Japan (high input of lower-cost labor) and New Zealand (low energy-intensive agriculture). Through reasons of national security Israel is probably in a class of its own. There is also some justification for considering Singapore part of group C.

Group D consists solely of the "big energy spenders" (U.S. and Canada). They are clearly on a different path than group C and are intermediate in trend between B and C. Oil-rich Kuwait is also in this category, but has not been included because of its small population. This group is characterized by luxury energy use and high private consumption. Heavy industry (especially smelting and mining, pulp and paper manufacture) would account for some of this high use.

Thus the United States and Canada are clearly on a track which implies great energy consumption per unit of GNP. Norway, New Zealand, and many European countries require far less energy per unit of GNP, even after correcting for the effect of temperature. Among the developing countries, also, great differences in national strategy can be identified. Venezuela and Trinidad, among others, are very energy-intensive, while many other developing nations use very little energy per unit of GNP.

Judging from the data, it becomes apparent that the difference between the so-called developed and underdeveloped world is not only on the basis of GNP/P (that is, those above and below U.S.$500 annual income would be the classical cutoff point) but even more, perhaps, on *the basis of energy consumption*.

A very important message follows from this graph and the preceding analysis. There is no single appropriate or "best" national economic-development strategy. Nations can develop using a large or a small amount of energy per unit of GNP. How much they use is determined not merely by need, or circumstances, but is largely influenced by cultural factors. Thus, for example, in the United States, where energy has been historically superabundant and cheap, it has come to be regarded as perfectly normal to use airplanes for very short trips. Not only is this behavior using energy in an enormously inefficient manner, but in cases where airport congestion is extreme (and those cases are frequent), even human time is being used inefficiently in spite of the purported time-saving value provided by air travel.

6
The Control of Information About the Environment

The previous chapters have shown that many environmental problems have arisen because the prevailing socioeconomic, cultural, and political values and systems have often failed to lead nations to operate in the long-term interests of humanity. The interests of the people are, admittedly, often difficult to discern. But governments have the responsibility to exhaust all possible means of identifying, analyzing, and responding to the public will and interest.

How the public arrives at an understanding of its own will and interest is one of the most important facets of the social process. The key ingredients, of course, are knowledge and information, two entities whose dissemination is predominantly under the control of government educational institutions, mass-media executives and editors, and/or the advertising industry. Since the knowledge and information disseminated to the public can effectively shape self-images, perceptions of reality, and indeed the very interests of the people, information manipulation and distortion can have severe effects on a society's ability to define, understand, and deal with environmental problems.

In contemporary society, information manipulation and distortion is widespread. Facts about the availability of resources are withheld from the public. Clandestine political activities, both within a nation's borders and internationally, are considered to be none of the public's business. The harmful effects of a product are suppressed until the truth is somehow exposed; and then a propaganda campaign, often using the appeals of sex, art, and humor, attempts to make light of the harmful effects.

Although examples of information control are numerous and diverse, we have chosen several issues that have special relevance to environmental concerns and, through a discussion of these issues, we will highlight instances of information distortion.

The first issue deals with the relationship between high rates of energy consumption per capita and the economic health of a society. An analysis of data on per capita consumption of energy and average annual rate of growth in GNP per capita among twenty-three developed countries between 1908 and 1973 (figure 6.1) indicates that the higher the per capita consumption of energy, the lower the average annual rate of growth of GNP per capita. Clearly the data from the developed parts of the world indicate that a country can have a higher rate of increase in GNP per capita without necessarily experiencing a sharp increase in energy consumption. Furthermore, the data reveal that steadily increasing rates of energy consumption per capita do not contribute to high rates of growth in GNP per capita. Some of the reasons behind these phenomena (already discussed in chapters 4 and 5) bear repeating. The history of industrial development indicates that technological inventions related to industrial productivity tend to favor an increasing rate of energy use. Machines are substituted for human labor to such an extent that unemployment, congestions, delays, pollution, and, above all, depletion of resources often result. Solution or amelioration of these problems absorbs capital that otherwise would contribute to economic growth.

So the facts are that high and rapidly rising rates of energy consumption do not increase, and indeed often lower, the rate of growth of GNP per capita. But the dominant technoculture's conventional wisdom leads the public to believe just the opposite, as evidenced by the following excerpt from Mobil Oil Corporation's advertisements.

> A time to choose—energy growth or economic stagnation . . . we . . . doubt that Americans are willing to—or need to—sacrifice their living standards. The million dollar study [of the Ford Foundation Energy Policy Project (EPP)] would have us substitute bicycles for cars, . . . [and] would even move more than one million people a year to new communities where they would work at jobs planned for them by the government.[1]

When one examines the EPP report in question, it becomes quite obvious that Mobil grossly distorted the report's findings and recommendations. The effect on the public of such blatant manipulation of information is to make energy conservation appear as a step toward massive inconvenience and Big Brother government control. But the actual thrust of the EPP report was that through simple, energy-saving behavior, the growth rate of energy can be reduced significantly. This slowing down in the rate of increase in energy use would then allow alternative sources of energy to be developed *before* present sources are depleted. But profits can be gained for the big oil and

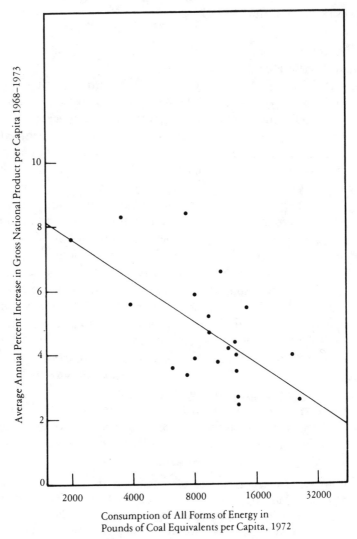

Figure 6.1. The Relationship between Average Annual Percent
Increase in GNP per Capita, 1968–1973, and the
Consumption of All Forms of Energy in Pounds of
Coal Equivalents, per Capita, for 1972

Each point represents one of the 21 countries that use large amounts of energy
per capita. The data are from *Statistical Abstract of the United States*, 1974,
tables 1363 and 1372. The fitted line was obtained from a regression analysis of
the form

$$y + a - b \ln x,$$

and accounts for 40 percent of the variance in *y* (i.e., this relation has a correlation coefficient of about .63).

   An explanation of this relationship was presented with the flow charts and
model in chapters 4 and 5.

utilities companies if rates of energy consumption move ever upward—thus the distortion of information is rationalized as a good business technique to promote sales.

Other examples of erroneous information concerning energy and healthy economic growth can be cited. W. Donham Crawford, president of the Edison Electric Institute, said that the several-year pause in new power plant sitings discussed in one of the EPP's scenarios would be "hazardous." And William Tavoulareas, president of Mobil, further characterized the EPP report mentioned above as "a formula for perpetual economic stagnation."[2]

Another instance of information distortion is seen in statements about nuclear energy and strip-mining of coal. As we have already mentioned, there are massive problems connected with use of either of these energy sources. For example, many technologically advanced countries are now committed to the notion that the salvation of mankind from the energy problem lies in the development of fast-breeder reactor technology. The fast breeder makes use of plutonium or uranium, substances that have an extremely long life (tens of thousands of years) and a very high level of potential hazard. Release of these substances into the environment in large quantities through reactor malfunction or accident would be extremely dangerous. Further, plutonium and uranium are used in atomic bombs, so that widespread distribution of these substances increases the dangers arising from their possible misuse. At Hiroshima and Nagasaki, the annual incidence rate of cancer in humans was roughly proportional to the exposure. Also, ten individuals in Japan occupationally exposed to high levels of radiation have had their deaths attributed to the exposure. So there can be no doubt that radioactive materials are toxic; the doubt is only about *how* toxic they are.[3]

Now we turn to an example of what numerous scientists, engineers, and corporation executives are saying about the issue. Dr. Hans Bethe, a noted physicist, has said that efforts to expand America's domestic supplies of energy are being crippled by organizations that oppose nuclear power, object to increased strip-mining of coal, and/or attempt to block stepped-up exploration for oil offshore. "If we follow the advice of these people," he says, "we might as well go back into the cave right away. There would be incredible unemployment, food production would be cut severely. In that direction lies catastrophe."[4]

This kind of scare tactic undoubtedly has an impact on a reading public whose knowledge of the energy debate has been kept so low that they feel obliged to rely on "expert" opinion. But if fright were to be put in its proper perspective regarding nuclear energy, it would be the risks of utilization, the chances of technical failure, and the complex precautions the use of breeder reactors necessitates that would worry and scare the public.

Two sobering incidents in the United States put these dangers in their proper perspective. In October 1966, a spectacular nuclear accident occurred at Detroit Edison's experimental Enrico Fermi Atomic Power Plant. Through minor mistakes and human errors, a partial melt-down of fuel in a fast-breeder reactor occurred, a process that could have destroyed the entire plant, released radioactive gas, and exposed thousands of people to harm and even death.[5]

On March 22, 1975, a fire at the Tennessee Valley Authority's Browns Ferry nuclear plant near Decatur, Alabama, set in motion a tense drama that exposed the inadequacy of standard emergency procedures, put out of commission the radiation monitors around the entire plant complex, and resulted in the failure of at least seven of the plant's twelve safety systems. Nuclear Regulatory Commission investigators identified some *eleven* particular deficiencies in the plant's safety precautions and handling of the accident.

But there are indications that representatives of the nuclear industry downplayed the seriousness of the accident and are lobbying strongly against increased governmental regulations that could cost the industry billions of dollars to make the fifty-six reactors around the nation safer.[6] Proponents of nuclear energy therefore lead the public to believe that the breeder reactor is a technically feasible, economically desirable source of energy, and consistently downplay the numerous dangers associated with nuclear energy.

Considerable misconception has also been created regarding the use of solar energy. To most people it no doubt seems reasonable that solar energy would be competitive with other forms of energy. After all, energy from the sun is free, inexhaustible, and does not pollute. It also seems logical that the negative effects of collecting and utilizing solar energy would be less potentially disruptive to weather and climate. Thus the public would seem on solid ground in favoring solar energy development, especially in the light of recent data on fossil fuel depletion and the overheating of the planet that could be caused by excessive fossil fuel use. In view of these dangers we are told that we must conserve fossil fuels, and that the economy of many countries is in danger of being destroyed because of the vast amounts of money needed to pay for imported crude oil or oil products. Clearly, the use of solar energy would conserve fossil fuel energy sources and would certainly have a beneficial effect on the international balance of trade and on the world economy.

Yet the official literature on energy issued by many governments (a notable example is information on Project Independence in the U.S.) treats solar energy as a minor item. This misleading presentation of such energy as a poor substitute for fossil fuels well serves the interests of the large oil and electric corporations who wish to maintain their monopoly over energy sources. The influence these corporations have with governments is well known and quite strong. For even though a U.S. National Science Foundation Report of 1973 stated that by 1976 the U.S. should be spending as much as $189 million for solar energy development, or at the very least a sum of $67.5 million, the 1976 budget for all solar and wind energy was only $57 million. This same budget allocated $1 billion for nuclear fission and $120 million for nuclear fusion.[7] A solar energy portable food cooking unit was developed in India, but has never been mass produced. Many small corporations who are successfully pushing ahead with speedy technological development of solar energy are starved for financial support, while the bulk of U.S. Federal money spent on solar energy goes to large corporations active in the sale of competing sources of energy. Westinghouse and General Electric, for example, are perhaps the two major companies in the field of nuclear power plant construction. Both are waiting for their multimillion dollar investments in nuclear power plants to pay dividends. Not surprisingly, GE's researchers found that "additional research is needed before solar heating/cooling systems become commercially viable"; and that "nuclear power and coal offer the most feasible means to meet energy needs for the foreseeable future."[8] This offers an interesting example of how money spent on promotion of solar energy may have actually worked against the very concept.

People are often led to believe that solar energy has a low priority because its costs are prohibitive, or because it raises formidable scientific and technological problems that cannot be solved for centuries. In fact, this is not the case.[9] It is true that direct conversion of solar energy into electrical energy depends heavily on advanced technology and materials, and thus is somewhat expensive. It is also true that the use of solar energy for chemical reduction is still in the basic research stage. However, an immense amount of research has been done on the technology and economics of heating and cooling buildings and of heating water with on-site solar energy collectors. It has been found that, at current fuel prices, solar energy for these purposes is competitive with other forms of energy; indeed, it is now cheaper, except in those regions with good hydroelectric power supplies and heavy cloud cover.[10]

Further, as this book was going to press, it appeared that a breakthrough in the cheap conversion of solar to electrical energy was imminent. A small company, the Consumers Solar Electric Power Corporation of Pacific Palisades, California, claimed that it would shortly be able to mass-produce solar cell arrays that would generate electricity at a capital construction cost of $250 per kilowatt peak generating capacity.[11] The fuel cost would, of course, be nonexistent. This compares with capital costs of $280 per kilowatt for nuclear steam, $210 for fossil steam, and $120 for gas turbine.[12] However, all of these latter three sources have significant fuel costs, which are rising constantly.

But this very large body of evidence does not serve the interest of electrical utilities companies or fossil fuel corporations; therefore one can hardly expect favorable testimony on their part. This observation is supported not only by innumerable instances of testimony before legislative committees,[13] but also in numerous publications. One such publication is a new book on energy written by a scholar working for an electrical utilities company.[14] The book seems quite misleading in that it leaves the reader with the impression that the harnessing of solar energy would best be done through the combustion of hay, a process that would lead to a fuel cost thirteen times that of electrical power generation from nuclear devices. The book does not deal with alternative processes involved in the heating and cooling of building space, or to the heating of water by solar energy, processes that would, of course, decrease the need for electrical energy from a central power station.

The manipulation of energy information also obscures an extremely important issue we have repeatedly emphasized: net energy. If the facts surrounding the net energy contribution of nuclear energy were made known, its appeal would diminish greatly. The most recently available calculations indicate that if nuclear energy use grew so rapidly that ten plants were under construction for each one operating, the costs would be so high that there might be a net energy loss from all eleven plants.[15]

Furthermore, it now appears that the cost to build atomic reactors will be six hundred 1975 U.S. dollars per kilowatt of output. Thus, to make the U.S. 50 percent dependent on nuclear power would cost twenty-two times the entire U.S. government budget in 1973. The capital cost of each nuclear fuel enrichment plant will be about a quarter of a billion dollars. Clearly, no country can possibly afford much atomic power at such a high cost. Some of the most recent estimates indicate that to obtain one unit of nuclear energy, .56 of a unit of energy from fossil fuel must be expended, just to keep the plant running.[16] Thus the net energy output from nuclear power may turn out to be very low because of the high energy costs of nuclear fuel enrichment, plant construction and operation, waste disposal, mining, and transportation.

In light of the research findings available, it is disappointing that prominent politicians rarely even mention solar energy. For example, in spite of the present consternation over the energy crisis, solar energy was not once mentioned by the president of the United States in the 1975 State of the Union address.

But examples of information manipulation are not limited to issues where there *might* be future dangers to humanity. In the case of Minamata, a small fishing town on the southern island of Kyushu in Japan, a horror story began to unfold in the 1950s. The hearing, sight, speech, and anatomical structure of bodies and limbs of the citizens of Minamata suffered serious impairment as a result of the mercury content of the fish they ate. The mercury compounds that polluted the water around Minamata were part of the waste discharged from the local factory of the Chisso Corporation. Chisso at first denied responsibility, and many of the leaders in government and industry, as well as university scientists, sided with the corporation and continued to speak in glowing terms of how industrial development would lead Japan to new glory. Soon, similar diseases broke out in Niigata and the Showa Denko Company was clearly confirmed as the polluter. Then the Itai-itai disease (as the Minamata people named it) appeared in Toyama in central Japan, slowly disintegrating bones, causing multiple fractures and excruciating pain. Still the proponents of industrial development minimized these tragedies and called for even more industries. Then quantities of rice bran cooking oil became contaminated, and arsenic was found in powdered milk, both the result of the expanded use of agricultural chemicals.

In the name of industrial and economic progress, information about the man-made causes of these fatal diseases was withheld, minimized, or distorted; perhaps no example better illustrates the seriousness of information manipulation.[17]

Numerous other incidents can be cited in which environmental information has been distorted, often by government agencies and spokesmen. Two well-documented examples are the major hydroelectric schemes at Lake Manapouri[18] in New Zealand and Lake Pedder in Tasmania.[19] Located in parts of national parks, both lakes are famous for their aesthetic, scientific, and wildlife attractions, and both have long been eyed eagerly by hydroelectricity developers. The harmful environmental impact of the proposed development projects, as well as the possible alternatives capable of conserving these two valuable lakes, has been conspicuously avoided in government information dissemination. Over the years the authorities concerned denied and distorted vital economic and environmental information required by the public. In the case of Lake Manapouri, the prolonged withholding of information ultimately generated a major controversy that became the watershed of the public conservation movement in New Zealand. In part it contributed to the electoral defeat of the incumbent government and the ultimate retention of the lake within its natural levels. But not all scenarios have outcomes this favorable to the environment.

Another example of information control involves the production of potentially harmful pesticides. As table 6.1 shows, U.S. production figures on nine pesticides were withheld at various times between 1968 and 1973.

The denial and distortion of information is just as acute in many developing countries, especially those anxious for foreign investment. Not only do many developing country governments offer tax incentives and other benefits to foreign investors, but they also downplay environmental issues that discourage the investor. The public is often informed only that the foreign investment policy is in the interests of the country's economy, and that through expansion of employment opportunity, business activity will be accelerated and government revenue will be increased.

But, as was mentioned in chapter 4, many foreign investment schemes actually have negative consequences for developing countries. A country's valuable and finite natural resources are often exploited and destroyed. The overexploitation of the forests of Indonesia is a case in point.[20] Foreign companies are given rights to timber extraction and management of forest areas. Usually the companies assume full control of the areas under the terms of the contract, and thus the forests become inaccessible to the local inhabitants. The information released to the public usually highlights only those terms of the agreement that relate to

> rules and regulations pertaining to the sustained yield principle, maintenance and reforestation of the cutover forest, aerial photography to produce an inventory of the concession area, submission of detailed annual as well as long-range working plans, and regulations ensuring that harvesting operations are carried out in accordance with the rules specifically prescribed for a particular forest.

Facts pertaining to soil erosion, shifts in climate, extermination of plant and animal life,[21] and siltation of fishing areas[22] that affect vital food sources are not made public.

This, however, is only part of the story of how foreign investment practices in developing countries are linked to information manipulation. Investors usually have one primary reason for investing: profit maximization. This motive leads to the establishment of consumer-oriented industries promoting superfluous consumption, such as soft drinks, beer, cigarets, noodles, ice cream, cars, motorcycles, cosmetics, and the like, instead of making significant, tangible contributions to the local economy. The use of information to create and increase consumption desires for those products bringing profit to the investors thus becomes a prevalent pattern. Advertising which discourages local societies from utilizing labor-intensive energy and processes not only increases the dependency of the people on the technology of the investor but also tends to degrade the cultural value of human labor.

The manipulation of information regarding pollution and other negative effects of industrialization is another prevalent pattern practiced by foreign investors in developing societies. Since the large corporations own much of the communications technology, it is quite easy for them either to withhold relevant information or to influence the way it is treated in the media.

There are numerous other instances in which institutions promulgate a distorted perception of their activities.[23] The way foreign aid is publicized by developed nations in their own countries is a good example. The donor nations create the impression that they are performing miracles for the underdeveloped world. However, if one visits the developing nations and is allowed to inspect development projects objectively, an entirely different perception often results. Projects that are publicized in the developed countries as being of great value may be almost unknown in the native village in Central America, say, where they are claimed to have effected a virtual economic revolution.[24]

The fact that foreign aid creates great indebtedness in recipient countries is also conveniently left unpublicized. Repayment of loans often forces recipient nations to borrow even more heavily from the donor nations. And, as was mentioned briefly in chapter 4, the knowledge that a large portion of all aid funds of an agency such as U.S. AID goes to purchase goods in the U.S.

TABLE 6.1   Chemicals Whose Production Figures Have Been Withheld, United States, 1968–1973

Item	1968	1969	1970	1971	1972	1973
Parathion	X	X	D	X	X	X
Nabam	X	D	X	X	X	X
Ferbam	D	X	X	X	X	X
Zineb	D	X	X	X	X	X
2, 4, 5-T	D	D	X	X	X	X
DDT	D	D	D	X	X	X
2, 4-Dacid	D	D	D	X	X	X
Methyl Bromide	D	D	D	X	D	D
Calcium Arsenate	D	D	D	D	X	NA

Source: Data from *Agricultural Statistics*, 1974, USDA; X = not disclosed; D = disclosed. NA = not available.

which are then loaned to foreign countries is not made clear to the public, especially in terms of who benefits most.

Thus institutions and interest groups use a variety of methods and techniques for information control and distortion, all of which ultimately affect the environment adversely. Problems are allowed to develop, intensify, and get out of hand without key personnel in policymaking positions knowing the full facts. And the potential power of the public is effectively neutralized by withholding or manipulating the knowledge essential to responsible dissent.

Advertising and Mass Media

Of the numerous specific instances that show how consumer information is manipulated, the systematic promulgation of environmentally destructive attitudes and beliefs through advertising and mass media is one of the most dangerous. Some years ago Vance Packard[25] pointed out that people were being encouraged to consume resources at an extraordinarily wasteful rate through the combination of advertising and planned obsolescence. Recent analyses of advertising techniques make it clear that advertising has now become much more sinister. Many people are becoming aware of the psychological tricks being played in automobile and cigaret advertising; but the use of sexually oriented subliminal messages, documented in a book by Wilson Key,[26] is not so obvious. Representing the outcome of extremely sophisticated market research on public attitudes and psychological behavior, the aim of this type of modern advertising is to induce people to consume resources. Through the use of various communication tricks, the target audience is manipulated without its knowledge.

Values can also be changed by the program content of television. Indeed, in many instances the medium sells not only merchandise and services, but also life-styles, value systems, and other cultural messages that are conducive to the promotion of a particular commodity. The fact that these values and commodities have harmful effects on the society as a whole is conveniently ignored. This issue becomes especially significant in the developing nations because of the enormous scale on which programs from developed countries are imported[27] together with package advertisements that bring subliminal messages having harmful impact on the society. The dangerous trend is to replace producership with consumership.[28]

As long as media operations are primarily dependent on advertising for their revenues, this unhealthy situation is likely to continue. Advertising is a much more important source of revenue for the media than is generally recognized. In 1970 twenty billion dollars were spent on advertising in the U.S.; and for several important British newspapers, income from advertising is about three times greater than income from circulation.[29] It is very tempting, therefore, for the media to be careful about using content that might be offensive to their main advertisers. A good example of how newspapers can be influenced occurred in 1966 when the *Washington Post* contracted with Louis Harris Associates to poll residents of the Washington metropolitan area on twenty issues, including crime, education, ghettos, jobs, public transportation, and road construction. The poll showed that more public transportation was given the highest priority of the twenty issues, and was considered more than twice as important as more roads. The poll also showed that thirteen other issues were considered more important than parking.[30] But parking and increased road construction are given a very high priority by Congress, the highway interest groups, and the powerful automobile industry. So when the results of the survey were published by the *Post*, the revelations were distorted by simply omitting the questions on transportation. Thus information that would further justify conversion to mass transit, thereby making more efficient use of energy and land, and cutting down on air pollution and congestion delays, was systematically suppressed.

This practice of withholding parts of stories or doctoring the information cannot be attributed solely to the editorial policy of a given medium. In many instances the public relations officers who are responsible for the release of information from a given institution produce one-sided information that guarantees the interest of that institution. For example, very cautious phrasing was used by the Institute of Oceanology in Jakarta in publishing their research findings on contamination of the oysters in the vicinity of Jakarta Bay. Although the actual findings showed that the polluted waters had caused a significant percentage of the oysters to be infested with coliform bacteria, an indicator of intestinal disease hazard, the published report minimized the adverse conclusions of the research. This selective treatment of research findings was due to the fact that a luxurious beach resort (where many of the upper-middle-class families of Jakarta spend weekends of enjoyment and leisure) had been constructed in the bay area by a company partly owned by the city. Furthermore, Jakarta Bay is still considered to be a potential source of fish and oysters for the local market. The possible health hazard of using the beach for swimming, and the potential danger of eating oysters from the bay, were downplayed in the report, and no clear warning to the public was issued. Similar practices appear in beach resorts and other tourist centers. Tourists are usually kept ignorant of possible health hazards incurred by swimming at such beautifully advertised beaches.

Another interesting example relates both to consumerism and to the manipulation of information so frequently perpetrated by large organizations. While this book was being written, the U.S. automobile industry and the U.S. government were deep in the throes of a major economic recession. Given the exalted place of the automobile industry in the U.S. economy, it was generally assumed that slumping car sales were playing a major role in deepening the recession. One of the remedies, then, was to increase sales. This was not easy, however, because the public was finally becoming aware that most models of U.S automobiles had consistently made inefficient use of fuel. (The average mileage per gallon of U.S. passenger cars dropped from 14.95 to 13.67 between 1950 and 1972.[31]) This awareness led many thinking people to realize that national fuel efficiency in the United States would be improved enormously if there were a significant shift of passengers from cars to more efficient means of travel, such as buses. To counteract this growing public awareness (an awareness that would obviously discourage auto sales), the automobile industry began an exhaustive media campaign.

On April 21, 1975, an article carried by Associated Press, datelined Detroit, appeared in U.S. newspapers. Executives of all four U.S. automobile manufacturers were at that time on a "speaking tour" and eager to supply quotes. General Motors Chairman Thomas A. Murphy said, "The economy has bottomed out, we already are seeing signs of a resurgence in our industry." Ford Motor Company President Lee A. Iacocca said in a speech, "I don't want to mislead anyone or spread false hopes—unemployment is awful. From the bottom of the trough we're in, it's a long climb back to business as usual. Even with all the qualification, however, things are getting better, not worse." But the sales figures covering the periods immediately before and after the Big Four speaking tour contradicted the statements of Murphy and Iacocca. As table 6.2 shows, car sales for the first twenty days of April 1975 were *down* 28.4 percent from April of the previous year, and down 27.7 percent in mid-May.

It is difficult to see what automobile executives were referring to when they said that business was showing "signs of a resurgence," or that "things are getting better." Since sales figures for the entire industry are typically available within 5 days of the close of a ten-day selling period, the executives would certainly have known by April 21 that early April sales did *not* indicate an improvement, but rather were at the lowest point in fourteen years. Furthermore, as sales figures for the thirty days immediately following their speeches indicate, it seems unlikely that there existed any firm information at the executives' disposal that could possibly have indicated to them that sales were going to improve significantly in the immediate future; and indeed sales did *not* improve significantly. Thus, it seems reasonable to interpret their remarks as a deliberate misrepresentation of facts. It does not seem

TABLE 6.2   Sales Figures for U.S. Automobiles
            (All Four Manufacturers)

| Period | No. Units | | Percent change, |
	1975	1974	1974 to 1975
March	523,000	654,000	−20.0
First 20 days of April	309,878	432,715	−28.4
Last 10 days of April	207,759	269,623	−22.9
First 10 days of May	162,046	204,505	−20.8
Second 10 days of May	180,423	249,394	−27.7

Source: Compiled from data in the *Wall Street Journal,* April and May 1975.

too much to ask of a nation's economic leaders to be truthful with the public and to point out the serious situation in a given industry. Such a forthright policy would make a valuable contribution to realistic perceptions, and to identifying priority problems and eventual solutions.

The Impact of Transnational Advertising

During the past twenty-five years, an "acceleration of history" has occurred in the lesser developed countries. The poor, rural, and largely illiterate populations have been suddenly exposed to print, film, radio, and television. This has given rise to the related phenomena of rising expectations and rising frustration.[32]

Television probably has as much impact on other cultures as does any other medium. As UNESCO has frequently pointed out, most of the television stations in the developing countries of Asia, Africa, and South America broadcast a large number of programs produced in the developed countries. The contents of American and Japanese programs are, generally speaking, consumption-oriented.[33] Advertisements usually show the materials of the "good life," Western style. An example is the advertising of Australian and American blue jeans in Southeast Asian countries. Young people in these countries are encouraged to believe that these foreign-made jeans are somehow better than locally made garments and consequently are worthy of a higher price. The fact is that the foreign-made jeans are usually less suitable for the heat and humidity of the local climate. And the high price cannot be attributed solely to the quality of the jeans, for advertising costs and profits taken out of the developing countries greatly increase prices.

Furthermore, nothing good is accomplished by encouraging young people in some parts of the world to go horseback riding in their jeans (as depicted in the advertisements) when there are no horses available in their communities. In the context of Southeast Asia, the advertisements merely help to distort further the cultural self-image of local young people. This example is typical of advertising devices used in lesser developed countries to push sales of commodities such as soft drinks, cosmetics, beer, and cigarets. The advertising always depicts a lavish life-style for happy, virile, beautiful people, subtly suggesting that the merchandise in itself will create a better life for the consumers.

Other examples show the extremes to which insidious advertising can go. Take the rich villager in rural Java who has been convinced by advertising that owning a shiny Japanese motorcycle will provide him with a worthy status symbol. So he buys the cycle, never learns how to operate it, and finds no practical use for it in his daily activities. But the cycle manufacturer gets his profit and consumerism receives another shot in the arm—with no concern for basic human needs, environmental stability, or development of local production and export.

Historically, there is evidence that this type of consumer-oriented advertising has led to an overemphasis upon the values of consumption rather than of productivity in lesser developed countries.[34] Although some Asian leaders like Mahatma Gandhi and Mao Tse-tung have urged self-reliance and promotion of locally made products, unless the whole economic system is made to operate in conformity with this goal, positive change will be sporadic at best. As long as governments allow advertising to promote luxury commodities such as air fresheners, electric stoves, body lotions, and the like, national efforts toward basic need satisfaction, conservation of resources, and indigenous productivity will continue to be thwarted.

The Cultural Implications

The effect that information dissemination has on cultures all over the world is indeed startling. In many societies traditional cultural values that emphasize ethnic identity, oneness with nature, cooperation, patience, and moderation are being weakened or destroyed by what can be aptly termed "cultural imperialism." Cultural imperialism as advanced by the technoculture pushes an image of man as primarily a consumer of material goods; an implication that resources are infinite, and ever-increasing desires can be satisfied; an emphasis upon individual advantages at the expense of collective harmony and mutual gain; a belief that wealth and luxury are synonymous with happiness; the gnawing, offensive attitude that nonindustrialized, low-consuming people are backward and inferior; and the implication that acceptance of the dominant economic development model means acceptance of the entire dominant culture. These far-reaching cultural messages, conveyed to the world's people through information systems controlled primarily by corporations and governments, have a powerful impact. Indeed, in some societies it has been estimated that fully 77 percent of the total sources of information about the environment and social problems, information that shapes public perception and action, comes from the mass media.[35]

The substance and style of present information dissemination channels penetrate into the psyche which can easily develop an impatient, often antirational consciousness. Indeed, much of what passes as information is only a bombardment of society with news about and pictures of the worst aspects of the human potential. With this kind of "information" dominating communication channels, it becomes increasingly difficult for people to identify objectively the major environmental problems, their interrelated causes, and the innovative steps, skills, and discipline necessary for solutions. Information and knowledge are precious resources in this age of complex social existence. Regular and easy access to objective facts, unhindered by the manipulation of desires and perceptions by special interests, thus becomes a right and indeed a need, if the masses are to have a voice in shaping the future.

Notes to Chapter 6

1. Graham Chedd, "How Mobil Confronts a Crisis."

2. Both quotes from the *New York Times*, 18 October 1974.

3. For a recent review discussing the case on both sides of the argument see Victor P. Bond, "Fuels for Power," pp. 257–308.

4. *New York Times*, 14 December 1974.

5. See John G. Fuller, *We Almost Lost Detroit*. See also "Incident at Browns Ferry," *Time*, 20 October 1975, pp. 113–114.

6. The information on the Browns Ferry incident comes from the article in *Time* referred to in note 5.

7. U.S. Senator Mike Gravel's "Energy Newsletter," June 1975, Washington, D.C.

8. Tom Zeman, "Solar Power Now," p. 55.

9. E. L. Ralph, "Large Scale Solar Electric Power Generation"; R. Ramakumar, H. J. Allison, and W. L. Hughes, "Prospects for Tapping Solar Energy on a Large Scale"; John A. Duffie and William A. Bechman, *Solar Energy Thermal Processes*.

10. G. O. G. Lof and R. A. Tybout, "Cost of House Heating with Solar Energy"; idem, "The Design and Cost of Optimized Systems for Residential Heating and Cooling by Solar Energy"; Filino Harahap, "The Prospect of Solar Utilization, The Indonesian Case" (unpublished paper).

11. News release from The Consumer's Solar Electric Power Corporation, 645 Las Lomas Avenue, Pacific Palisades, California 90272.

12. Data from John C. Fisher, *Energy Crises in Perspective*, p. 135, table 14.1.

13. An example of misleading testimony is that given before the Legislation and Military Operations Subcommittee of the U.S. House of Representatives Committee on Government Operations, 27, 28 and 29 November 1974, concerning the Energy Reorganization Act of 1973 (H.R. 11510). Virtually all points of view concerning energy in the United States were represented at the hearing. One of the people giving testimony was Dr. Chauncey Starr, President, Electric Power Research Institute. Regarding energy use, Dr. Starr stated, "I think the most important thing we should recognize is that for the foreseeable future, and certainly beyond the year 2000, the demand for energy in the United States will grow no matter what is done to conserve or constrain such energy consumption" (found on p. 34 of the testimony). Starr not only indicated that limiting demand would be impossible, he also indicated that the consequences would be harmful if such limitation were attempted (pp. 34–35). "Now, there are three approaches to managing a future increase in energy demand. One would be to place a ceiling on the total energy availability in the United States. . . . The effect of any such action, even if it were accomplished with great wisdom, would be to seriously limit the improvement in the quality of life of the great mass in the population that now does not have all the material goods and recreational options which the upper economic sector of our country enjoy. . . . There is an additional difficulty with such administrative limitations on energy consumption; that is, the very act of doing this distorts a rational approach to a permanent solution." These statements by Dr. Starr quite obviously ignore the possibility of using either income redistribution policies or increases in the efficiency with which energy is used to improve the lot of the middle or lower classes. The testimony of John Love, at that time Director of the Energy Policy Office, pointed out another misleading aspect of Starr's statement. In response to Representative Moorhead's question, ". . . is the only solution in the short term the reducing of demand?" Governor Love replied, "I believe that to be true" (p. 186). On the specific question of solar energy, Dr. Starr had this to say: "The development of the new conversion systems which the newspapers are always discussing, such as thermonuclear fusion, solar power, and other energy sources, is also very important. Because of the time required for such development, however, these cannot be considered as solutions for our near term problems. They are obviously very important for the long range" (p. 34). The contrast is rather striking between this statement and the following statement by John Steinhart, Professor of Geology and Environmental Studies, University of Wisconsin: "We have, in fact, missed the boat. The fact that the Japanese have more than 2 million solar water heaters suggests they may know something we don't know. Australia has more square feet of solar collectors than that, and Israel's water is heated with little else. The technologies for solar hot water heating and solar space heating, including commercial spaces, are really well understood . . ." (pp. 240–241). This position would appear to be supported by the following statement from the director of the National Science Foundation: "Because of our active role in sponsoring research on terrestrial uses of solar energy, the Foundation is well on its way to carrying out a carefully organized, fast-paced plan which is designed to bring solar heating and cooling systems for buildings through the proof-of-concept phase to the development, demonstration and commercial design stages in 1975" (p. 310). Does this sound like an energy source that cannot be considered as a solution for our short-range problems?

14. Fisher, *Energy Crises*.

15. F. Hippel, M. Fels, and H. Krugman, "The Net Energy from Nuclear Reactors." Also see the September 1974 issue of *Energy Policy* for a series of articles by Peter Chapman and others on "energy budgets."
It is only fair to point out that in the debate over the nuclear net energy issue, arguments charging that nuclear power requires many years to pay back its energy investment must recognize the diversion of effort and materials for military purposes, the changes in management to maximize military objectives, and the relatively short time in which past investment has had a chance to produce outputs. However, we contend that nuclear energy has not

demonstrated a net energy contribution, and that given its costs, susceptibility to military co-option, and extreme dangers, nuclear energy is highly overrated as an efficient and positive energy source.

16. The data in this paragraph come from Harold Morse, "N Power Called Wasteful Energy."

17. For a good discussion of these incidents, see Geoffrey Murray, "Jun Ui: A Different Kind of Japanese Radical."

18. Much of the documentation of government propaganda and misinformation regarding the Lake Manapouri proposal is contained in the fifty written submissions from private societies and citizens presented to the Manapouri Commission. These are listed in *Report of Commission to Inquire into the Proposal to Raise the Level of Lake Manapouri. . . .* Other information is contained in: Jeremy Pope, "Manapouri Report Illustrates Limitations of Lawyers"; R. F. McLean, "Hydro Development"; and P. Lusk, "Comalco, Manapouri and the Bluff Smelter."

19. The background to the Lake Pedder controversy is outlined in *Lake Pedder: Why a National Park Must be Saved*, by Dick Johnson. A more detailed analysis of the decision-making procedure and misstatements employed by the Hydroelectricity Commission of Tasmania has been presented in detail by Keith McKenry, "A History and Critical Analysis of the Controversy Concerning the Gordon River Power Scheme," pp. 9–39.

20. Kuswata Kartawinata, *Report on the State of Knowledge on Tropical Forest Ecosystems in Indonesia.*

21. S. Sastrapradja and D. S. Sastrapradja, "Development and Conservation of Plant Genetic Resources in Indonesia."

22. Aprilani Soegiarto, "Aquatic Resources in Indonesia, Their Problems and Management."

23. William Paddock and Elizabeth Paddock, *We Don't Know How: An Independent Audit of What They Call Success in Foreign Assistance.*

24. Ibid.

25. Vance Packard, *The Waste Makers.*

26. Wilson Bryan Key, *Subliminal Seduction.*

27. Herbert I. Schiller, *Mass Communications and American Empire.*

28. Hidetoshi Kato, "Global Instantaneousness and Instant Globalism."

29. Fred Inglis, *The Imagery of Power.*

30. Helen Leavitt, *Superhighway—Superhoax.*

31. *Statistical Abstract of the United States 1974*, table 938.

32. Daniel Lerner, "Technology, Communication and Change."

33. Kato, "Global Instantaneousness."

34. Lerner, "Technology, Communication and Change."

35. Institute for Future Technology, "The International Comparative Beliefs Study."

7
An Option for a
New Environmental Order

The knowledge and insights provided in the preceding chapters argue strongly for immediate and fundamental changes in political, economic, and social policies; for evidence clearly shows that without such changes the quality of life in many sectors of society will deteriorate rapidly.

Most of the suggestions and proposals offered in this final section are intended as immediately applicable, feasible steps that can improve a society's chances of solving the most crucial problems now confronting humanity. Rather than providing a rigid blueprint for a future world order, these ideas seek to generate a policy context in which each society can better pursue the future it needs without jeopardizing the future of the larger global society. Such a context must not only deal with the most immediate and severe of our problems, but must also anticipate and move to prevent the future difficulties competent analysis can reveal as being most probable.

As stated earlier, several major environmental problems of both a physical and social nature are now threatening the quality of life of contemporary mankind. These problems have been caused in large measure by the failure of societies to recognize that an improved quality of life cannot be maintained unless material growth is held accountable to the needs of a society's people and to the limitations of a finite environment. We have attempted to show that the problem of instability has been greatly intensified, and in many cases created, by the absence or deficiency of planned homeostatic controls. Poverty has in part resulted from a disregard for equity in the distribution of the fruits of growth, and has increased as the widening amplitude of fluctuation throughout societies has made need-meeting services more difficult. Inequity continues to persist as a result of policies that favor the already powerful and wealthy. And misconceptions of man's interdependent relationship with nature, and of the facts of socioeconomic complexities, are created and perpetuated by a lack and manipulation of information.

Thus many of the causes of these problems can be traced to the attitudes and structures that dominate the major political-economic sectors of contemporary world relations. Although these sectors most certainly overlap frequently, four general categories can be identified: government, the market, transnational corporations, and the public. The priorities and mechanisms used by the first three of these sectors to accomplish their goals virtually define the socioeconomic systems within which the world's people have access to interaction.

It has already been noted that the first sector, government, has contributed substantially to environmental problems. As our proposals will show, it is upon government's shoulders that a large portion of the responsibility must fall if conditions of homeostasis are to be attained. But the government action we advocate is not merely more application of the same governmental policies that have added so greatly to our problems. On the contrary, what we advocate is a government that anticipates the total consequences of seemingly unrelated decisions rather than retaining tunnel vision perception, and that constructs policies to integrate quality of life components into an organic growth process of human development. It is a government that not only listens more attentively to expressions of public need, but also refrains from and restricts practices that condition the public to seek the perpetuation of policies that ultimately obstruct need satisfaction and harm the quality of life.

The market, the second sector of present world political economy, is definitely a dependent factor, and as such will undergo alteration as the other sectors are changed. But unless four basic pillars of the market economy—competition, unlimited profits, material incentives, and monopoly property—are significantly restructured by direct action, it is unlikely that the major environmental problems can be adequately handled.

The third of the world's major political-economic sectors, the transnational corporation (TNC), has accumulated such enormous power that numerous scholars now see it as perhaps the dominant global economic force.[1] In fact, it well may be that the most influential planning now undertaken in world affairs is by the TNC, not by governments. As was discussed in chapters 4 and 6, the effect of TNC activity on the market and on world development potential is quite strong, especially in policies of price fixing, consumer manipulation, labor strategies, and the transfer of technology and capital. Thus no set of proposals that seeks to improve the quality of life can ignore transnational corporations.

And finally, it is in the fourth major sector, the public, that we hope the greatest political and economic power might be developed; for a society guided by public need and the collective welfare provides the ultimate framework for the alternative future we seek. Changes that result in the dissemination of more objective information, improved access to participation in identifying needs and goals, and the increased monitoring by the public of the other sectors of the society represent those improvements we feel are most pertinent in the public sector.

Priority Goals of Structural Change[2]

In the design of social change strategies, there is value in pointing out goals and priorities even if designs of specific alternative structures are left imprecise. Such an approach in no way suggests that structural power is of minimal importance. To the contrary, it well may be that a structural transformation of global society is necessary if major world problems are to be solved to the benefit of all mankind. In this context, four major structural themes seem not only to speak to the most serious problems of today, but also lend themselves to cross-cultural adaptation and application. These major themes are:

(1) Systems integration and impact planning,
(2) Reallocation of resources,
(3) Collective interest representation, and
(4) Factual information compilation and dissemination.

Within the systems integration theme, two areas—the political and the educational—are especially important. In the political area, one of the most serious obstacles to problem-solving is the fragmented, often special-interest nature of present governmental structures. One department, enclosed within its own restricted mind-set and its own vested interests, often makes policy decisions that affect other departments without any interdepartmental exchange of information. One simple yet illustrative example shows the waste and senselessness such nonintegrative structures can produce. The department responsible for road construction decides to resurface a particular street. At the same time, the public works department decides to put a new sewer under the same street. The street is resurfaced in March and then the street is torn up again and the sewer is installed in April. When far more important issues are involved, issues such as ecosystem balance, health care, food crops, and wage-price synchronization, the need for interdepartmental policy integration becomes crucial.

One potentially effective means for assuring more integrative policies would be to give great responsibility to impact planners, whose sole job it is to analyze which sectors of society will be affected by which policies. With a thorough knowledge of the programs planned by various departments, impact planners could serve as the communication links within bureaucracies. Furthermore, these key planners, trained and directed to approach every issue in terms of short- and long-term impacts, could discover potential consequences to numerous, seemingly unrelated areas of the environment and society. Many ultimately harmful policies could thus be avoided.

Within many contemporary educational systems we find a degree of fragmentation just as severe as that found in government. Knowledge is artificially divided into "disciplines," a division that not only creates in students the tendency to overlook holistic interrelationships, but also makes it difficult for people to gain the diverse knowledge about the whole society that prepares them to anticipate, understand, and act upon interrelated phenomena. All the disciplines currently taught could fit within a more holistic framework without weakening the valuable contribution to knowledge each discipline provides. One example of such a framework is discussed later in this chapter.

The reallocation of resources is the second major priority theme. The following priorities in the allocation of a society's time, efforts, and capital seem most crucial: equitable redistribution of benefits; environmentally safe expansion of food production; inexpensive health-care and housing facilities; massive integrative and practical education programs; solar energy development by smaller enterprises and local home/community collectives; mass transportation expansion and curtailment of private automobile production and use; expanded programs for conservation of natural areas and wildlife; and funds for training impact planners and for instituting a systems-wide impact-planning apparatus. If implemented, there is strong reason to believe that these reallocation efforts could be instrumental in helping to solve pressing global problems.

Collective interest representation is the third priority objective. In many societies only vested special interests have access to decision-making. The masses of people, whose lives are greatly affected by the decisions of their leaders, have no structural means of determining their own destiny, short of highly dangerous efforts at revolution. With advances in communications encircling the globe, there is no excuse for denying mass collective interests their rightful voice in decision-making. Governments and corporations can institute intensive apparatus to collect information on needs and goals as defined by those people and groups who may not have the money, connections, status, and shrewd knowledge of the system that are now the major prerequisites for substantive influence on decision-making.

This effort to broaden participation in decision-making introduces the final priority goal: the compilation and dissemination of factual information. One of the excuses sometimes used to deny the masses a participatory role in decisions is that the vast majority of the public is uninformed, uninterested, and incapable of dealing with the complex affairs of a society. Such a misleading generalization allows the dominant elite to increase their monopolization over power, resources, and benefits. That some people do indeed wish to ignore cumbersome data on complex issues in no way relieves governments, institutions, and industries from the responsibility of making factual information available. If some people then disregard the information, at least the opportunity will have been provided.

The substance of information is as important as its accessibility. Objective facts concerning the environment, the workings of the socioeconomic and political system, the opportunities available in education and labor, and knowledge of self-reliant health care and practical maintenance skills—all need to be disseminated regularly. Armed with factual knowledge about disruptions of the environment, misuses of power, and self-reliant skills, the alleged uninterested and incapable public can become concerned and highly capable of effecting change.

Thus, it is to fundamental changes in the priorities and structures of all four sectors of the contemporary political economy—government, the market, corporations, and the public—that proposals must be directed. We suggest that the following ideas, if implemented, can promote homeostasis and help channel growth toward an improved quality of life.

GOVERNMENT STRUCTURES AND ACTIONS
The Planning Function

One of the first innovations needed within the governments of all nation-states is a competent planning apparatus. To be sure, many governments already have a system of planning. But far too often the type of planning utilized has remained locked into conventional and obsolete thought patterns. Competent planning, on the other hand, involves far-sighted analysis aimed at policies for the future.[3]

The planning function of government needs to formulate explicit conceptualizations and comprehensible statements of national goals, goals that are based not only on the knowledge and expertise of the planners but also on the collection and analysis of public expressions of needs, objectives, and priorities. The legislative and executive organs of government can then use this information in the drafting of specific policies, which, after extensive public debate, can ultimately be voted upon by the people. Although each society should base the identification of its own goals and priorities on criteria specific to its own needs, culture, and resources, we contend that homeostatic organic growth in any society requires attention to the following priority goals: the avoidance of major socio-political-economic-environmental instability; the meeting of basic human needs; the avoidance of resource waste, whether it be human or otherwise; a management of distribution that not only meets basic needs but also prevents degrees of inequality that give particular interests manipulative control over the rest of society; the maintenance of a system that serves the people with full and accurate information; the maintenance of a decision-making apparatus that responds to the public will; and the development of a planning competence that is capable of discerning forthcoming major systems breaks that might damage the quality of life.

As already stated, present planning is usually done on a short-term basis by a disjointed variety of governmental agencies that often lift a portion of a problem out of the context of the total system of which it is a part. Although this short-term, poorly coordinated type of planning is often seen to be a result of the short terms of office of government leaders, a more fundamental cause is the fact that many societies have not regarded long-term planning as a desirable or necessary function of government. But a new element has now come into the human condition. We are confronted with many problems that require long lead times to put solutions into operation. Thus a solution must be initiated now for a problem that will not be acute for perhaps twenty or thirty years. For example, major national conversions from automobiles to public transportation, or from fossil fuel to solar power energy systems, may take a long time. But severe problems will result unless much of the conversion is completed in three decades. Therefore, governments in all countries need an integrated planning branch with the mandate, capability, and perspective necessary to look far into the future. Within this planning structure great care should be taken to avoid the prevalent pattern of having a policy that is decided by a special department be totally ignored or distorted by a "higher" department whose knowledge in the particular area with which the policy deals is quite limited.

Another specific approach that can improve planning in some societies is the one utilized by the second Club of Rome team,[4] one in which comprehensive mathematical models of various countries were formulated, based on statistical analyses of data. By this method computer simulations or scenario projections can be used to explore the consequences of taking alternate policy options to attain goals. Public participation at all stages of the goal and strategy definition process would, in our opinion, be important to the development of legitimate policies.

But regardless of which methods and structures are utilized, there are certain kinds of issues directly related to environmental problems that government planning needs to address. Twelve of these key issues are discussed below.

1. The maintenance of a condition of homeostatic stability is of such importance to a healthy relationship between man and his environment that the analysis and advocacy of political and economic policy should place great weight on ecosystem stability criteria. The well-known feedback loop in which the birth, growth, and survival rate of any organism decrease as its density increases serves as a good biological example of ecosystem concepts that should be an essential part of planning knowledge.

2. Rational, long-term-oriented methods for making fiscal allocation decisions is a vital contribution planning should make. For example, we have already pointed out that at present there is overcapitalization of the automobile freeway system and the breeder-reactor program, while there is undercapitalization of solar- and wind-power development and mass transit. Government planning should point out how such allocation imbalances often stem from conflicts of interest arising in part from the failure to separate development from regulation within government. A good case in point is the atomic energy commissions which sometimes have authority and responsibility not only over research, development, and maintenance of installations, but also over the promotion and regulation of atomic energy use.

3. The planning branch of government should explore new means of improving the matching of land-use functions to the characteristics of soil, slope, and site features. It should explore the efficacy of various techniques for obtaining more aggressive down-zoning than we now have, in order to get top-quality yet presently idle farmland at city edges and elsewhere back into farm production.

4. Planning should explore the feasibility and effectiveness of various means for attaining a more rational pricing system for labor and resources than most societies presently have. The goal would be to break the cycle in which cheap energy replaces expensive labor and contributes to unemployment.

5. The planning branch should make a careful analysis of the phenomenon of competition and assess the detrimental consequences competition has on today's world. More specifically, instances in which the number of competitors is suboptimal with respect to various measures of benefits/costs should be pointed out. As Thayer[5] has noted, while we live in a society that pays lip service to competition as a positive value, government action, or inaction, often allows competition to result in increased social cost without any corresponding increase in benefits. One example is the government regula-

tion of airlines that influences too many lines to compete on a particular run so that the only real competition is in the number of empty seats, a service of no utility to riders.

6. Planning might also investigate innovative communal patterns of ownership and develop scenarios to explore the consequences. For example, rarely used equipment could be owned by the community and lent or rented out to the citizenry. Services could also come totally under the aegis of the community, thereby limiting the likelihood of human needs being exploited by private, profit-seeking service organizations.

7. A new system of incentives can be another goal of planning branches. Financial incentives could be used not only to encourage conservation and cleanup of recreation areas, but also to contain the use of common property resources within reasonable consumption ranges. Incentives for the development of on-the-job day care centers is another mild example. But far more significant would be the commitment to discover and implement nonmaterial incentives to replace the detrimental reliance on material profit as a major motivation.

8. Great attention to the population problem is another crucial task of government planning. Means of encouraging population limitation through policies operating on seemingly unrelated parts of the socioeconomic system need to be explored. For instance, self-reliant home electrification units that allow for evening reading, radio listening, and so on, might be one approach. Cradle to the grave social security might also reduce birth rates by lessening the dependence on a large number of children for ensuring a comfortable and secure old age. But government planning should also consider the vast resource human population provides, especially in societies where imported technology has an ultimately negative effect on the public welfare. In other words, planning is needed that realizes the population problem can be one of inadequate utilization as well as one of too great a number.

9. As a counterforce to population concentration in a few big cities, planning organizations need to plot innovative techniques for promoting economic development in areas that get "left behind." This would require the cessation of those present policies that now give aid to areas on the basis of their "contribution" to the national economy. This criterion discriminates against those areas where resources essential to making a significant contribution are in short supply, rather than providing needed assistance.

10. Planners also need to deal with the fact that in many respects mankind is incapable of changing rapidly. For example, humans have evolved to breathe a certain combination of gas and to drink water of a certain chemical composition; thus they cannot make a rapid adaptation to an environment

with trace (but biologically dangerous) lead concentrations. Also, if it appears to planners that events are likely to change faster than institutions as presently structured can respond, then the institutions have to be restructured.

11. Much more thought needs to be given to the structure of planning commissions and boards. Ecologists, systems analysts, and representatives of other disciplines need to be added to such groups. People concerned about energy use in society and the net energy problem, as well as people knowledgeable about the stability of complex biological systems, should be represented. We note a disturbing tendency for governments to staff planning groups with people who are often quite unrealistic in their projections. We think a variety of points of view is required so that planning boards will be able to advise governments in time, if strenuous preparations are required to ward off impending disaster. Rather than having a staff made up exclusively of unrealistic optimists who, for example, rejoice at the decreasing rate with which unemployment is rising, society might be better served by having a large number of planners who would urge strong measures because unemployment is indeed *still* rising, even though at a slightly decreased rate.

12. Planning organizations must have their activities designed so that they can learn from mistakes. There must be regular reports by the planning agency, especially emphasizing answers to "Why did we fail to hit a target?" There must be postaudit investigations. "Why did the silt load exceed expectations?" "Why did the rate of economic decline or the unemployment rate exceed expectations?" "Why did we overestimate the availability of rice supply, or underestimate the climatic hazards that caused crop failure?" "Why did a decline in birth rates fail to occur?" "Why did car sales collapse?" "Why were energy-cost predictions too low?" "What can we discover about how to improve planning and forecasting methodology from our past errors?" In seeking answers to these questions, social planners must be willing to challenge even the most sacred institutions and patterns of a society; for it well may be that it is in those entrenched assumptions and structures that the causes of many problems will be found.

In carrying out all these planning functions, one helpful and basic step is to ask those questions most pertinent to a complete understanding of the major issues. For example, planners should regularly ask themselves, "What really nasty surprises might occur in future?" Then realistic scenarios showing how the country might respond should be formulated. To illustrate, what happens if Saudi Arabia, Venezuela, and Iran decide to cut oil production in half? What happens if hail in India, frost in Canada, the U.S., China, and Russia, and floods in Argentina and Australia wipe out one complete season of grain production, worldwide? Where computer technology exists, models should be used to discover, through simulation, the relative sensitivity of different subsystems in the economy to very large perturbations of this type. Where are the weak links in society which need to be strengthened so as to withstand such shocks? Which parts are relatively so insensitive to such shocks that any strengthening applied to them would represent wasted money? Planners need to study the statistics of extremes, and the detailed behaviors of all subsystems in such extreme cases. One of the most ubiquitous nasty surprises we see coming worldwide is that employees will be laid off in the interests of economic efficiency. Thus, there needs to be highly innovative planning for new labor-intensive industries to take up the slack. Education of all types will do some of this, if properly fostered by government (perhaps implying added taxes), but many new and diverse ideas may be called for: cultivation of exotic foods, the raising of orchids and fish for hobbyists, innovations in mariculture and aquaculture, subsidies for home solar-energy units and do-it-yourself shelter programs, and many others of a much more radical nature.

Planners must constantly be alert for critical limits that can turn into surprising bottlenecks for the whole socioeconomic system. How can a country prevent, get around, or respond to critical shortages of rice, water, seeds, naphtha, phosphate, pipe for refineries and irrigation, petroleum, and storage bins? Could transportation capacity in future limit shipment of food or fuel, or a critical industrial raw material? For example, there is a widely held view in many countries that the oceans can supply any amount of metal, fish, and shellfish. What happens if this turns out not to be so?

How could complete surprises from other countries affect one's own country? How is one country critically dependent on the world system, and what plans does that imply? What if another country does something analogous to closing the Suez Canal, or forming an OPEC-like cartel for another raw material? What happens to a resource-rich developing country if it does *not* form a cartel? What happens if the major export commodity of a country drops drastically in world market value? How could a society respond to a sequence of consequences flowing from one subsystem to another in a domino effect? Could there be synergistic effects if two or more subsystems in society failed simultaneously? Planners need to look at the coupling between sectors; at present, they typically look at sectors lifted out of context. For example, a domino effect is occurring in several regions because the new "miracle" strains of grain have less chaff than previous strains. Thus, cattle have less food and are more emaciated, so there is less milk and its products as well as less dung for fuel. Also, if a country uses up all its forests, extensive chain reactions can result. Supplies of pulpwood become inadequate so that wood or paper must be imported. This has implications not only for the balance of trade, but the country may also become so short of paper that there is not enough for schoolbooks, thus impairing the educational program. Furthermore, floods and drought will most likely result from erosion, loss of forest cover, poor water-holding capacity of watersheds, and alteration in water moisture exchange with the air. Wind velocities will also be higher close to the ground, so that evaporation off crop plant surfaces will be greater, lowering productivity.

Planners can discover systems breaks by asking additional key questions. How are requirements for new investment now affected by extending the future time horizon for planning to sixty from twenty years? Does the extended look ahead to A.D. 2035 reveal a systems break (for example, exhaustion of coal supply) that would have to be dealt with at that time by a strategy that we must begin to design now? Does our short-term planning conform to our long-term objectives and long-term problems?

How do alternate solutions measure up when reexamined in terms of the net energy issue? Many activities that seem feasible, and potentially highly profitable, take on a different appearance when viewed in terms of the energy output relative to the energy input. For example, catching fish and whales in the open ocean was energy-efficient when free power from the wind drove sailing vessels, and was still cheap when crude-oil derivatives were used for fuel. But as crude oil becomes more expensive, and substitutes become even more expensive, attention will be attracted to the energy cost of open-ocean fishing, relative to the energy gain. Some people think we can get enormous quantities of food from the ocean by annihilating all the large predators (fish, whales, squid) and harvesting the small organisms which they eat. But this ignores the great energy expenditure by predators in finding their food (which in the open ocean may exist at very low densities), an expenditure of energy humans would then have to make to harvest the small organisms.

All the numerous questions we have been posing suggest that the utilization of new social indicators in formulating and evaluating policy is essential to the planning function. As was emphasized in chapter 1, a new list of indicators should begin with the identification of the most important components of the quality of life. We have suggested that present-day problems argue strongly for the inclusion of at least three primary components: ecosystem balance, basic human needs, and equity. Indicators based on these components stand in opposition to the present, most widely used economic measure of systems performance—the money output versus money input formula of profitability. As we have shown, profitability is one of the most environmentally damaging of the many possible output/input measures of systems performance. A very large number of other measures could be used, and the implications for society of using these measures would be extremely significant. For example, in the transportation planning field, a more socially desirable measure is

$$\frac{\text{distance traveled per unit time spent traveling}}{\text{energy cost to build, maintain, and operate transportation system}}$$

This measure rejects profitability as the main criterion for systems and, instead, focuses on the speed with which people can be moved around relative to the energy cost of attaining that speed. Consistent use of such a measure would put great emphasis on eliminating traffic congestion through novel public mass-transportation systems.

A major reason for doing away with profitability as a social management criterion is that purely economic arguments rarely, if ever, give any reasons for conserving anything, whether it be whales, petroleum, or the earth itself. Since man as a species presumably wants to live on this planet for more than a few additional decades, other measures of social utility that attach a value to conservation must be proposed. As we have noted earlier that the present type of socioeconomic resource system shows a tendency toward instability, stability criteria should also be included in the indicator set, replacing economic efficiency arguments that ultimately destroy economics.

We propose, therefore, that planning organizations explore the possibility of using a wide variety of output/input measures as criteria for evaluating alternate policy options. A few of these are

$$\frac{\text{reduction in instabilty}}{\text{energy expenditure to attain that degree of reduction}}$$

$$\frac{\text{energy output}}{\text{energy input}}$$

$$\frac{\text{increase in biological diversity in a wildlife area}}{\text{energy cost of increase in diversity}}$$

While these and many other indices which we could propose may sound exotic, in fact they may be easy to compute since they require no new measurements and are calculable from existing data. Stability can be calculated from time trends in existing data series, and diversity can be calculated from existing collection data.

More complex areas can also be explored. For example, diverse international cross-cultural accounting systems must be developed to ensure that useful value systems in one country are not being eroded by goods or communications from one or more other countries. Also, since the demand inputs from the public to the political system are such vital ingredients of participation, indicators need to be devised that assist the public in focusing its demands both on key system defects and on the particular decision-makers responsible for particular policies.

Indicators thus play a significant role in determining priorities and in setting and evaluating policies. Stability, diversity, efficient energy use, lowered rates of resource depletion, wise land use, humane uses of time, and movement toward a long-term steady state can all be encouraged through the use of more relevant indicators.[6]

Questions of central versus local planning, and rigidity versus flexibility, always arise when governmental planning is advocated. Regardless of how a society resolves these questions, one fundamental need seems clearly apparent in these times—long-range, systems-wide impact planning. The creation and training of impact planners suggested in the section on priority goals is a significant structural change that offers promise for most all societies. With a new set of indicators and questions, with knowledge of systems instability theory, and with a sensitivity to quality of life goals, these planners could trim waste and add competence to the planning function. A new policy context would thus be generated in which the planning function of goverment serves as a major link between the identification and implementation of quality of life goals.

The Service Function

A government that plans and sets policy on quality of life criteria necessarily devotes much energy to its service function. Since most governments in existence today engage in at least some degree of service-oriented activity, we are concerned in this section with which services are now badly neglected and which deserve major emphasis.

As with all social concerns, we begin with basic human needs. In chapter 4 the depth of need deprivation was made abundantly clear. To overcome these insufficiencies in nutrition, health care, housing, work conditions, and recreation, government at various levels needs to allocate much more energy and resources to service programs, particularly in the setting of minimums and the expansion of free and/or low cost services. The concept of minimums (or floors) is based on the principle that all humans have a right to a survival-plus standard of living regardless of their status in a society. A guaranteed minimum income, the right of and access to at least a minimum quality and quantity of nutritional intake, of employment and/or social contribution, to hectares of land, to square meters of living space, and to recreational time and space could all be determined by a society on the basis of available resources. Using these minimums, coupled with a consistent program of ceilings (see the next section on regulation), each society should be able to set a reasonable range of living conditions conducive to the general welfare.

In the provision of basic need services, public access is a paramount objective. Health care costs that soar beyond the financial capabilities of low-income groups are exploitative and have no place in a system that is committed to improving the quality of life. Housing prices that allow access only to the upper-middle and high income strata lead to social instability and depression of basic need satisfaction. Thus the service function of government must do what the free market has proven incapable of doing and provide free and/or low-cost health care and housing. Government-funded paramedical training centers, where young and old are taught the skills of providing basic health care free to members of communities, is one positive plan. Encouragement and funding of very low-cost housing units designed to be constructed by individuals is another. Greatly expanded zoning of natural areas as recreation spaces, and the upgrading of low-cost housing areas to provide greater opportunities for physical, psychosocial, and cultural enrichment are two other examples of service functions governments can undertake.

Beyond these important services, numerous other priorities deserve attention. As chapter 6 pointed out, the suppression and manipulation of information has a detrimental effect on a society's overall cohesion. Consequently, the dissemination of factual information, undistorted to favor special interests, should be an important service provided regularly by government. The rapid advancements in communications technology can be used to provide such a service with strong public and legal checks placed on the manipulation of information by government. Advertising, political propaganda, sensationalist news, and violent programs need to be replaced by the objective treatment of issues, diverse cultural presentations, and educational programs.

Recent data from Japan and elsewhere suggest that in those cases where the public has had access to objective information, public opinion is incisive and, quite often, opposed to the growthmania policies of their governments. For example, in a survey of two thousand people (over age eighteen and dispersed widely throughout Japan), 54 percent indicated government policy "should make much greater effort to protect the environment than to push for more economic growth,'' while only 15 percent favored more efforts for economic growth than for environmental protection. Further, the survey showed that 47 percent of the respondents felt that ''there are serious environmental problems for the present and the future,'' 13 percent felt there were serious problems for the future but not for the present, and only 3 percent felt there were no serious problems either for the present or the future. In order to clean up one environmental problem, pollution, 42 percent felt that additional fees or price increases in use of electricity would be required, while 41 percent felt that increases would be needed in automobile-related energy use.[7]

With adequate information, the public is better prepared to participate in the affairs of society. Even in the midst of conflicting ideologies regarding the role of public participation in policy decisions, we contend that it is to every society's advantage to maximize public input. Only those governments whose values and objectives stand in contradiction to the welfare of the people would suggest that input from the public on needs and goals is incidental. Thus we suggest that a perpetually operating apparatus for public need-goal gathering and analysis become a major responsibility of government. More government commitment to expose to a public vote the policies that are, hopefully, based on the gathered public input, is a logical corollary suggestion.

Transportation offers yet another example of the expanded service function of government. Perhaps an initial step would be to increase greatly the allocation of funds to develop mass bus and rail systems at low cost to the public. But as a long-range program, alternatives to the internal combustion engine need to be extensively researched, developed, and implemented while, at the same time, stringent tax burdens should be placed on the manufacture, consumption, and use of automobiles.

The above examples of government's service function only scratch the surface. But at least they can serve to illustrate the necessity for service programs that aid, not obstruct, the realization of basic need satisfaction, ecosystem balance, and homeostatic organic growth.

The Regulatory Function

An ideal social system would be one in which no policy that did not improve the quality of life would be given priority. Few if any such ideal systems exist. Rather, we find that one of the problems in bringing about social change is the unwillingness of people to let go of certain convenient, near-sacred slogans (such as ''freedom of unlimited accumulation'' and ''free competition''), even after the slogans have been proven detrimental to the quality of life.

To move closer to the ideal stated above, we recommend that significant changes be made in the regulatory function of government. Present arrangements far too often facilitate regulation procedures that either serve the interests of those industries they are supposed to regulate, or operate so irrationally that they benefit no one. Some type of regulatory organization is needed that is more responsive to the public will and has as its goal the maintenance of those conditions a society has identified as its quality of life criteria. The people working in this organization should, ideally, be elected by the public, and their decisions should be monitored closely by citizen groups such as those discussed later in this chapter.

Within the regulatory function there would need to be at least three divisions; one would deal with the regulation of wealth, one with control of transnational corporations, and the third with the regulation of energy.

As we have demonstrated, the trickle-down theory of the free enterprise market system simply has not worked. Increased wealth will *not* automatically find its way into the hands of the mass of the population. Rather, increased wealth often widens the gap between rich and poor as the rich use existent wealth and power to control the distribution of new wealth.

To break this pattern, two types of controls seem most appropriate. The first system of controls, wealth ceilings, meets head-on the detrimental obsession with freedom of accumulation that has come to justify the monopolization of wealth. (Inequitable wealth distribution has reached such staggering proportions in the U.S. since World War II that the poorest fifth of families receives 6 percent of money income while the richest fifth receives 40 percent.[8]) Under the guidance of the regulatory agency, upper limits on land holding, income, profits, and consumption need to be set, beyond which no member of society would be permitted to go. Such a suggestion will inevitably raise protests from those societies, groups, and individuals who have profited from unrestricted accumulation, and the familiar banners of freedom and individualism will again be waved. But the facts of the present system are (1) that resources are *not* infinite, and (2) that the overwhelming majority of the human race is *not* "free" to compete for society's benefits, primarily because the knowledge, power, skills, and access essential to gaining benefits are monopolized by a very few nations, families, and corporations. Thus if any semblance of an equitable distribution of resources and benefits is to exist, the monopoly hold over power and wealth must be broken. The setting of ceilings is one way to accomplish such a break.

The second major program within the regulation of wealth function would deal with wealth *after* distribution, primarily in the area of taxation. Most present tax structures simply have too many loopholes to serve as effective checks on excessive wealth. From U.S. statistical data on income tax for

1962, we find that the income share of the top fifth of the population declined from a pretax 45.5 percent to 43.7 percent after taxes. The lowest three-fifths raised their share by only 1.4 percent (from 31.8 percent to 33.2 percent).[9] Capital gains, percentage depletion allowances, depreciation allowances, exclusion of interest on bonds, inheritance and estate tax benefits—nontaxable "power-money" held in foundations run by the very wealthy—all severely limit the effect income taxes have on the redistribution of wealth. For although the listed tax rate for top income brackets is between 50 and 70 percent, "the effective rate of tax paid in 1967 by the top 1 percent was only 26 percent of their total reported income, including all of their realized capital gains."[10] And the inequality gap widens even further when we add to the income tax picture the fact that some social security payroll and local taxes are so structured that low-income families pay a greater percentage of their income than do high-income families.

Thus, to begin with, taxation policies need to close the loopholes that benefit the rich, especially in capital gains. But far more drastic alterations should also be pursued. A 100 percent tax on revenue gained through the use of computers could not only raise billions of dollars for social services in technologically highly developed societies, but might also decrease the growthmania obsession with automation. A tax on both private and public nonrenewable resources would also be a positive step.

Another potential for equity would be some type of "social management tax," the specifics of which could be designed by each society to operate institutions where, for example, the marketplace sets a price so low as to be socially damaging. If flexible enough, such a tax could dampen cycles of over- and under-investment, and mitigate against intractable fluctuations in resource demand and/or wasteful overinvestment in unnecessary capital stock (such as fleets of aircraft or supertankers and excessive construction of luxury hotels).

The third section within the regulatory organization would deal exclusively with energy. When considered as a whole, energy is the capacity for producing an effect. In this context, energy includes not only the power of the sun, of combustion, and of fission and fusion, but of human effort as well. Thus any branch of government that is intended as a regulator of energy must deal with research on, development of, and costs of energy sources; with human labor and employment; and with the goals, methods, and consequences of energy utilization.

As is true with all other functions of government, the regulation of energy needs to be based on one major criterion: the improvement of the quality of life. Put into energy-specific terms, this means that net energy, full employment, and maintenance of ecosystem balance become the principles upon which policies need to be based. Thus growth for profit becomes a low-priority concern, and technology devoted to rampant automation is no longer the objective of research and development. The wasteful expenditure of research and development on military hardware is seen as a foolish net-energy loss, and efficiency based solely on economic considerations gives way to more qualitative efficiency measures.

In more specific terms, the regulation of energy can operate on several fronts, the first being in consumption. Even the most elementary study of world data reveals the extreme inequity of energy consumption. In 1972 the United States (with only 5.5 percent of the world's population) consumed 31.5 percent of all coal, lignite, petroleum products, natural gas, and hydro- and nuclear electricity consumed in the world. When energy consumption is computed, we find that the U.S. *per capita* figure is 345 times that of Ethiopia, more than 60 times that of India, 23 times that of Turkey, and some 2½ times that of the U.S.S.R. Further, when the ten nations with the highest per capita consumption of energy are combined (in order, the U.S., Canada, Czechoslovakia, Belgium, the German Democratic Republic, Sweden, the Netherlands, Australia, the United Kingdom, and the Federal Republic of Germany), we find that they consume more than half of all the world's energy, although they comprise only 11 percent of the world's population.[11]

Note that we have consistently argued that increasing the rate of energy flow through a system does not necessarily lead to an increase in the rate of GNP per capita, or to increased benefits for the whole of a society. We have also echoed numerous other works in pointing out both the depletion and pollution consequences of excessive energy use, and the possibility of accidents involving nuclear energy. Thus, in the technologically developed countries, regulations that reduce energy consumption seem necessary. The suppliers of energy could be taxed heavily if they made too much available beyond reasonable needs. Consumers could be charged higher costs per unit whenever their own consumption (of gasoline, gas, electricity, water) exceeds standards set as "reasonable," according to needs and the availability of resources. And the exorbitant profits of major oil and electricity monopolists could be taxed heavily, in addition to being made subject to income-ceiling regulations.

In developing countries, different kinds of problems involving energy must be confronted. In order to get more energy, or power, citizens in these countries can turn to more work animals, more children, electric power in central stations, some fossil fuel sources, or the more basic sources such as sun, water, wind, and human and animal waste. Although many leaders of developing societies seem to be intent on following the technoculture's model, it seems extremely important for the basic sources to be given top priority. Regulations and programs making these sources more attractive and available thus cry out for attention. Continued dependence on processed energy from outside sources plays right into the hands of the resource monopolization practices of the technologically developed countries and the transnational corporations.

In a paper on transition to the future,[12] Kenneth E. F. Watt discusses the overall energy situation, and concludes that the way out of the dilemma " . . . is to manage growth, not try to accommodate it. Accommodation is the road to ruin." Watt also points out that we must dare to try radically new solutions. "Solar and wind energy, using sophisticated modern physics and engineering, are most promising, contrary to the conventional wisdom. . . . At present, great quantities of energy are generated in immediately useable or stored form at a limited number of sites (generating plants, refineries, and the like), then are distributed to a very large number of sites to be used. A major change would be to generate a sharply increased proportion of the energy we use at the sites where it is used, by means of solar and wind systems. This has the interesting systems property that energy losses down electrical transmission lines, or in hauling crude oil and gasoline, are avoided. However, the most interesting consequences of a change in the energy system from a central plant to a generation at use site concept would come via the scale effect. . . . if you are generating energy at a central site, then because of economies of scale, you have a strong motive to increase use. However, if each family generates much of its own energy using solar and wind collectors, then it has a powerful motive to economize: more use means a greater investment in collecting surfaces or equipment."

The major role we have given to government in planning, services, and regulation no doubt will prove unsettling to many readers. Indeed we ourselves are convinced that more and bigger government is not the answer to environmental problems. But given the present situation in which transnational economic interests bent on corporate growth and profit maximization are gaining greater power over governmental policy, we feel that an improved quality of life can be better accomplished if certain planning and regulatory powers rest, for the time being, in the hands of a government that is responsive to the public need. This does not mean to imply that no governments as presently constituted are totally unresponsive to the needs of the public. But we are convinced that the dominant values and priorities evident in many governments (representing diverse ideological persuasions) are in need of change if the quality of life is to be improved.

Ensuring that government does in fact represent the will of the people is a complex problem as old as social organization itself. This book does not purport to supply any precise answers to this major question, but instead attempts to point to structures and actions that might add to the potential power of a public which has knowledge of and commitment to qualitative development needs.

Public Structures and Action

Without diligent and responsible action in the public sector, an increase in government activity can easily go against human and environmental requisites. In order to be most effective in meeting the needs of society, the public should utilize objective information about the society as a whole. But the specific ways in which information and knowledge are utilized by the public is a distinctly different issue, one that varies from culture to culture and individual to individual. There are some individuals and cultures who feel burdened by a large quantity of information. If enough knowledge to pursue their private lives and work is available, many people are quite happy. All of the numerous complex problems of society are thus seen as the responsibility of those few who desire leadership power. Other individuals and cultures reject such a passive role in the affairs of society and demand a full flow of information on most every issue.

Regardless of which of these views one holds, it seems highly probable that information directly affecting one's survival and basic development needs will, if made available, be of concern to almost every human being. Since we are dealing with environmental problems that relate directly to life-support systems and policies, we feel confident in advocating information availability for all societies, realizing, of course, that the amounts and types of information utilized will be somewhat determined by individual and cultural preferences.

How well informed the public becomes is primarily determined by the substance and methodologies of the single most important instrument in dealing with contemporary problems: education. But, for education to fulfill its vast potential for improving the quality of life, it must undergo a profound transformation. Rather than shaping learners to conform to the existing norms of a society (as is now the general case), education must become an instrument of far-sighted change that exposes learners to those values, experiences, and structures essential to a qualitative-growth approach to human development.

The chances are slim that the regnant powers controlling institutionalized education will put schools in the vanguard of fundamental social change. For this reason, and many others, the ultimate needs of the world's people and environment might be better served through informal education programs conceived and run by community action groups. But since institutionalized education will obviously persist for the foreseeable future, and will continue to play an important role in value and attitude formation, changes *within* the system must be proposed and implemented. And it is upon individual teachers, students, and administrators that the brunt of the load will fall.

Again, it is important to point out that we realize education systems will vary from culture to culture. But as with most of the other proposals suggested throughout this chapter, we feel that certain educational priorities are of such an integral value to ecosystem balance and human need satisfaction that they can be advocated as general parameters for human society. One educator[13] has developed what he calls a "Pedagogy for Qualitative Development" that combines into a curriculum most of the priority educational substance we advocate. A brief outline of this pedagogy is as follows.

Pedagogy for Qualitative Development[14]

I. The Conceptual Framework
  A. Visions of the future—dislodging the conventional mind-set by imagining ideal alternative futures and their underlying values
  B. Extending the learner's time horizons—developing the tendency and ability to perceive present actions in terms of consequences they might have for the future
  C. Understanding the earth's ecosystem—emphasizing ecosystem balance, interdependency, and finiteness
  D. Understanding the human being as but one component in the total ecosystem
  E. Understanding contemporary human society
    1. Basic human needs, their undersatisfaction and oversatisfaction
    2. Environmental needs and problems
    3. The dominant patterns and structures that contribute to ecosystem disruption, poverty, inequity, dependence, etc.
  F. Understanding the values and perceptions underlying the dominant patterns, structures, and resultant problems
  G. Understanding alternative values and perceptions

II. The Action Framework
  A. Understanding that the need for change in contemporary times involves a fundamental transformation of the polsocioeconomic patterns and structures of society
  B. Experiencing the design and planning of social change

1. Conceptual readiness and value identification
2. Structural change techniques
3. Self-reliant development techniques
C. Experiencing personal involvement in change actions

If successful, education should help develop a consciousness of skill readiness that leads the public to identify and act upon those policies most supportive of qualitative survival and development. One structure that might be significant in directing public action toward priority goals is what can be termed a People's Action Program (PAP). Organized at the community level, PAPs should operate as free as possible from influence exerted by government and special interests. Let us now turn our attention to a discussion of how People's Action Programs might operate.

People's Action Programs[15]

The major functions of PAPs are to:
(1) Oversee government operations
(2) Provide information to the public
(3) Organize public action on pertinent issues
(4) Protect the consumer's welfare
(5) Promote cultural arts expression
(6) Promote informal education

In overseeing the operations of government, People's Action Programs need to make sure that governmental priorities, personnel, and structures are consistent with the current needs of society. In a general sense, this would mean that a society's quality of life indicators be perpetually called to the attention of all government agencies. More specifically, several foci seem to merit particular emphasis by PAPs.

The redundancy of governmental bureaucracy; patterns of nepotism in official appointments; linkages of personnel and interests between government leaders and corporations, specialized industries, and land utilization projects; excessive expenditures and wastes in the military sector; invasion of public rights by governmental agencies; disregard of equal employment opportunity guidelines; mishandling of aid provisions; misuse of communication media to propagandize and misrepresent issues and policies; and programs that result in environmentally destructive consequences, such as deforestation, pollution, wildlife extinction, and radiation leakage—these are but a few of the present governmental malpractices that PAPs could monitor, expose, and perhaps change.

The exposé activity just mentioned brings us to the information dissemination role of PAPs. Well-developed communication systems that bring to the attention of the public diverse approaches to major issues, detailed incidents of governmental and corporation antipublic behavior, and opportunities for self-reliant development activities should be a priority endeavor of PAPs. Vigilant watchdog committees should monitor all media output and not only publicize which media outlets and personnel are producing antipublic information, but also assist the appropriate PAP committee in targeting public protest. The media should be challenged to provide access to well-organized, creative PAP presentations. By utilizing problem identification, multiple-option, problem-solving experiences, value education, and the exposés already mentioned, these PAP media programs could provide a worthwhile outlet for numerous professionals who now refuse to work in advertising or other commercialized misuses of their talent.

Organizing public action on pertinent issues is the third function of PAPs. Without strong, persistent pressure from the public, many power-holders will continue to utilize political and economic structures for their own exclusive benefit. Numerous well-known precedents have proven the power of organized public action. Economic boycotts, labor strikes, antiwar mobilization, and popular uprisings have all resulted in significant changes in governmental policies. These tactics should be intensified and better organized to work upon the most vulnerable and the most critical pockets of antienvironment, antipublic power. The potentially divisive nature inherent in the multiple interests of the citizenry can be minimized by the use of small learning groups in which the particulars of the long-range negative or positive consequences of a given issue to *all* segments of the society are clearly outlined.

The fourth function of People's Action Programs focuses on the consumer. Although consumerism has been heavily criticized in our preceding chapters, we realize that within a moderate range, consuming is a necessary fact of life. Thus we applaud the efforts of consumer protection groups throughout the world and advocate a much stronger public role in consumer protection. Preventing dangerous products from ever reaching the market; encouraging the manufacture of more durable goods to replace planned obsolescence; deemphasising luxury goods production; weakening and a fundamental reform of the advertising industry; and seeking full disclosure on labels on foods, not only of the ingredients but also of the distribution of the sale price to various producing sectors (for example, how much of the price of a can of tuna goes to the fishermen)—all are examples of how PAPs might actively inform and protect the consumer.

Perhaps the two most important of these activities involve control over advertising, and determination of which consumer goods are put on the market. Using as the primary criteria need and quality rather than desire and quantity, advertising and production must be held accountable to the public. As Galbraith and numerous other economists point out,[16] the desires of the public market are greatly shaped by the advertising industry. Thus the claims that the public or the market is the independent determinant of what goods are produced are highly misleading and false. Therefore, in those societies where advertising is powerful, new means of public control must be implemented. The boycott and exposé tactics already discussed are important, but more stringent measures may be necessary. On all products specific standards need to be set that insist on high minimum durability, high reusability, strict nonpolluting properties, and so on. Merchants, consumers, and manufacturing firm workers should all refuse to contribute to any product that violates these standards.

The revolution in advertising we advocate may require fundamental changes in the basic concept and structure of the market system. When compared to the values of ecosystem balance and basic human need satisfaction, access to diverse forms of material consumption becomes a very low priority. This low priority status drops even further when one realizes that the advertising and consumption patterns of the market system often actually harm ecosystem balance, and obstruct basic need satisfaction. To assume that human happiness and well-being are somehow enhanced by a saturation of superfluous material goods is to define the human being as primarily a creature who craves and consumes material things. We do not accept this image of humanity and thus argue for a system in which government and public alike insist that resources involved in the production of wasteful products, such as military weapons and toys of violence, aerosol sprays, nonbiodegradable containers, nonnutritious foods, be reallocated to mass-transit vehicles, more durable need-goods, free-clinic funding, and a host of other positive uses. People's Action Programs need to demonstrate to business and government that the public insists upon advertising that merely informs the consumer of the quality, uses, and price of the product without the deception, sexual overtones, and subliminal manipulation that now characterize so much of the advertising effort.

The fifth function of PAPs is the promotion of cultural activities. We see diversity both in environmental and cultural dimensions as worthy of preservation and development. It follows, then, that one PAP function stresses the use of media and community meetings for increasing cultural understanding. Music, art, dance, handicrafts, language, social organization, and customs can all be shared by traveling troupes on a regular basis. Free publicity and use of meeting places, and the allocation of funds for the

maintenance of cultural organizations are obvious examples of how community governments might contribute.

In a more substantive sense, the type of information disseminated by
cultural organizations can emphasize and try to develop an appreciation of
the mutually beneficial contributions various cultures can make to each
other, rather than emphasizing competition and the historical dominance of
one culture over another. Cultural stereotypes can be confronted head-on
and exposed as misleading generalizations. Historical similarities and common ancestry can be emphasized, showing how it was often fleeting political
and/or economic influences that caused one culture to become the
"enemy" of another culture.

And finally, People's Action Programs need to provide the type of education so badly lacking in formal schooling contexts. In numerous societies we
see informal education programs already functioning in ashrams, "free
schools," sensitivity groups, and criticism cells. These formats offer great
potential for learning experiences that go far beyond the institutionalization
of values and conformity so replete in modern education. Using concepts
and approaches suggested in numerous works on pedagogical alternatives,[17]
PAPs could be instrumental in facilitating public learning and disseminating
the knowledge generated.

The organizational structure and support of People's Action Programs
would naturally vary from society to society. One possible means of financial
support in those societies where income and sales taxes exist would be a new
PAP tax. A portion of every tax unit paid could automatically go to the national or local PAP budget to be allocated to various PAPs according to the
size of the population they serve. In societies where no tax system exists, the
national and/or local budget would need to include a category for People's
Action Programs in an amount equal, for example, to the state education
budget.

Depending upon the cultural and political setting, the people responsible
for maintaining PAPs could be chosen in special local elections or otherwise.
Governed by extremely strict campaign regulations, the PAP candidates
could run for special committees and communicate their capabilities and
plans to the public by submitting detailed program projections as a mandatory part of campaigning.

One example of how public action in a nongovernmental role can make a
significant impact is the Sarvodaya ("multiple effort") movement in Sri
Lanka. Under the leadership of A. J. Ariyaratne, this private community
development organization is involved in numerous rural development programs. Surviving on the donations from communities, Sarvodaya utilizes the

energy and skill of urban and rural citizens in such projects as road construction and credit union formation. The Sarvodaya program has had an impact on the national development scheme of the Sri Lanka government, serving as a constant reminder of the potential effectiveness of direct-action programs which cut through much of the usual red tape of bureaucratic government.[18]

It cannot be assumed, of course, that PAPs would automatically possess the holistic, long-range perceptions advocated throughout this book. However, the potential for developing such perceptions and actions in the public sector must be realized and enlivened. But regardless of how energetic People's Action Programs or any other public sector structure might be, it seems painfully obvious that in many societies public action will usually end in failure. Due to the concentration of power in the hands of a closely linked political-economic-social monopoly, due to the pressure these powers can use to scare off or buy off key change agents, and due to a "leave-it-to-the-experts" attitude often prevalent among the masses, investing great hope in public action programs may seem foolish. But we repeat that we believe that a courageous public, educated to identify and pursue goals of qualitative, equitable development, has a good chance of using these troubled times to seize a consequential degree of power by adamantly refusing to acquiesce in a system that destroys the environment, subordinates basic human needs to excessive material growth, and misrepresents these actions to the people most negatively affected. It is to this end that the proposals just discussed are directed.

GLOBAL STRATEGIES

The interdependent nature of present human society demands that proposals for the future give attention to global strategies. Although we remain firm in our support of the right and value of political, economic, and social diversity, we strongly contend that certain fundamental global structures and actions can and must be implemented if the quality of human life is to be improved. For regardless of how one envisions the specifics of a new world order, there is growing acceptance of the need for strategies of change beyond just national and regional scales. The global setting in which these macro strategies must occur is characterized by several conditions. One is that the nation-state, in spite of its numerous shortcomings, will persist for some time as the dominant unit of world political organization. Consequently, global strategies of change will be forced to respect national sovereignty. Second, present world interaction patterns reveal in many nations a serious separation between the ruling powers and the masses in values and priorities.

This separation is often exacerbated by a closer harmony of interests between the center in one nation and the center in another nation than between the center and periphery of the same nation. Global strategies need to respond directly to this phenomenon. And third, global interaction is now predominantly economic, with politics and culture increasingly subordinated to perceived economic theory and interests. Thus global strategies of change need to point toward a new international economic order.

The major dilemma usually confronting proposals of fundamental global change stems from the ineffectiveness of enforcement structures. How to accomplish international strategies and still allow full national sovereignty becomes a problem of seemingly insurmountable proportions. Nations strong in economic, political, and technological power can simply refuse to alter their environmentally damaging policies, and the majority of the world has no recourse but to acquiesce. The United Nations, although valuable as a beginning step toward international communication and cooperation on global concerns, has proven only minimally effective in implementing most of its change strategies, regardless of how positive many of these programs may be.

Thus, for those societies that do not wield dominant power in world interactions, several general steps seem absolutely essential. As growing numbers of Third and Fourth World nations are demonstrating, unified stands on wide-ranging issues must be forged and maintained. Cartelization on products much in demand by technologically advanced nations needs to expand on the successes of the Organization of Petroleum Exporting Countries. With the increased revenues resource-rich developing countries would gain from such activity, the design and implementation of indigenous paths to development need to be funded on a major scale throughout the developing world. Ties of dependency on the dominant powers such as the U.S., the U.S.S.R., Japan, and those of Western Europe, can consequently be loosened and cut.

But world public opinion has not been a strong enough force to pressure the dominant nations to agree to a more equitable economic order. In instances where exploitive domination has been broken, firm independent acts such as nationalization and confiscation of excessive wealth and property have proven necessary. An increase in these measures, plus a continued weakening of the power of the Security Council of the UN vis-à-vis the General Assembly, seems to represent at least minor advances toward operationalizing the goals of a new economic order.

In more specific terms, a new international political economy that points toward an improved quality of environmental life needs to include the objectives and strategies outlined below. Many of these have been suggested before; some have not. But the fact that many of these suggestions are now familiar should in no way detract from their value. Indeed, as this book goes to press, some of the main themes underlying these proposals have finally found their way into a major policy statement by the United States to the UN General Assembly. Of course, the sincerity and commitment of the U.S. and other dominant powers to significant structural changes in the relations among rich and poor nations has yet to be translated into direct action. But at least some sense of change may be in the air. Thus, in an attempt to highlight a few of the goals and actions crucial to those structural changes most in need of implementation, we offer the following list of general suggestions.[19]

1. Structures to alleviate food problems
    a. Emergency relief to famine areas without political or economic strings of any sort.
    b. Reclamation and development of now dormant land, based on ecological studies and on a reasonable balance between labor-intensive and mechanized agricultural goals.
    c. International programs to avert problems such as salination and desertification, with complete transfer to developing countries of the technology required to accomplish such tasks.
    d. Rigorous policies protecting natural resources and food resources from pollution and harmful chemicals, necessarily including limits on harmful fertilizers and better utilization of night soil.

2. Terms of trade favorable to developing countries
    a. Stabilization of world markets for primary products and raw materials at prices significantly above present levels.
    b. Removal of developed countries' tariff barriers and other restrictive policies that obstruct developing countries in the processing and export of finished products.
    c. Utilization of customs duties and taxes charged by developed countries on imports from the least-developed world to stock a UN development fund to be allocated for development projects solely determined by the peoples of the least-developed countries.
    d. Diversification of exports from developing countries and rigorous restrictions on those foreign policies obstructing diversification.
    e. Limitations on the manufacture of synthetic materials when renewable natural materials can be utilized.
    f. Realignment of pricing policies to favor the least-developed countries.

g. Dissolution of shipping monopolies and inflated shipping costs to reduce the disadvantages caused to the least-developed countries.

h. Greatly increased trade exclusively among the developing and least-developed countries.

3. Restructured programs of development aid

a. Fundamental alteration of the International Monetary Fund and World Bank to lessen the influence of developed societies in the determination of aid allocation and use.

b. Implementation of no-interest loan policies with long-term repayment schedules.

c. Full transfer of technology so that independent development can be attained.

d. Greatly increased aid programs from resource-rich developing societies to least-developed nations to break aid links with the highly developed world.

e. Industrialization programs that acknowledge the serious implications to the physical and social environment of overemphasizing industrial growth at the expense of labor-intensive and ecologically sound growth policies.

f. Strict limitations on the political, cultural, and economic manipulation that accompanies many aid programs.

g. Technology transfer policies that allow recipient nations to determine completely the substance of research and development.

4. Regulation of transnational corporations (TNCs)

a. Prohibition of TNCs from being founders or cofounders of any business enterprise in developing societies.

b. Ultimate management power placed in the hands of developing country workers, with the TNC having equal representation on a body (similar to Yugoslavia's Joint Operations Board) whose power is only recommendatory.

c. Limitations on foreign investment to less than 40 percent (we recommend a maximum figure much closer to 20 percent) of the total investment of any enterprise.

d. Stringent limitations on a foreign investor's share of profits.

e. Policies that force a high percentage of products made by enterprises using foreign investment to be exported so as to bring foreign exchange to developing nations.

f. A policy whereby the determination of products and advertising rests with the local government and, most especially, with the local workers who make the product.

    g. Requirements that all the technology utilized in a particular enterprise be transferred to the developing country to prevent the TNC from holding back several elements that are essential to independent development.

    h. Cartelization of numerous resources (tin, copper, bauxite, coffee, uranium, plutonium, and others).

    i. Severe penalties (such as expulsion or massive fines) on any TNC payoffs to developing country officials.

    j. Requirements that a high percentage of all positions at all levels be filled by local citizens.

    k. Policies that make wages in developing countries comparable to wages of counterpart workers in highly developed societies.

    l. Actions that break up TNC control over local firms.

5. Other general suggestions

    a. A UN–administered plan that distributes the resources of the oceans according to need.

    b. Full academic freedom within the new United Nations University, and the active involvement of young people (especially from the developing world) in determining the focus of UNU research.

    c. The development of a college for impact planning, and a college for conflict resolution within the framework of the UN University.

    d. Exhaustive programs of analysis that attempt to ascertain the needs and goals of the frequently ignored masses.

    e. Research and education programs that identify and encourage concepts of ceilings and floors regarding consumption and wealth.

    f. Independent development of an increasing number of experimental communities in which alternatives to present dominant values are used as the basis of community organization.

    g. Greatly increased exposé activity by mass media and public groups to reveal antipublic behavior of political and economic leaders.

    h. Greatly increased transnational efforts to devise and implement educational programs that develop global consciousness, environmental awareness, and more egalitarian structures and institutions.

The implementation of these measures can be aided by UN actions of censure, boycott, and embargo, and by intense public opinion pressure against violator nations. Governments of developing nations can be instrumental in bringing these objectives to fruition by refusing to play any longer the overly dependent role in the dominant global system that obstructs their development. The governments of the highly developed nations can serve the ultimate interests of all humanity by relinquishing their monopolistic grip on the benefits of international interaction, and by firmly restricting the exploitive activities of corporations. Governments all over the world can make objective information concerning environmental problems available to the citizenry. The public can take this information and mobilize movements to secure fundamental needs and protect a reciprocally beneficial balance between man and the environment.

All these actions *can* aid in the establishment of a more healthy international system. But, for numerous and complex reasons, of which inaccurate and self-interested perceptions and planning are two of the most important, the direction and pace of essential attitudinal and structural changes are proving incapable of keeping up with the rate at which new problems arise and old ones intensify. There seems no workable method of ensuring that developed nations will cease their exploitation, that leaders of developing countries will place priority on basic need-meeting services instead of the purchase of armaments, that corporations will deemphasize their profit-maximization ethos, that the resources of the oceans will be distributed equitably among all inhabitants of the planet, or that the earth's environment will be spared the distortion and destruction wrought by man's obsession with excessive quantitative growth.

But those people who urgently appeal for a process of qualitative growth, in which ecosystem balance is maintained and basic human needs are met, must continue to point out the ultimately disastrous consequences brought to all sectors of society when the quality of life is subordinated to the material values of excessive growth. In this book we have shown that greater energy consumption decreases growth. We have demonstrated a relationship between cheap energy, automation, unemployment, dependency, crime, alienation, and social disharmony. We have shown that pollution, depletion, and short-sighted policies greatly limit the total diversity in the plant- and animal-life systems of the planet, a diversity that enhances the adaptability and balance of the entire ecosystem. We have demonstrated that the great inequity evident in the distribution of life's benefits, and the unrestricted overaccumulation on the part of the affluent few, are depleting the earth's finite resources while also contributing to the impoverishment of the world's masses. We have pointed to the powerful effect certain cultural beliefs have on the way human development is perceived, priorities are set, and structures are devised. And we have attempted to point out the inter-relationship of all these factors in contributing to an instability that greatly diminishes a society's will and ability to solve major problems.

Beyond the illumination of these environmental problems and their complex causal pathways, we have also suggested possible solutions. Although we have repeatedly said that each culture's identity will determine the efficacy of these proposals within that culture, we argue strongly that the values and policies necessary to maintain ecosystem balance, develop homeostatic mechanisms, and meet basic human needs are universal survival requirements for all societies. A full commitment to these goals will need to be made by the public, by governments, and by corporations if we are to stand a chance of solving environmental problems and improving the quality of life.

Notes to Chapter 7

1. See the writings of Richard Barnet, Ronald Muller, John Kenneth Galbraith, Robert Stauffer, and many others.

2. This section is condensed from Dudley Weeks, "Learning Alternative Futures."

3. As an example of a general outline of the functions of competent planning, Soetjipto Wirosardjono suggests the following:
   1. Assessment and comprehension of the problem
   2. Establishment of reasonable goals and objectives
   3. Determination of alternative means of reaching goals and objectives
   4. Determination of the consequences related to pursuance of each alternative, with specific emphasis on social and environmental consequences, and on internalized costs and benefits
   5. Determination of one desirable alternative after study of the consequences and an analysis of the "public will"
   6. Implementation of the plan
   7. Follow-up analysis of the effects external factors have on the plan, with attention given to how the goals and objectives have been altered, and to the magnitude of social, environmental, and economic costs
   8. Implementation of necessary adjustments

4. Mihajlo Mesarovic and Edward Pestel, *Mankind at the Turning Point*. It should be noted of course, that false conclusions can also be drawn from highly mathematical approaches. There is also a place for meso-scale mathematical modeling in which the holism is supplied by subjective control of the use of the model.

5. Frederick Thayer, *An End to Hierarchy!*

6. The World Indicators Project (Univ. of Oslo, P.O. Box 1070, Oslo 3, Norway) is one of the most valuable programs presently involved in work with new indicators. Johan Galtung and his international team are developing indices in a wide range of areas from "gross national pollution" to "gross national happiness," demonstrating the wealth of potentialities available in the design of new measures for the quality of a society's life.

7. These and other interesting data of Japanese perceptions are contained in a report of the Institute for Future Technology entitled "The International Comparative Beliefs Study," brought to our attention by Yosaku Hasegawa.

8. From U.S. Census Bureau data, cited in Letitia Upton and Nancy Lyons, *Distribution of Personal Income and Wealth in the United States*, p. 1.

9. Edward C. Budd, ed., *Inequality and Poverty*, pp. xii, xvi.

10. Joseph Pechman, "The Rich, the Poor and the Taxes They Pay," p. 27.

11. Compiled from data in *Statistical Abstract of the United States 1974*, table 1372 (pp. 829–830) and table 1356 (pp. 815–817).

12. Kenneth E. F. Watt, "Critically Important Determinants of the Transition to the Future."

13. Dudley Weeks developed the pedagogy outlined in the text. Examples of other relevant curricula can be obtained from numerous sources, including the Institute for World Order (1140 Ave. of the Americas, New York, N.Y. 10036); Center for War/Peace Studies (218 E. 18th St., New York, N.Y. 10003); Movement for a New Society (1006 S. 46th St., Philadelphia, Pa. 19143); and Institute of Cultural Action (27 Chemin des Crêts, 1218 Grand Saconnex, Geneva, Switzerland).

14. The complete "Pedagogy for Qualitative Development" appears in Dudley Weeks, "Learning Alternative Futures."

15. The People's Action Program concept is developed further in the dissertation mentioned in footnote 14. Similar structural emphases concerning social assemblies and anticipatory democracy appear in the writings of Alvin Toffler. George Lakey's *Strategy for a Living Revolution* and Saul Alinsky's *Rules for Radicals* are also valuable.

16. See John Kenneth Galbraith's *New Industrial State*, and the writings of R. L. Heilbroner, Fred Thayer, Paul Baran, Paul Sweezy, and others.

17. See, for example, the well-known works of Elsie Boulding, Paul Goodman, Ivan Illich, and Paulo Freire, plus recent publications such as George Kent "World Order Design: What Could Be More Practical?"; and William H. Boyer *Alternative Futures: Designs for Social Change*.

18. Recent developments in Sri Lanka evidence a definite attempt by government to make local development more self-determined. Most of the district revenue officers, who serve as perhaps the main catalysts in rural development, originally come from rural areas, undergo training, then return to work with local inhabitants in development programs. Resources are surveyed by the people in a village, and local structures, resources, and patterns are retained when possible, with input of new technology and methodology being used mainly to make the local structures more efficient, productive, and ultimately self-reliant. District development councils have a direct link to the member of Parliament representing a particular district, and that MP has authority to approve projects for his or her own district.

But even this improved governmental structure has a difficult time combating the impact of the dominant technological culture's emphasis on ever-increasing growth and consumption. As Renton deAlwis, an agricultural economist from Sri Lanka, has expressed it, "My culture has many of the negative feedback loops needed to discourage the dominant model of 'growth'. The slow pace of life, the extended family concept, strong community and cooperative traditions favoring the group over individual desires, the Buddhist idea of Karma, wealth defined as land—all should help us view the growth rat race with restraint. But many people have been conditioned by the media and tales of riches to dream of getting where the 'developed' world is now, and the harmful consequences this can bring are often ignored."

19. This list is taken from Dudley Weeks, "Learning Alternative Futures." It combines many of the goals now being actively pursued by the less developed and the developing nations in the UN.

Bibliography

Abrams, Charles. *Man's Struggle for Shelter in an Urbanizing World.* Cambridge, Mass.: M.I.T. Press, 1964.

Adelman, Irma. "Growth, Income Distribution and Equity-Oriented Development Strategies." *World Development* 3, nos. 2 & 3 (February–March 1975): 67–76.

Alexander, Richard D. "Natural Enemies in Place of Poisons." *Natural History,* January 1975, pp. 92–95.

Alinsky, Saul. *Rules for Radicals.* New York: Random House, Vintage Books, 1972.

Allen, Robert. "Woodman, Spare Those Trees." *Development Forum,* April 1975, pp. 6–7.

Barber, Arthur. "Toward World Corporate Structures." *Current,* no. 102 (December 1968): 61–64.

Barber, James D. *The Presidential Character: Predicting Performance in the White House.* Englewood Cliffs, N.J.: Prentice-Hall, 1973.

Barnet, Richard J., and Muller, Ronald E. *Global Reach: The Power of the Multinational Corporations.* New York: Simon & Schuster, 1974.

Bartlett, H. H. "Fire, Primitive Agriculture and Grazing in the Tropics." In *Man's Role in Changing the Face of the Earth,* William L. Thomas, Jr., ed. Chicago: Chicago University Press, 1956.

Bellman, Richard E. *Adaptive Control Processes: A Guided Tour.* Princeton: Princeton University Press, 1961.

———. *Dynamic Programming.* Princeton: Princeton University Press, 1957.

Bellman, Richard E., and Dreyfus, S. E. *Applied Dynamic Programming.* Princeton: Princeton University Press, 1962.

Bennett, Hugh Hammond. *Soil Conservation.* New York: McGraw-Hill Co., 1939.

Birch, David L., et al. *America's Housing Needs, 1970 to 1980.* Cambridge, Mass.: Joint Center for Urban Studies of Massachusetts Institute of Technology and Harvard University, 1973.

Bond, Victor P. "Fuels for Power: Costs, Benefits and Risks in Perspective." In *Energy Crisis: Danger and Opportunity,* Victor John Yannacone, Jr., ed. St. Paul, Minn.: West Publishing Co., 1974.

Borgstrom, Georg. "The Breach in the Flow of Mineral Nutrients." *Ambio* 2, no. 5 (1973):129–136.

———. *The Food and People Dilemma.* North Scituate, Mass.: Duxbury Press, 1973.

———. "Food, Feed and Energy." *Ambio* 2, no. 6 (1973):213–220.

———. *Harvesting the Earth.* New York: Abelard-Schuman, 1973.

Borlaug, Norman, and Ewell, Raymon. "The Shrinking Margin." *Ceres, FAO Review on Development,* March–April 1974, p. 55.

Boyer, William H. *Alternative Futures: Designs for Social Change.* Dubuque, Iowa: Kendall/Hunt Publishing Co., 1975.

Brown, Graham, and Stellon, Pete. "The Energy Cost of a House." In *Rational Technology Unit 73–4.* London: Architectural Association, 1974.

Budd, Edward C., ed. *Inequality and Poverty.* New York: W. W. Norton & Co., 1968.

Burkitt, D.; Walker, A. R. P.; and Painter, N. S. "Dietary Fiber and Disease," *Journal of the American Medical Association* 229 (1974):1068–1074.

Butzer, Karl W. "Accelerated Soil Erosion: A Problem of Man-Land Relationships." In *Perspectives on Environment,* Ian R. Manners and Marvin W. Mikesell, eds. Washington, D.C.: Association of American Geographers, 1974.

Carter, Vernon Gill, and Dale, Tom. *Topsoil and Civilization.* Rev. ed. Norman, Okla.: University of Oklahoma Press, 1974.

Chang, Jen-hu. *Climate and Agriculture: An Ecological Survey.* Chicago: Aldine Publishing Co., 1968.

Chedd, Graham. "How Mobil Confronts a Crisis." *Not Man Apart* 4, no. 17 (December 1974):5.

Cicerone, Ralph J.; Stolarski, R. S.; and Walters, Stacy. "Stratospheric Ozone Destruction by Man-Made Chlorofluoromethanes." *Science,* 27 September 1974, pp. 1165–1167.

Clark, Andrew H. "The Impact of Exotic Invasion on the Remaining New World Mid-Latitude Grasslands." In *Man's Role in Changing the Face of the Earth,* William L. Thomas, Jr., ed. Chicago: University of Chicago Press, 1956.

Clark, Colin. "Economics and Population Growth." In *Exploding Humanity: The Crisis of Numbers,* H. Regier and J. B. Falls, eds. Toronto: Anansi Press, 1969.

Cleaver, Harry M., Jr. "The Contradictions of the Green Revolution." *American Economic Review* 62, no. 2 (May 1972):177–186.

Conklin, Harold C. "An Ethnoecological Approach to Shifting Agriculture." *Transactions of the New York Academy of Sciences,* 2nd ser., 17 (1954):133–142.

Conway, Gordon R. "Better Methods of Pest Control." In *Environment: Resources, Pollution and Society,* William W. Murdoch, ed. Stamford, Conn.: Sinauer Associates, 1971.

_____. "Ecological Aspects of Pest Control in Malaysia." In *The Careless Technology: Ecology and International Development,* M. Taghi Farvar and John P. Milton, eds. Garden City, N.Y.: Natural History Press, 1972.

Cowan, I. M. "Ecology and Discretion." In *Exploding Humanity: The Crisis of Numbers,* H. Regier and J. B. Falls, eds. Toronto: Anansi Press, 1969.

Culbertson, John M. *Economic Development: An Ecological Approach.* New York: Alfred A. Knopf, 1971.

Curry-Lindahl, Kai. "Projecting the Future in the Worldwide National Park Movement." In *Second World Conference on National Parks,* Sir Hugh Elliott, ed. Morges, Switzerland: International Union for the Conservation of Nature and Natural Resources, 1974.

Daly, Herman E. "The Steady-State Economy: Toward a Political Economy of Biophysical Equilibrium and Moral Growth." In *Toward a Steady-State Economy,* Herman E. Daly, ed. San Francisco: W. H. Freeman & Co., 1973.

Daly, Herman E., ed. *Toward a Steady-State Economy.* San Francisco: W. H. Freeman & Co., 1973.

Dary, D. A. *The Buffalo Book: The Full Saga of the American Animal.* Chicago: Swallow Press, Sage Books, 1974.

Dasmann, Raymond F. "A Rationale for Preserving Natural Areas." *Journal of Soil and Water Conservation* 28 (1973):114–117.

_____. "Towards a System for Classifying Natural Regions of the World and Their

Representation by National Parks and Reserves." *Biological Conservation* 4, no. 4 (July 1972):247–255.

Dasmann, Raymond F.; Milton, John P.; and Freeman, Peter H. *Ecological Principles for Economic Development*. New York and London: John Wiley & Sons, 1973.

Davis, Kingsley. "The Urbanization of the Human Population." In *Cities*, a Scientific American book. New York: Alfred A. Knopf, 1965.

Djojohadikusumo, Sumitro. *Indonesia Towards the Year 2000* (Jakarta, February 1975).

Duffie, John A., and Bechman, William A. *Solar Energy Thermal Processes*. New York: Wiley-Interscience, 1974.

Dumond, D. E. "Swidden Agriculture and the Rise of Maya Civilization." In *Environment and Cultural Behavior: Ecological Studies in Cultural Anthropology*, Andrew P. Vayda, ed. New York: Natural History Press, 1969.

Easterlin, R. A. *Population, Labor Force, and Long Swings in Economic Growth: The American Experience*. New York: Columbia University Press, 1968.

Ellul, Jacques. *The Technological Society*. Translated by John Wilkinson. New York: Alfred A. Knopf, 1964.

Engel, Heinrich. *The Japanese House: Tradition for Contemporary Architecture*. Rutland, Vt.: Charles E. Tuttle Co., 1964.

"Experimental Low Cost Housing Project—Peru." *Architectural Design* (London), April 1970, pp.187–205.

Farvar, M. Taghi, and Milton, John P., eds. *The Careless Technology: Ecology and International Development*. Garden City, N.Y.: Natural History Press, 1972.

Fatemi, Nasrollah, and Williams, Gail. *Multinational Corporations*. London: Barnes & Co., 1975.

Fathy, Hasan. *Architecture for the Poor*. Chicago: University of Chicago Press, 1969.

Felix, Fremont. *World Markets of Tomorrow*. New York: Harper & Row, 1971.

Fennelly, J. F. *Twilight of the Evening Lands*. Brookdale Press, 1972.

Fiering, M. B., and Holling, C. S. *Management and Standards for Perturbed Ecosystems*. Laxenburg, Austria: International Institute for Applied Systems Analysis, Research Report RR–74–3 (1974).

Fisher, James; Simon, Noel; and Vincent, Jack. *Wildlife in Danger*. New York: Viking Press, 1969.

Fisher, John C. *Energy Crises in Perspective*. New York: Wiley-Interscience, 1974.

Food and Agriculture Organization of the United Nations *Production Yearbook*, 1973.

Fosberg, F. R. "Temperate Zone Influence on Tropical Forest Land Use: A Plea for Sanity." In *Tropical Forest Ecosystems in Africa and South America: A Comparative Review*, Betty J. Meggers, Edward S. Ayensu, and W. Donald Ducksworth, eds. Washington D.C.: Smithsonian Institution Press, 1973.

Frank, Andre G. *Capitalism and Underdevelopment in Latin America*. New York: Monthly Review Press, 1969.

Franklin, Jerry F.; Jenkins, Robert E.; and Romancier, Robert M. "Research Natural Areas: Contributors to Environmental Quality Programs." *Journal of Environmental Quality* 1, no. 2 (1972):133–139.

Frederiksen, Harald. "Feedbacks in Economic and Demographic Transition." *Science*, 14 November 1969, pp. 837–847.

Freeman, Christopher. "Malthus with a Computer." In *Thinking about the Future: A Critique of "The Limits to Growth,"* H. S. D. Cole, Christopher Freeman, Marie Jahoda, and K. L. R. Pavitt, eds. London: Chatto & Windus, 1973.

Frejka, Tomas. "Reflections on the Demographic Conditions Needed to Establish a U.S. Stationary Population Growth." *Population Studies* 22 (1968):378–397.

Fuller, John G. *We Almost Lost Detroit*. New York: Reader's Digest Press, 1975.

Fuller, R. Buckminster. *Synergetics*. New York: Macmillan Co., 1975.

Galbraith, John Kenneth. *The New Industrial State*. Boston: Houghton Mifflin, 1967.

Galtung, Johan. "A Structural Theory of Imperialism." *Journal of Peace Research* 8 (1971):81–118.

Gandhi, Mohandas K. *Man v. Machine*. Pocket Gandhi Series, no. 15, Anand T. Hingorani, ed. Bombay: Bharatiya Vidya Bhavan, 1966.

_____. *Modern v. Ancient Civilization*. Pocket Gandhi Series, no. 19, Anand T. Hingorani, ed. Bombay: Bharatiya Vidya Bhavan, 1970.

Gans, Herbert J. *The Urban Villagers: Group and Class in the Life of Italian Americans*. New York: Free Press, 1962.

Gardner, Mark R., and Ashby, W. Ross. "Connectance of Large Dynamic (Cybernetic) Systems: Critical Values for Stability." *Nature,* 21 November 1970, p. 784.

Georgescu-Roegen, Nicholas. "The Entropy Law and the Economic Problem." In *Toward a Steady-State Economy,* Herman E. Daly, ed. San Francisco: W. H. Freeman & Co., 1973.

Gibbs, H. S., and Raeside, J. D. *Soil Erosion in the High Country of the South Island,* New Zealand Department of Scientific and Industrial Research, Bulletin no. 92 (1945).

Gofman, John W., and Tamplin, Arthur R. *Poisoned Power: The Case Against Nuclear Power Plants*. New York: New American Library, 1974.

Griffin, Keith. "The International Transmission of Inequity." *World Development* 2, no. 3 (March 1974), p. 6.

Grigg, David B. *The Harsh Lands: A Study in Agricultural Development*. London: Macmillan & Co., 1970.

Harahap, Filino. "The Prospect of Solar Utilization, The Indonesia Case." Unpublished paper.

Hayter, Teresa. *Aid as Imperialism*. Harmondsworth, England: Penguin Books, 1971.

Heichel, G. H. *Comparative Efficiency of Energy Use in Crop Production*. Connecticut Agricultural Experiment Station, Bulletin 739 (November 1973).

Held, R. Burnell, and Clawson, Marion. *Soil Conservation in Perspective*. Baltimore: Resources for the Future, 1965.

Hickling, Lee. "N-Plants Face a Shutdown." *Honolulu Star-Bulletin,* 8 May 1975.

Hippel, F.; Fels, M.; and Krugmann, H. "The Net Energy from Nuclear Reactors." *FAS Professional Bulletin* 3, no. 4.

Hohenemser, Kurt H. "The Failsafe Risk." *Environment* 17, no. 1 (Jan.–Feb.1975):6–10.

Holling, C. S. "Resilience and Stability of Ecological Systems." *Annual Review of Ecology and Systematics* 4 (1973):1–23.

Hubbert, M. King. "Energy Resources." In *Energy Crisis: Danger and Opportunity,* Victor John Yannacone, Jr., ed. St. Paul, Minn.: West Publishing Co., 1974.

_____. "Energy Resources." In *Resources and Man: A Study and Recommendations by the Committee on Resources and Man,* National Academy of Sciences and National Research Council. San Francisco: W. H. Freeman & Co., 1969.

Hutchinson, Joseph. *Farming and Food Supply: The Interdependence of Countryside and Town*. Cambridge: At the University Press, 1972.

Hyams, Edward S. *Soil and Civilization*. London: Thames & Hudson, 1952.

Illich, Ivan. *Energy and Equity*. New York: Harper & Row, 1974.

India Pocket Book of Economic Information. Government of India, Ministry of Finance, Department of Economic Affairs, 1971.

Inglis, Fred. *The Imagery of Power: A Critique of Advertising*. London: Heinemann, 1972.

Institute for Future Technology, Tokyo. "The International Comparative Beliefs Study, Perceptions of Environmental Quality." March 1975.

Intermediate Technology Group. *Kit 5, Planning and the Contractor*. London, n.d.

International Criminal Police Organization. *International Crime Statistics*. Paris, 1973.

International Road Federation. *World Road Statistics*. Washington, D.C., 1973.

IUCN, International Commission on National Parks. *United Nations List of National Parks and Equivalent Reserves.* 2nd ed. Brussels: Hayez, 1971; and Morges, Switzerland: IUCN, 1974.

IUCN, Survival Service Commission. *Red Data Book.* Morges, Switzerland, 1966.

Jacks, Graham V., and Whyte, Robert O. *Vanishing Lands: A World Survey of Soil Erosion.* 1939. Reprint. New York: Arno Press, 1972.

Jacobs, Jane. *The Death and Life of Great American Cities.* New York: Random House, 1961.

———. *The Economy of Cities.* New York: Random House, 1969.

Jalee, Pierre. *The Third World in World Economy.* New York: Monthly Review Press, Modern Reader Paperbacks, 1969.

Janzen, Daniel H. "Tropical Agroecosystems." *Science* 21 December 1973, pp. 1212–1219.

Johnson, Dick. *Lake Pedder: Why a National Park Must be Saved.* Published by the Lake Pedder Action Committees of Victoria and Tasmania and the Australian Union of Students, July 1972.

Johnson, Harry G. "Thrust and Response: The Multinational Corporation as a Development Agent." *Columbia Journal of World Business* 5, no. 3 (May–June 1970):25–30.

Kahn, Lloyd, ed. *Shelter.* Bodega Bay, Calif.: Shelter Publications, 1973.

Kartawinata, Kuswata. *Report on the State of Knowledge on Tropical Forest Ecosystems in Indonesia.* Indonesian National Committee on the Programme on Man and the Biosphere, National Biological Institute, Bogor, Indonesia, 1975.

Kato, Hidetoshi. "Global Instantaneousness and Instant Globalism: Some Observations on the Significance of Popular Culture in Developing Countries." Paper presented at the Conference on Communication and Change, East-West Center Communication Institute, Honolulu, 12–17 January 1975. (Available at the East-West Center, Honolulu.)

Kent, George. "World Order Design: What Could Be More Practical?" *Peace and Change* 2, no. 3 (1974):3–9.

Key, Wilson Bryan. *Subliminal Seduction: Ad Media's Manipulation of a Not So Innocent America.* Englewood Cliffs, N.J.: Prentice-Hall, 1973.

Kindleberger, Charles P. *American Business Abroad: Six Lectures on Direct Investment.* New Haven, Conn.: Yale Univ. Press, 1969.

Knight, C. Gregory. "Ethnogeography and Change." *Journal of Geography* 70 (January 1971):47–51.

Kuznets, Simon. *Economic Change: Selected Essays in Business Cycles, National Income, and Economic Growth.* New York: W. W. Norton & Co., 1953.

———. *Economic Growth and Structure.* New York: W. W. Norton & Co., 1965.

Lakey, George. *Strategy for a Living Revolution.* San Francisco, Calif.: W. H. Freeman & Co., 1973.

Landsberg, Helmut. "Man-Made Climatic Changes." In *Man's Natural Environment: A Systems Approach,* L. H. Russwurm and Edward Sommerville, eds. North Scituate, Mass.: Duxbury Press, 1974.

Lappé, Frances Moore. *Diet for a Small Planet.* New York: Ballentine Books, 1971.

———. "Fantasies of Famine." *Harper's,* February 1975, p. 51.

Laquaian, Aprodicio A. *Slums Are for People.* Manila: Local Government Center, College of Public Administration, University of the Philippines, 1969.

Leavitt, Helen. *Superhighway—Superhoax.* Garden City, N.Y.: Doubleday & Co., 1970.

Lerner, Daniel. "Technology, Communication and Change." Discussion paper presented at the Conference on Communication and Change, East-West Center Communication Institute, Honolulu, 12–17 January 1975. (Available at the East-West Center.)

Likens, Gene E., and Bormann, F. Herbert. "Effects of Forest Clearing on the Northern Hardwood Forest Ecosystem and Its Biochemistry." In *Proceedings of 1st International Congress of Ecology.* The Hague, Netherlands, September 1974.

Lof, G. O. G., and Tybout, R. A. "Cost of House Heating with Solar Energy." *Solar Energy* 14 (1972):253–278.

———. "The Design and Cost of Optimized Systems for Residential Heating and Cooling by Solar Energy." *Solar Energy* 16 (1974):9–18.

Lusk, P. "Comalco, Manapouri and the Bluff Smelter." *New Zealand Environment* 4, no. 3 (March 1975):18–25.

MacArthur, Robert. "Fluctuations of Animal Populations, and a Measure of Community Stability." *Ecology* 36 (1955):533–536.

Magdoff, Harry. *The Age of Imperialism: The Economics of U.S. Foreign Policy.* New York: Monthly Review Press, Modern Reader Paperbacks, 1969.

Manners, Ian R. "Environmental Impact of Modern Agricultural Technologies." In *Perspectives on Environment,* Ian R. Manners and Marvin W. Mikesell, eds. Washington, D.C.: Association of American Geographers, 1974.

Manners, Ian R., and Mikesell, Marvin W., eds. *Perspectives on Environment.* Washington, D.C.: Association of American Geographers, 1974.

Man's Impact on the Global Environment: Assessment and Recommendations for Action. Report of the Study of Critical Environmental Problems (SCEP). Cambridge, Mass.: M.I.T. Press, 1970.

Marsh, George Perkins. *Man and Nature.* 1864. Reprint. Cambridge, Mass.: Harvard University Press, Belknap Press, 1965.

Marx, Karl. "Alienated Labor." In *The Capitalist System: A Radical Analysis of American Society,* Richard C. Edwards, Michael Reich, and Thomas E. Weisskopf, eds. Englewood Cliffs, N.J.: Prentice-Hall, 1972.

May, Robert M. *Stability and Complexity in Model Ecosystems.* Princeton: Princeton University Press, 1973.

McCaskill, L. W. *Hold This Land: A History of Soil Conservation in New Zealand.* Wellington, N.Z.: Reed, 1973.

McKenry, Keith. "A History and Critical Analysis of the Controversy Concerning the Gordon River Power Scheme." In *Pedder Papers: Anatomy of a Decision.* Melbourne: Australian Conservation Foundation, 1972.

McLean, R. F. "Hydro Development." Paper presented at Seminar on "Our Environment— Does the Public Have Control?" Wellington, N.Z., published by New Zealand Conference on Environment and Conservation, 11 November 1972.

Mead, Margaret, ed. *Cultural Patterns and Technical Change.* New York: New American Library, 1955.

Meadows, Donella H.; Meadows, D. L.; Randers, J.; and Behrens, W. W., III. *The Limits to Growth.* New York: New American Library, 1972.

Mesarovic, Mihajlo, and Pestel, Edward. *Mankind at the Turning Point.* New York: Reader's Digest Press, 1974.

Mick, Stephen S. "The Foreign Medical Graduate." *Scientific American,* February 1975, pp. 14–21.

Molloy, L. F., comp. *A Critique of the Environmental Impact Report on the Proposed Utilization of South Island Beech Forests to the Officials Committee for the Environment.* Wellington: New Zealand Ecological Society, 1973.

Moore, Norman W. "A Synopsis of the Pesticide Problem." In *Advances in Ecological Research,* J. B. Cragg, ed. New York: Academic Press, 1967.

Morse, Harold. "N Power Called Wasteful Energy." *Honolulu Star-Bulletin,* 2 February 1975.

Mostert, N. "The Age of the Oilberg." *Audubon,* May 1975, pp. 18–45.

Muller, Ronald. "The Multinational Corporation and the Underdevelopment of the Third World." In *The Political Economy of Development and Underdevelopment,* Charles Wilber, ed. New York: Random House, 1973.

Murphy, Earl F. *On Governing Nature.* New York: Quadrangle/The New York Times Co., 1967.

Murray, Geoffrey. "Jun Ui: A Different Kind of Japanese Radical." *PHP* (Tokyo), June 1975, pp. 35–43.

Myers, Norman. "National Parks in Savannah Africa." *Science,* 22 December 1972, pp. 1255–1263.

Myrdal, Gunnar. *Asian Drama: An Inquiry into the Poverty of Nations.* 3 vols. New York: Random House, 1968.

Nicholson, E. Max. *Handbook to the Conservation Section of the International Biological Programme.* IBP Handbook no. 5. Oxford: Blackwell, 1968.

_____. "What Is Wrong with the National Park Movement?" In *Second World Conference on National Parks,* Sir Hugh Elliott, ed. Morges, Switzerland: IUCN, 1974.

Norman, Colin. "The Little Nipper Who Cost the South a Fortune." *Nature,* 8 May 1975, pp. 94–95.

Odum, Eugene P. "The Strategy of Ecosystem Development." *Science,* 18 April 1969, pp. 264–265.

Odum, Howard T. *Environment, Power, and Society.* New York: Wiley-Interscience, 1971.

Odum, Howard T., and Odum, E. C. *Energy Basis for Man and Nature: Energy Growth to Steady State.* New York: McGraw-Hill Co., forthcoming.

Oliver, Paul, ed. *Shelter in Africa.* Springfield, Mass.: Praeger, 1971.

Ominde, S. H. "Environmental Problems of the Developing Countries." Paper presented at the United Nations ECOSOC Symposium on Population, Resources, and Environment, Stockholm, 26 September–5 October 1973.

Oregon, State of, Office of Energy Resources and Planning, Office of the Governor. *Transition: A Report to the Oregon Energy Council.* 1975.

Ortega y Gasset, José. *The Revolt of the Masses.* New York: W. W. Norton & Co., 1932.

Oshima, Harry T. "Development and Mass Communication: A Re-examination." Paper presented at the Conference on Communication and Change, East-West Center Communication Institute, Honolulu, 12–17 January 1975.

Packard, Vance. *The Waste Makers.* New York: David McKay Co., 1960.

Paddock, William, and Paddock, Elizabeth. *We Don't Know How: An Independent Audit of What They Call Success in Foreign Assistance.* Ames, Iowa: Iowa State University Press, 1973.

Page, R. W. "The Non-renewable Resources Sub-system." In *Thinking about the Future: A Critique of "The Limits to Growth,"* H. S. D. Cole, Christopher Freeman, Marie Jahoda, and K. L. R. Pavitt, eds. London: Chatto & Windus, 1973.

Pechman, Joseph. "The Rich, the Poor, and the Taxes They Pay." *Public Interest,* no. 17 (Fall 1969):21–43.

Pelzer, K. J. *Pioneer Settlement in the Asiatic Tropics.* Institute of Pacific Relations, American Geographical Society, Special Publication no. 29. New York, 1945.

Pimentel, David; Hurd, L. E.; Bellotti, A. C.; Forster, M. J.; Oka, I. N.; Sholes, O. D.; and Whitman, R. J. "Food Production and the Energy Crisis." *Science,* 2 November 1973, pp. 443–449.

Pope, Jeremy. "Manapouri Report Illustrates Limitations of Lawyers." *New Zealand National Business Review* 16 (November 1970):5.

Preston, Samuel H.; Keyfitz, Nathan; and Schoen, Robert. *Causes of Death: Life Tables for National Populations.* New York: Seminar Press, 1972.

Puffer, R. R., and Serrano, C. V. "Patterns of Mortality in Childhood." Washington D.C.: Scientific Publication No. 262, Pan American Health Organization, Pan American Sanitary Bureau, Regional Office of the World Health Organization, 1973.

Ralph, E. L. "Large Scale Solar Electric Power Generation." *Solar Energy* 14 (1972):11–20.

Ramakumar, R.; Allison, H. J.; and Hughes, W. L. "Prospects for Tapping Solar Energy on a Large Scale." *Solar Energy* 16 (1974):107–115.

Rappaport, R. A. *Pigs for the Ancestors: Ritual in the Ecology of a New Guinea People.* New Haven: Yale University Press, 1968.

Redistribution with Growth: Policies to Improve Income Distribution in Developing Countries in the Context of Economic Growth, a joint study commissioned by the World Bank's Development Centre and the Institute of Development, University of Sussex. Oxford University Press, 1974.

Report of Commission to Inquire into the Proposal to Raise the Level of Lake Manapouri for the Purpose of Generating Electricity. New Zealand Government Printer, 1970.

Revelle, Roger. "Food and Population." *Scientific American,* September 1974, pp. 161–170.

Rostow, W. W. *The Stages of Economic Growth: A Non-Communist Manifesto.* 2nd ed. Cambridge: At the University Press, 1971.

Royal Commission to Enquire into and Report upon the Sheep Farming Industry in New Zealand. Wellington, N.Z.: Government Printer, 1949.

Rudofsky, Bernard. *Architecture Without Architects.* Garden City, N.Y.: Doubleday & Co., 1964.

Sastrapradja, S., and Sastrapradja, D. S. "Development and Conservation of Plant Genetic Resources in Indonesia." Paper submitted to the Symposium on Energy Resources and the Environment, Jakarta, 25–28 February 1975.

Sauer, Carl O. "The Agency of Man on Earth." In *Man's Role in Changing the Face of the Earth,* William L. Thomas, Jr., ed. Chicago: University of Chicago Press, 1956.

Schiller, Herbert I. *Mass Communications and American Empire.* Boston: Beacon Press, 1971.

Schneider, Kenneth R. *Autokind vs. Mankind.* New York: W. W. Norton & Co., 1971.

Schumacher, E. F. "Buddhist Economics." In *Toward a Steady-State Economy,* Herman E. Daly, ed. San Francisco: W. H. Freeman & Co., 1973.

_____. *Small is Beautiful: Economics as if People Mattered.* New York: Harper & Row, Harper Torchbooks, 1973.

Schwartz, Eugene S. *Overskill: Technology and the Myth of Efficiency.* New York: Quadrangle/The New York Times Co., 1971.

Searle, Graham. *Rush to Destruction.* Wellington, New Zealand: Reed, 1975.

Shuman, James B., and Rosenau, David. *The Kondratieff Wave: The Future of America until 1984 and Beyond.* New York: Dell Publishing Co., 1974.

Smith, Ray F., and van den Bosch, R. "Integrated Control." In *Pest Control: Biological, Physical and Selected Chemical Methods,* W. W. Kilgore and R. L. Doutt, eds. New York: Academic Press, 1967.

Soegiarto, Aprilani. "Aquatic Resources in Indonesia, Their Problems and Management." Paper submitted to the Symposium on Energy Resources and the Environment, Jakarta, 25–28 February 1975.

Sorokin, Pitirim A. *Social and Cultural Dynamics.* Boston: Sargent, Porter, 1957.

Spengler, Oswald. *The Decline of the West.* Translated by Charles Francis Atkinson. Vol. 2, *Perspectives of World History.* New York: A. A. Knopf, 1929.

_____. *The Hour of Decision.* Translated by Charles Francis Atkinson. New York: A. A. Knopf, 1934.

Spurgeon, David. "Strategy for Survival: 2: The Green Revolution." *Nature,* 20/27 December 1974, pp. 624–625.

"Stamp Out Food Faddism." *Science,* 16 May 1975, p. 714.

Statistical Pocketbook, Indonesia, 1972/73. Jakarta, Indonesia: Biro Pusat Statistik.

Stauffer, Robert. *Nation Building in a Global Economy: The Role of the Multinational Corporations.* Beverly Hills, Calif.: Sage Publications, 1973.

Steinhart, John S., and Steinhart, Carol E. "Energy Use in the U.S. Food System." *Science,* 19 April 1974, pp. 307–316.

Stone, Michael E. "Federal Housing Policy: A Political-Economic Analysis." In *Housing Urban America,* Jon Pynoos, Robert Schafer, and Chester W. Hartman, eds. Chicago: Aldine Publishing Co., 1973.

Thayer, Frederick C. *An End to Hierarchy! An End to Competition! Organizing the Politics and Economics of Survival.* New York: Franklin Watts, New Viewpoints, 1973.

Thomas, William L., Jr., ed. *Man's Role in Changing the Face of the Earth*. Chicago: University of Chicago Press, 1956.

Thomson, A. D., ed. *Beech Research News* (Christchurch, New Zealand: DSIR), no. 1 (June 1974); no. 2 (December 1974).

Tieh, T. Min. "Soil Erosion in China." *Geographical Review* 31 (1941):570–590.

Toffler, Alvin. *The Eco-Spasm Report: Why Our Economy Is Running Out of Control*. New York: Bantam Books, 1975.

Tolstoy, Leo. *War and Peace*. New York: New American Library, 1968. Epilogue, pp. 1351–1455.

Toynbee, Arnold. *A Study of History*. New ed. revised and abridged by the author and Jane Caplan. London: Oxford University Press, 1972.

Turner, John F. C. "The People Build with Their Hands." In *Environment and Change: The Next Fifty Years*, William R. Ewald, Jr., ed. Bloomington, Ind.: Indiana University Press, 1971.

Turner, John F. C., and Fichter, Roberts, eds. *Freedom to Build*. New York: Macmillan Co., Collier Books, 1973.

UNESCO. *Criteria and Guidelines for the Choice and Establishment of Biosphere Reserves*. Program on Man and the Biosphere Report Series no. 22. Paris, 20–24 May 1974.

United Nations. *Compendium of Social Statistics 1967*. Statistical Papers Series K, no. 3.

United Nations, Conference on Trade and Development. *Review of International Trade and Development*. 1967.

United Nations, Department of Economic and Social Affairs, Statistical Office. *Demographic Yearbook*.

United Nations, Department of Economic and Social Affairs. *The Use of Bamboo and Reeds in Building Construction*. New York, 1972.

United Nations, Environment Program. *Fact Sheet* no. 4. Nairobi, Kenya, 1975.

United Nations. *Science and Technology for Development: Prosposals for the Second UN Development Decade*. 1970.

United Nations, Secretariat, Department of Economic and Social Affairs, Population Division. *Total Population Estimates for World, Regions, and Countries Each Year*, 1950–1985 (ESA/P/WP.34), 16 October 1970.

United Nations. *Statistical Yearbook*.

U.S., Arms Control and Disarmament Agency. *World Military Expenditure*, 1971.

U.S., Atomic Energy Commission. *Brookhaven Report*. 1957.

U.S., Department of Agriculture. *World Agricultural Situation*. Dec. 1973.

U.S., Department of Commerce, Bureau of the Census. *Historical Statistics of the United States*.

_____. *Statistical Abstract of the United States*.

U.S., Department of the Interior, National Park Service. *The Spirit of Kaloko-Honokohau*. 1974.

Upton, Letitia, and Lyons, Nancy. *Distribution of Personal Income and Wealth in the United States*. Cambridge Institute, 1972.

Vacca, Roberto. *The Coming Dark Age*. Garden City, N.Y.: Doubleday & Co., 1973.

Varshney, C. K. "Food Potential of India." *Tropical Ecology* 13, no. 1 (June 1972):120–121.

Vernon, Raymond. *Sovereignty at Bay: The Multinational Spread of U.S. Enterprises*. New York: Basic Books, 1971.

Wade, Nicholas. "Green Revolution (I): A Just Technology, Often Unjust in Use." *Science*, 20 December 1974, pp. 1093–1096.

_____. "Green Revolution (II): Problems of Adapting a Western Technology." *Science*, 27 December 1974, pp. 1186–1188.

Watt, Kenneth E. F. "Critically Important Determinants of the Transition to the Future." University of California, Davis, 1974.

_____. *Principles of Environmental Science*. New York: McGraw-Hill, 1973.

_____. *The Titanic Effect.* Stamford, Conn.: Sinauer Associates, 1974.

Weeks, Dudley. "The Dominant Network of Exploitation: A Technoculture in the Making." Paper presented at the Inter-University Center of Post-Graduate Studies, Dubrovnik, Yugoslavia, February 1975.

_____. "Learning Alternative Futures: The Dominant Conceptual, Behavioral, and Structural Patterns of Contemporary Human Society and the Design of Polsocioeconomic Alternatives." Doctoral dissertation, University of Hawaii, 1976.

Widdowson, J. P.; Yeats, G. W.; and Healy, W. B.. "The Effect of Root Nematodes on the Utilisation of Phosphorus by White Clover on a Yellow-Brown Loam." *New Zealand Journal of Agricultural Research* 16, no. 1 (February 1973):77–80.

Winkelstein, Warren, Jr., and French, Fern E. "The Role of Ecology in the Design of a Health Care System." *California Medicine* 9 (November 1970):7.

Wong, Luke S. K. "An Overview of Housing Provision and Housing Needs in Hong Kong." In *Housing in Hong Kong,* edited by Luke S. K. Wong. Monograph prepared for the South East Asia Low Cost Housing Study sponsored by the International Development Research Center, Ottawa, Canada, 1975.

Wood, B. J. "Integrated Control: Critical Assessment of Case Histories in Developing Economies." In *Insects: Studies in Population Management.* Memoirs 1. Canberra: Ecological Society of Australia, 1973.

World Bank Atlas of Per Capita Product and Population. IBRD, 1966.

World Bank Atlas: Population, Per Capita Product and Growth Rates, 1974.

World Health Organization. *Health Hazards of the Human Environment.* Geneva, 1972.

World Health Organization. *The Place of DDT in Operations Against Malaria and Other Vector Borne Diseases.* Geneva, 1971.

World Health Organization. "Health Trends and Prospects, 1950–2000."*World Health Statistics Report* 27 (1974):670–706.

Yeates, G. W.; Healy, W. B.; and Widdowson, J. P. "The Influence of Nematodes on Growth of Plots of White Clover on a Yellow-Brown Loam." *New Zealand Journal of Agricultural Research* 18 (November 1975).

Yudelman, Montague; Butler, Gavan; and Banerji, Ranadev. *Technological Change, Agriculture and Employment in Developing Countries.* Organization of Economic Cooperation and Development, Development Centre Studies, Employment Series no. 4. Paris, 1971.

Zeman, Tom. "Solar Power Now." *Ramparts.* April 1975, p. 21.

Zon, Raphael. *Forests and Water in the Light of Scientific Investigation.* U.S. Forest Service. Washington, D.C.: Government Printing Office, 1927.

Index

Systemic phenomenon, society as a, 19
Systems integration and impact planning, 244

Takeoff period, 5
Technique, 27
Technoculture belief system, 12
Technological fix, 94–95
Technology, 38; transfer of, 39
Tolstoy hypothesis, 200, 201
Toynbee, A., 24, 200
Trade acreage balance, food, 117, 181
Traditional way of life, 16
Tragedy, 21
Transnational corporations, 170–172, 243

Unemployment, 33, 85–86, 185, 187, 188, 236
Unrealism, 213–217
Urbanization, 13, 24, 31, 132–136

Vacca, R., 38

Wage rates, 34, 185
Wealth ceilings, 257
Will of the populace, aggregate, 21
Wood, B. J., 37
World environmental problems, interrelationships of, 3

Yudelman, M., 34, 39

☮ Production Notes

The text of this book was designed by Roger J. Eggers and typeset on the Unified Composing System by the design and production staff of The University Press of Hawaii.

The text typeface is Garamond No. 49; display face is Serif Gothic.

Jacket design is by Steve Reoutt.

Offset presswork and binding is the work of The Maple Press Company. Text paper is Glatfelter P & S Offset, basis 55.